IMAGES
of America

BELMONT

On the Cover: Belmont High School Band's letter girls lead the band in the 1951 Belmont Christmas parade. This annual event draws a large crowd each year. The Belmont High School Band performed in many civic events, such as the dedication of bridges, the awarding of Army-Navy Es for outstanding production in support of the World War II war effort, and other happenings. It has also participated in sporting events through the years. (Courtesy of Allen Millican.)

IMAGES
of America

BELMONT

Allen Millican, Gearl-Dean Page,
and Jack Page

ARCADIA
PUBLISHING

ISBN 978-1-4671-3373-9

Published by Arcadia Publishing
Charleston, South Carolina

Printed in the United States of America

Library of Congress Control Number: 2016930457

For all general information, please contact Arcadia Publishing:
Telephone 843-853-2070
Fax 843-853-0044
E-mail sales@arcadiapublishing.com
For customer service and orders:
Toll-Free 1-888-313-2665

Visit us on the Internet at www.arcadiapublishing.com

We dedicate this book to the Belmont Historical Society and its founders, supporters, and volunteers, all of whom have made significant contributions to the discovery, presentation, and explanation of Belmont's past. Also, to Belmont's newcomers who will share in building a sterling future built on our historic past.

Contents

ACKNOWLEDGMENTS

The authors wish to thank all the many patrons who, through the years, have shared old photographs with Allen Millican, whose business is restoring photographs, keeping them on file, and making them available to people who may wish to purchase them. It is because of his vast array of pictures that he was able to find these that pertain to Belmont's history. Unless indicated otherwise, all images are courtesy of the Millican Pictorial History Museum.

INTRODUCTION

The land that Belmont occupies lies between the South Fork River to the west and the Catawba River to the east and forms what has recently become known as the South Point Peninsula. This area was occupied for thousands of years by nomadic Native Americans. When Europeans explored this area, they found the land occupied by the Catawba Indians. By the mid 1700s, Scotch-Irish and German immigrants came down the "old wagon road" from Pennsylvania and Virginia and moved into the area. The rich red soil, heavily timbered forests, moderate climate, and plenty of water enabled them to make an adequate living as subsistence farmers.

The Revolutionary War found men from "the Point" led by Maj. William Chronicle engaged against the Tories and the British in the Battle of Kings Mountain. Major Chronicle was killed in this battle.

The general orientation of travel at that time was north and south. The main thoroughfare ran from the confluence of the South Fork and the Catawba Rivers northward through present Belmont, Catawba Heights, Mount Holly, and on to River Bend. Fording the rivers to the east and west was difficult, and at high water, it was impossible.

Unsatisfied with the limited opportunities of a farm economy and observing the construction of textile mills along the rivers, Jasper and Edwin Stowe, sons of Larkin Stowe, constructed a cotton textile mill on the banks of the South Fork River. The Civil War's outcome extinguished early efforts to establish manufacturing, curbed retail trade, and left the area in poverty. Farming, distilling, and crafts related to agriculture were relied upon for subsistence.

With the construction of the Atlanta and Charlotte Air Line Railway in 1872 and its water tank and refueling station, a focal point was established around which commercial and social activities centered. Named for John Garibaldi, construction foreman for the Mecklenburg Ironworks that built the water tower, Garibaldi the community began to grow. General stores, a post office, and a school were built.

Churches had been important centers of worship and social life early. Most groups would worship in brush arbors until a building could be constructed. Goshen Presbyterian, established in 1764, is believed to be the earliest church built west of the Catawba River. In 1876, the Benedictine Order founded a monastery: Maryhelp. By 1895, there were Catholic schools that would evolve into Belmont Abbey College and Sacred Heart College.

Garibaldi became Belmont with a name change in 1886. The town was incorporated on March 6, 1895, with W.B. Puett as its first mayor. By this time, there were several businesses along Main Street, including J.W. Armstrong's store, the Stowe and Puett store, and some private residences. By 1910, the town boasted a hotel, a bank, a mill office, a railway station with telegraph, and perhaps a half mile of paved roadway.

The success of post-construction cotton mills in the area inspired brothers Robert Lee and Samuel Pinckney Stowe to organize their own cotton mill in Belmont. In 1902, the Chronicle Mill, named for Maj. William Chronicle, began operations. In 1907, Belmont's second mill, the Imperial, began operations using electric power. Mills soon to follow were the Majestic, the National Yarn Mill, the Climax, the Acme I, the Perfection, the Linford, the Sterling, the Crescent, Eagle Yarn Mills, Stowe Spinning, South Fork, Acme II, the Aberfoyle, Piedmont Processing, and the Stowe Thread Corporation.

Some diversification was accomplished by the construction of various knitting operations, including Hatch Full Fashioned Hosiery, Knit Products, and Belmont Hosiery Mills, Inc. Further diversification was established by the addition of three knit fabric industries—Beltex, Knitcraft, and Swagknit.

Belmont's first public schoolhouse was originally built as a commissary for the railroad workers who built the Atlanta and Charlotte Air Line Railway through this area. About 1870, when it was no longer needed, it was moved to a site near Smith's Graveyard. There was, however, a schoolhouse known as the Gingles School prior to that time, but it was a tuition school. The first of a series of schools on the corner of Central Avenue and Main Street was built around 1880. In charge was Frank P. Hall, a Davidson College graduate. R.L. Stowe was one of the early teachers. Hall later became Gaston County Schools superintendent and held that post until 1937.

Belmont's first high school was on the same site as the Central Schools. In 1939, a modern high school was built on the corner of Central Avenue and Myrtle Street. When the high school was moved to South Point Road, the 1939 building became a junior high school. The property has been improved several times and is today one of the most beautiful schools in the state.

Elementary schools were subsequently built in North Belmont, East Belmont, Catawba Heights, and New Hope. The black schools, led for many years by Prof. Charles Jesse Reid, produced many outstanding students and citizens. The Reid Schools, named in honor of Professor Reid, were integrated with the other schools in the area in 1966. Two years later, the Gaston County schools, including those in Belmont, were consolidated with the Gastonia City schools and the Cherryville schools to create a single system of public schools in Gaston County.

For many years, social life in Belmont centered around the churches, schools, and communities nearest where one lived. For many, it was a community of houses clustered around a manufacturing plant—a "mill hill." As the years have passed, businesses downtown and in East Belmont have undergone change. Outlying shopping malls have, to a large extent, turned Belmont's downtown commercial area into a cluster of eating establishments and specialty shops. The local churches have evolved into attractive places of worship with up-to-date sanctuaries. The greatest transformation within the city limits, however, is apparent in what were the mill villages. Most mill houses have been either modernized and sold to individuals or razed. Areas outside the city limits have been changed from farmlands into upscale residential developments.

—Jack Page

One

Early Settlers and Landowners 1700s–1900s

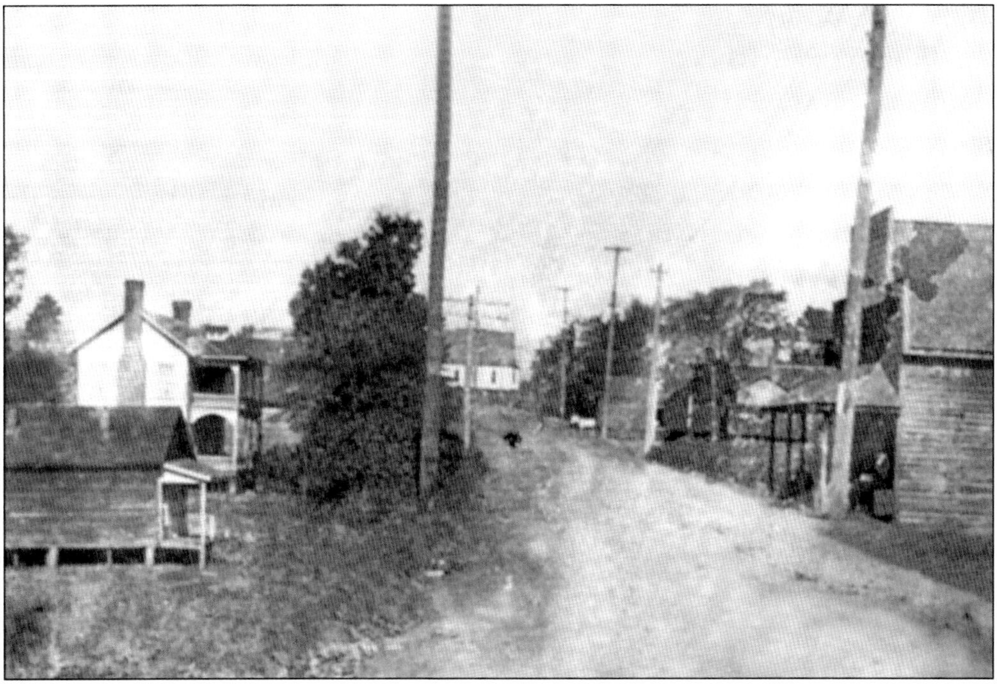

Oldest Picture of Belmont's Main Street. From around 1850, this photograph is thought to be the oldest picture of the community, which was first called Garibaldi and later renamed Belmont. The community was incorporated in 1895. The view in this photograph faces north on what became Main Street. At the very top of the street is the first Presbyterian church built in Belmont. This church was later moved east one block to the corner of Catawba Street and Glenway Street. It was rebuilt as a brick structure, and this move made room for the mill office. The church has in recent years moved once again and a new building was constructed on the corner of Main Street and Central Avenue. (Courtesy of Millican Pictorial History Museum.)

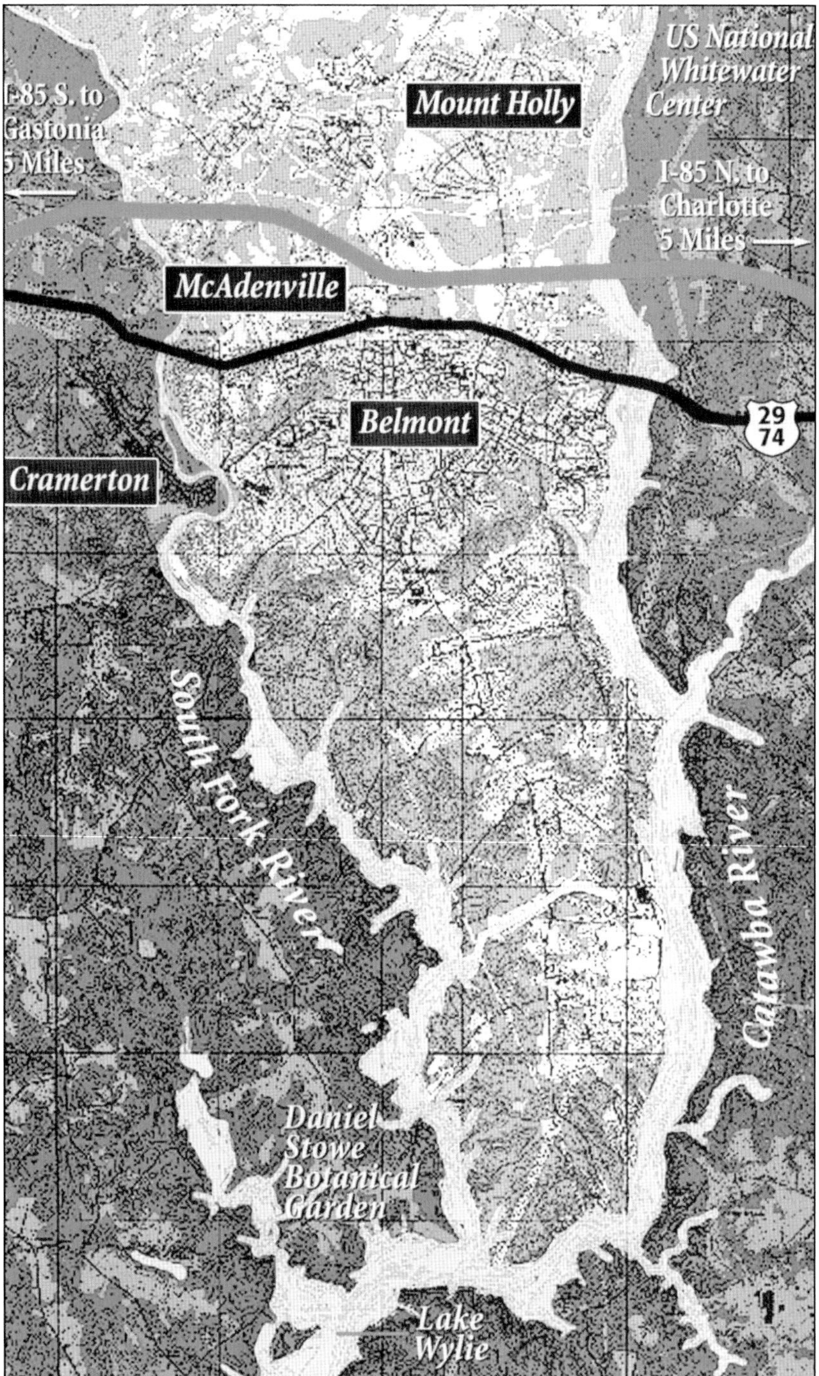

Map of South Point Peninsula. The land between the South Fork River and the Catawba River has been recently referred to as the South Point Peninsula. These two rivers were once smaller streams; however, they comprise Lake Wylie today. The most productive farmland has now been covered by the lake. The loss of this fertile land forced farmers to seek other employment to support their families. (Courtesy of Millican Pictorial History Museum.)

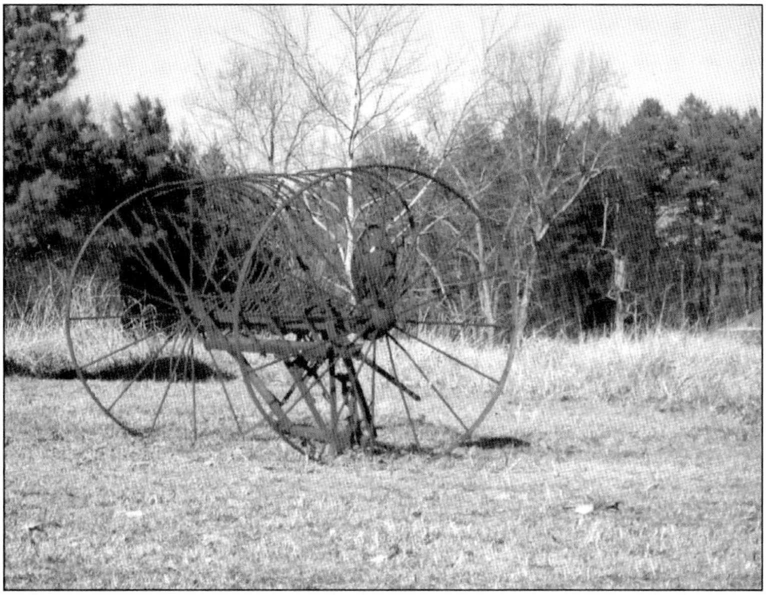

Abandoned Hay Rake. This hay rake sits idle with its tongue missing and seat sitting akimbo. For many years, farmers on "the Point" used machinery like this to bring in their crops. This hay rake was powered by a pair of horses, but today, there are no fields of hay to be gathered and no more farm horses to be seen. (Courtesy of Jack Page.)

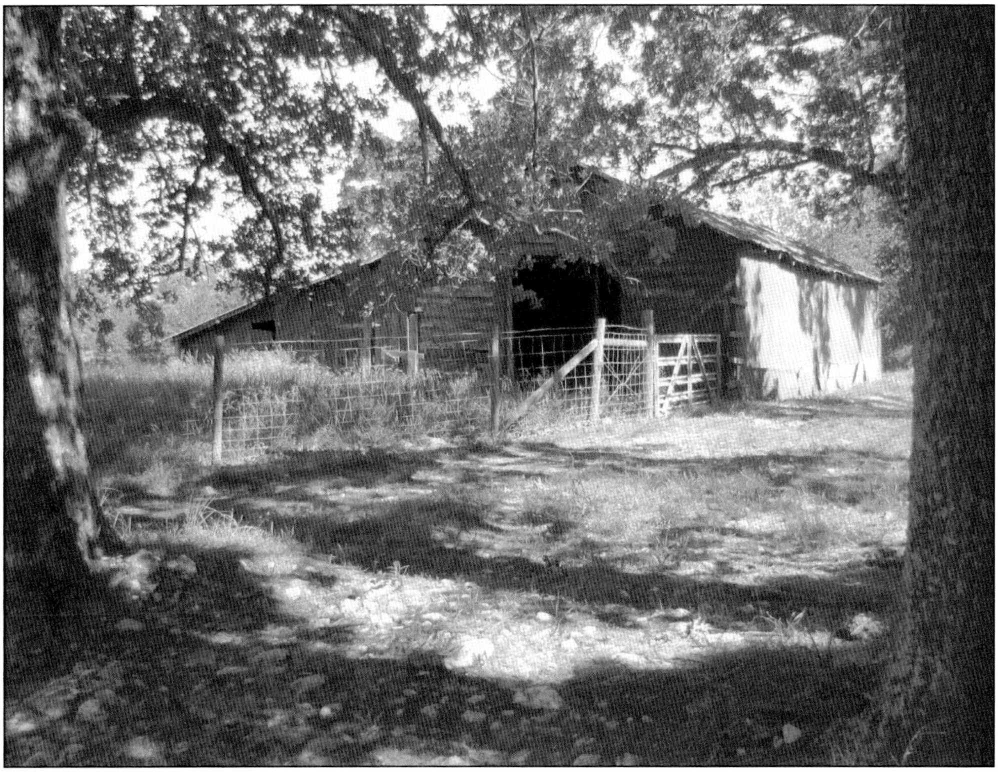

Dixon Dairy Farm. As space for field crops diminished, many farmers converted their fields to pastureland. Some farmers, like Palmer Dixon, became dairymen. Some of these dairymen bottled their milk and established routes that supplied milk to customers throughout the Belmont area. Some dairymen placed their milk in large milk containers and put the containers beside the road to be picked up and delivered to a milk processing plant in Shelby, North Carolina. (Photograph by Jack Page.)

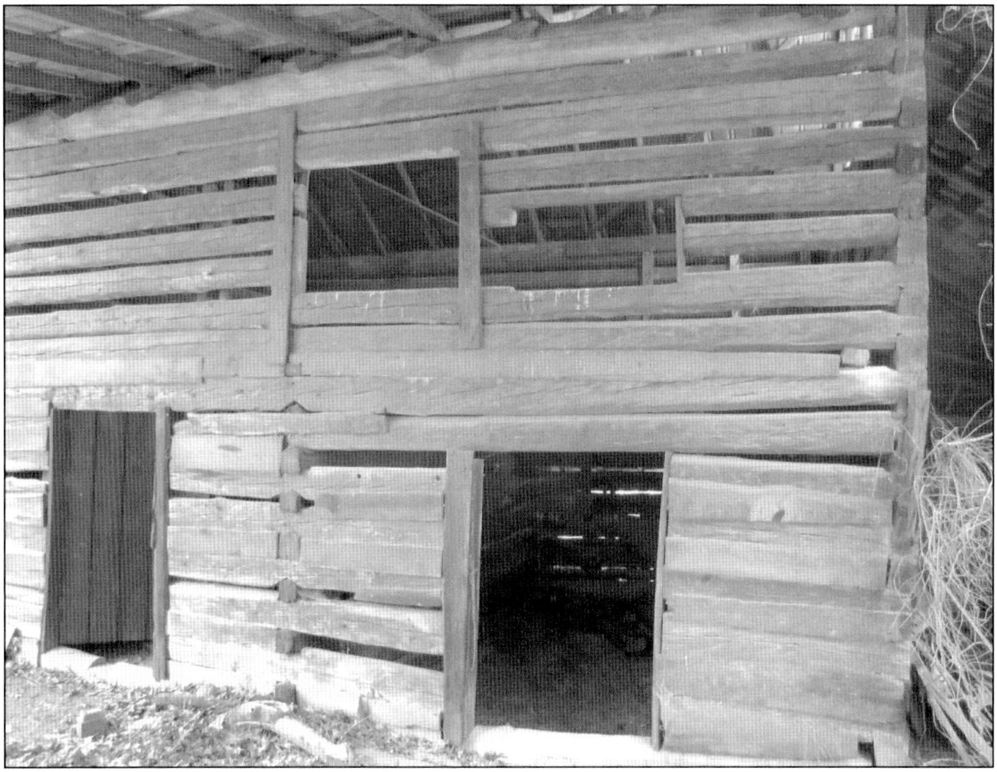

Typical South Point Construction. A.A. Cathey's stable lies deserted along the lower Armstrong Road. Cathey was noted as an efficient farmer. All of his children attended college, and several of them became teachers in the Gaston County school system. (Photograph by Jack Page.)

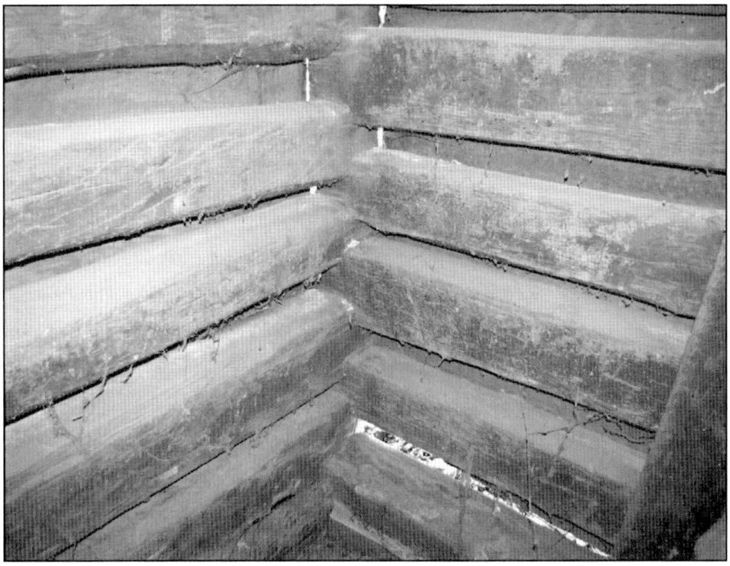

Typical South Point Construction Technique. This technique of joining logs at corners has been handed down for many generations. It was popular throughout the South for its efficiency and ease of construction. (Photograph by Jack Page.)

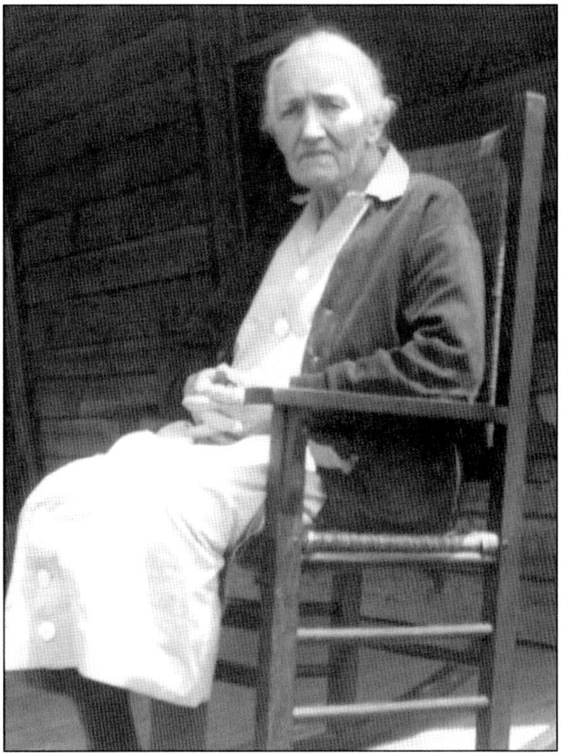

Emma Jane Leeper Wilson. Emma Wilson was the widow of Samuel W. Wilson. The Leeper family of the South Point community is one of the oldest families that settled the South Point area. Robert Leeper, a great uncle of hers, was one of the first known settlers of the land near the junction of the South Fork and the Catawba Rivers, on 350 acres issued in 1750. Robert was one of the four residents on the Point who helped construct a log fort near the junction of the two rivers. (Courtesy of Millican Pictorial History Museum.)

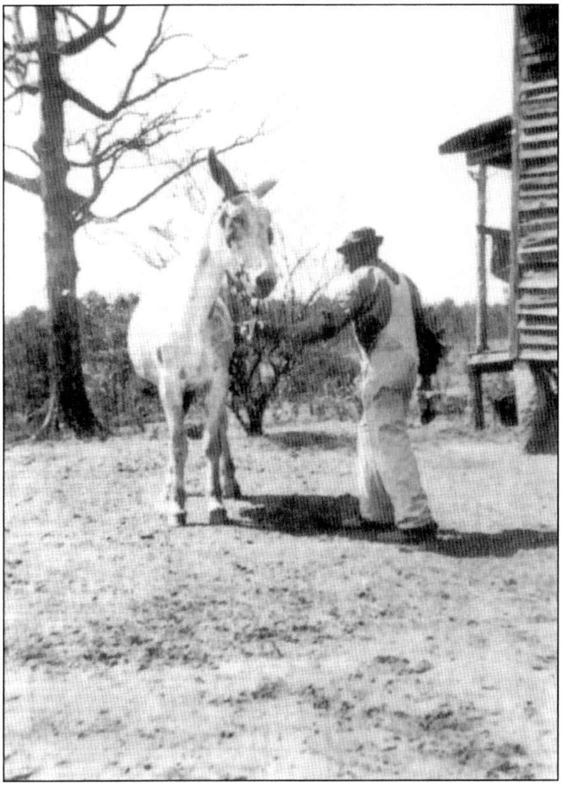

Green Hand. Green Hand raised a large family and was noted for his religious fervor, having served in various capacities in more than one church. His work ethic was passed on to his children, several of whom have distinguished themselves through hard work, higher education, and outstanding citizenship. (Courtesy of Millican Pictorial History Museum.)

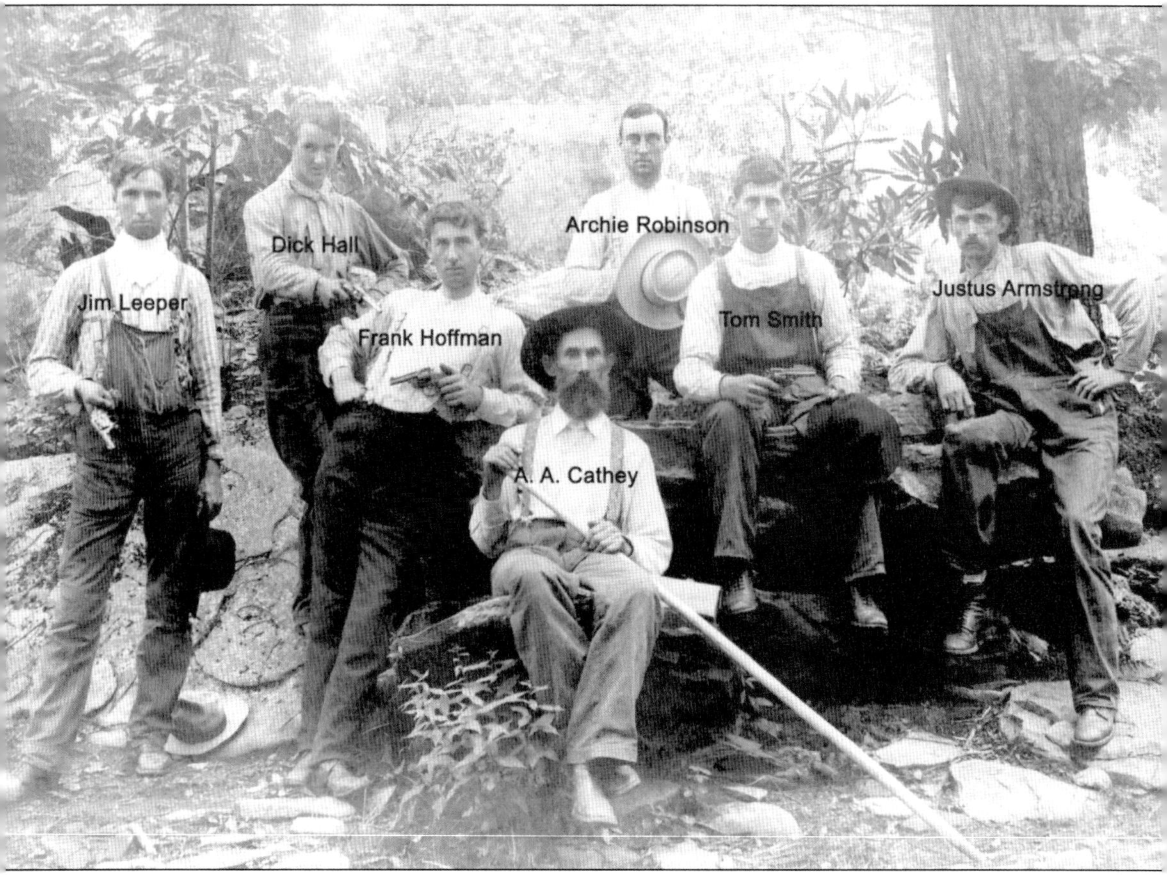

Early Residents of South Point, Belmont. This group of South Point farmers has gathered for a social event: marksmanship practice. From left to right are Jim Leeper, Dick Hall, Frank Hoffman, A.A. Cathey (foreground), Archie Robinson, Tom Smith, and Justus Armstrong. The surnames of these men are very familiar because their descendants became prominent citizens in Gaston County for many years. (Courtesy of Millican Pictorial History Museum.)

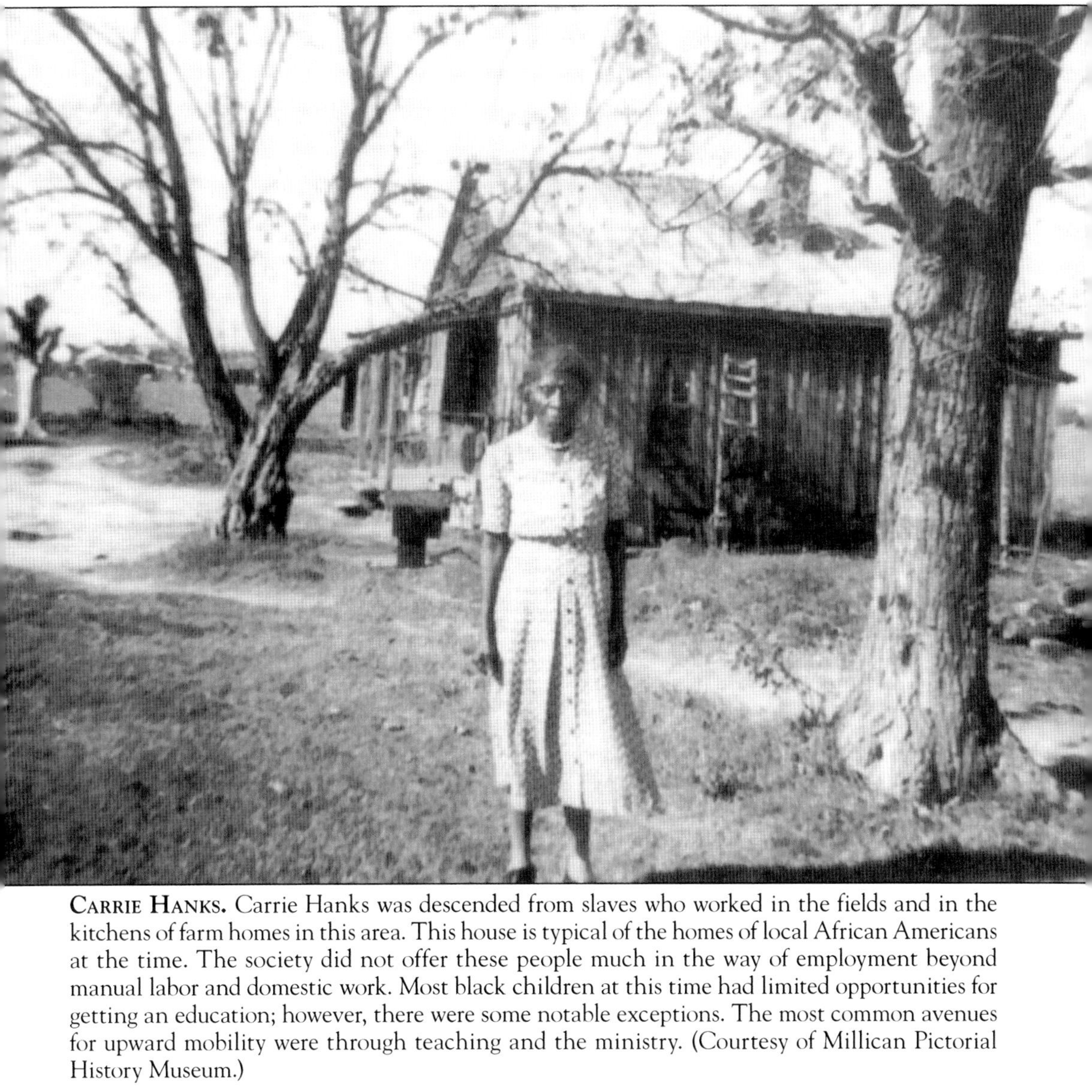

CARRIE HANKS. Carrie Hanks was descended from slaves who worked in the fields and in the kitchens of farm homes in this area. This house is typical of the homes of local African Americans at the time. The society did not offer these people much in the way of employment beyond manual labor and domestic work. Most black children at this time had limited opportunities for getting an education; however, there were some notable exceptions. The most common avenues for upward mobility were through teaching and the ministry. (Courtesy of Millican Pictorial History Museum.)

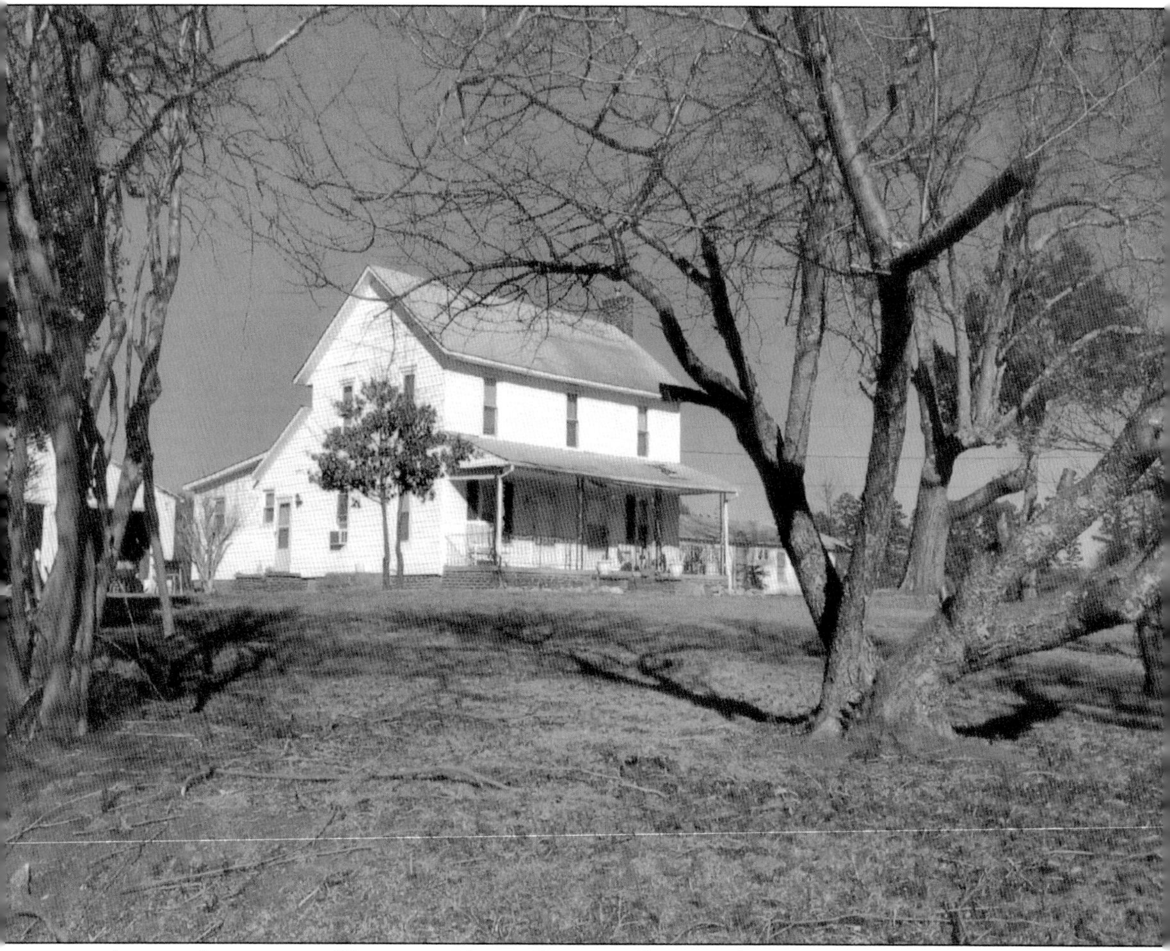

Albert Armstrong House on Nixon Road. Following the pattern of farmhouses all over Piedmont North Carolina, the Albert Armstrong house remains empty today. This design had a long hallway down its center and bedrooms on the second floor. The kitchen is located at the rear of the house, and indoor plumbing is a retrofit to these homes, which commonly had outhouses. This particular house lost a chimney on the left side to Hurricane Hugo, but the remaining chimney is a duplicate to the one lost. (Photograph by Jack Page.)

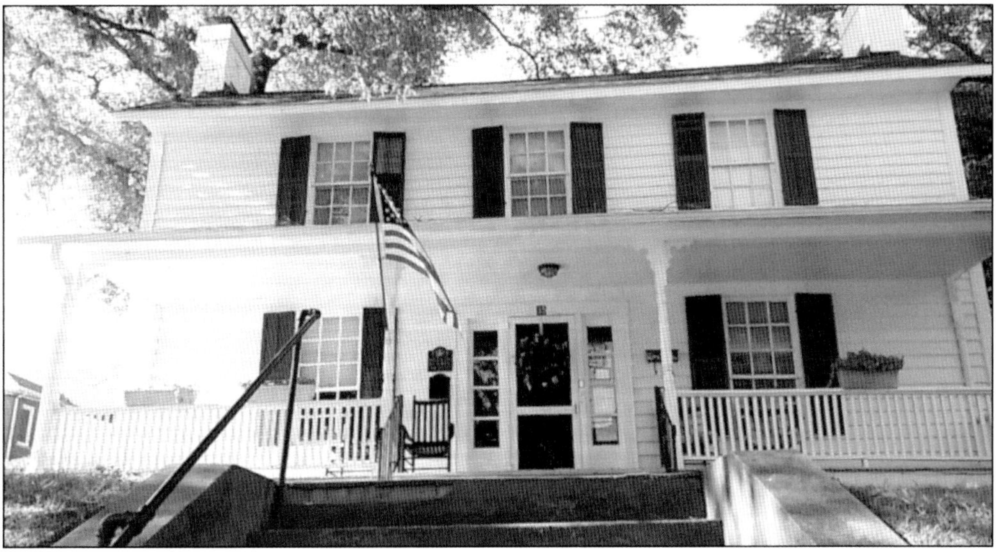

Abram Stowe House. The oldest known surviving structure in Belmont, the Abram Stowe House was built around 1868. This is a log structure later covered with clapboards. Stowe was the second postmaster, taking over after Alex Beaty. He was the first mayor of Garibaldi and also the first depot agent. Stowe had a country store and was a contractor for the Atlanta and Charlotte Air Line Railway to manage the wood supply for the train. (Courtesy of Millican Pictorial History Museum.)

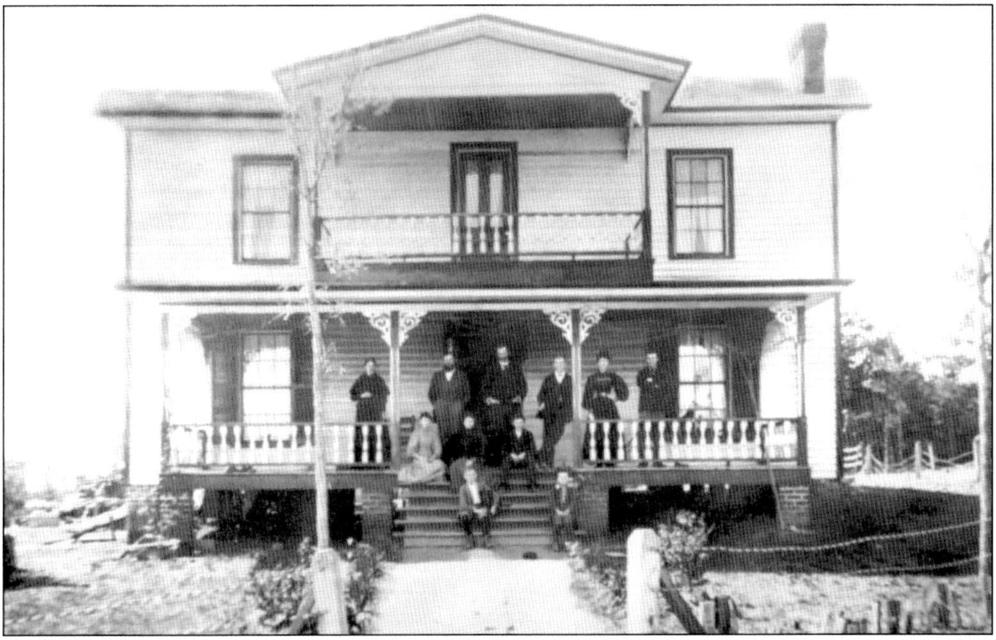

James P. Stowe House. The second-oldest house in Belmont was built for James P. Stowe and was located where city hall now stands. The Stowes took in boarders, one of whom was R.B. Suggs Sr., who married one of James Stowe's daughters. Sometime later, the house became known as the Suggs Apartments. In 1939, the structure was relocated just behind where it had been to make room for the new post office building, which is now city hall. (Courtesy of Millican Pictorial History Museum.)

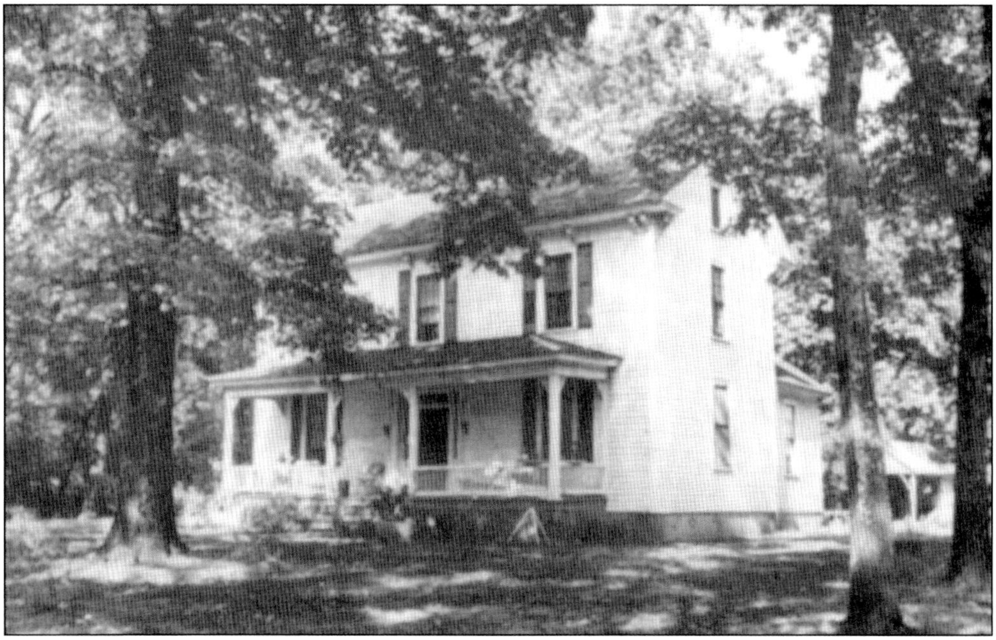

CHARLES THEODORE STOWE HOME, 1880. This is the Charles Theodore Stowe Home, often called the "Dory" Stowe home. This house replaced the log home of Samuel L. "Uncle Sammy" Ewing, with whom Dory and his family lived. For many years, this residence stood at the end of the Amity Acres development on Stowe Road. In recent years, many upscale homes have been built in the eastern section of the Dory Stowe property. It is from this home that Robert L. Stowe Sr. left to move into his house on Catawba Street, the present home of the Belmont Historical Society. (Courtesy of Millican Pictorial History Museum.)

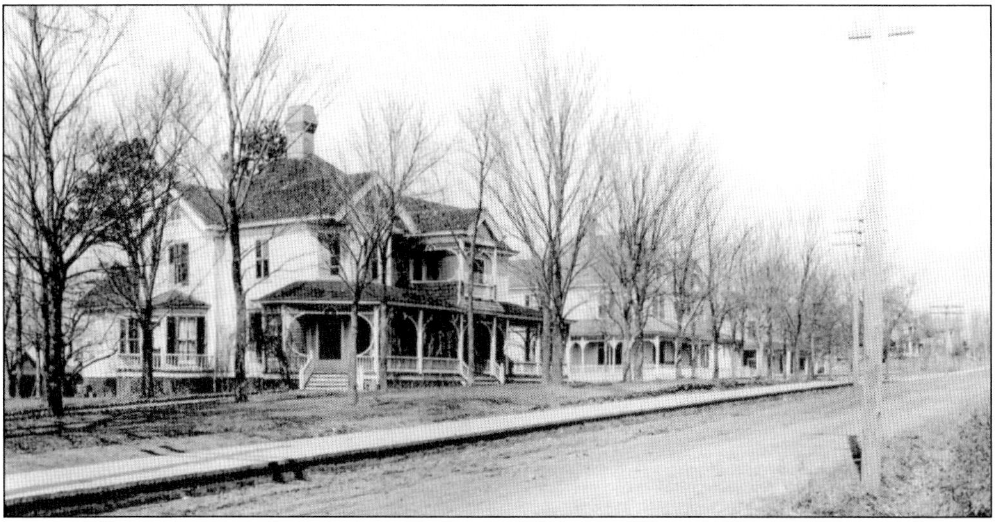

LOOKING NORTH ON MAIN STREET. The first house on Main Street is the Will Puett house, to the right is the Gullick house. Puett, having come to Belmont as a telegraph operator, married Minnie Stowe. He eventually became cashier at the Bank of Belmont. George Gullick, at the request of leading citizens, constructed the hotel building on Main Street. Both families were prominent citizens and investors in the fledging textile industry. (Courtesy of Millican Pictorial History Museum.)

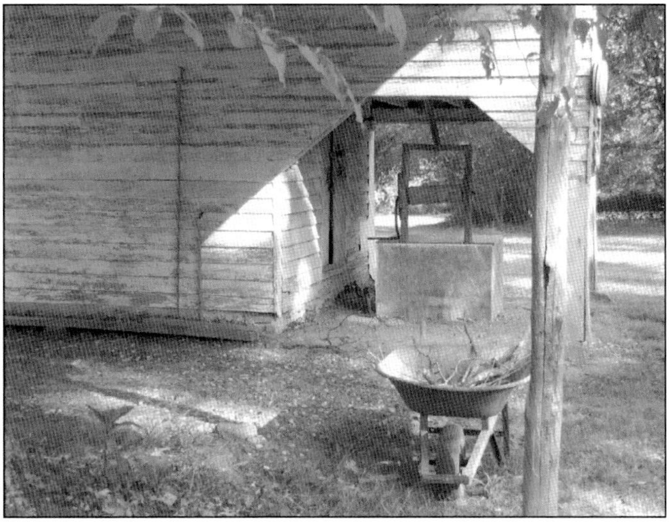

Well House on New Hope Road. The water source for farms in rural areas of the Point had to be dug wells. Often, a well house sheltered the well head. Notice the windlass that raised and lowered the bucket of water. This was toilsome labor for women who had to obtain water for all household uses, including watering stock, laundering clothes, and bathing the family. This building was used for outside storage. (Photograph by Jack Page.)

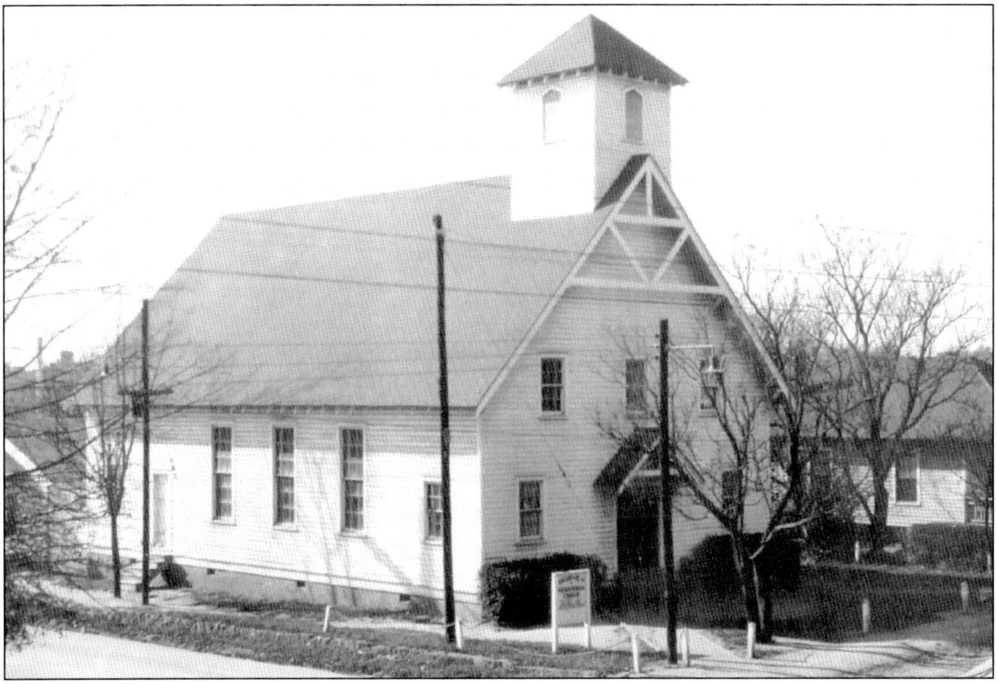

Goshen Presbyterian Church. Goshen Presbyterian Church, organized in 1764, is the region's oldest house of worship—believed to be the first in North Carolina west of the Catawba River. Located in North Belmont, it is the mother church of First Presbyterian Church in downtown Belmont as well as the mother church of several other Presbyterian churches in the area. It has had several buildings on different locations over the years. (Courtesy of Millican Pictorial History Museum.)

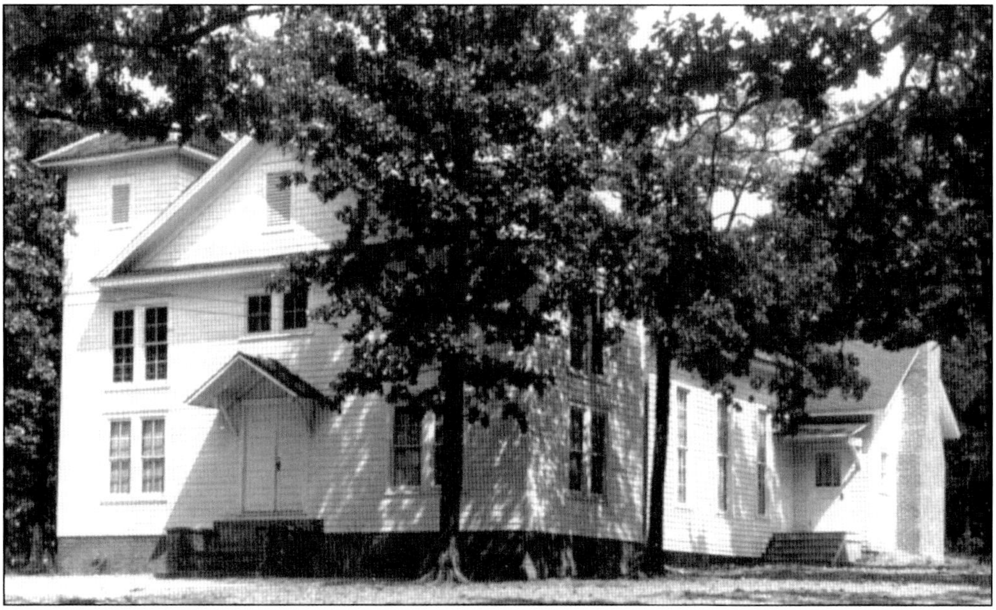

EBENEZER UNITED METHODIST CHURCH. The Ebenezer United Methodist Church in Catawba Heights was founded in 1790, making it over 200 years old. In this picture, the church has a clapboard exterior; however, the present church is made of brick. Just to the right side of the church is a cemetery (not pictured). (Courtesy of Millican Pictorial History Museum.)

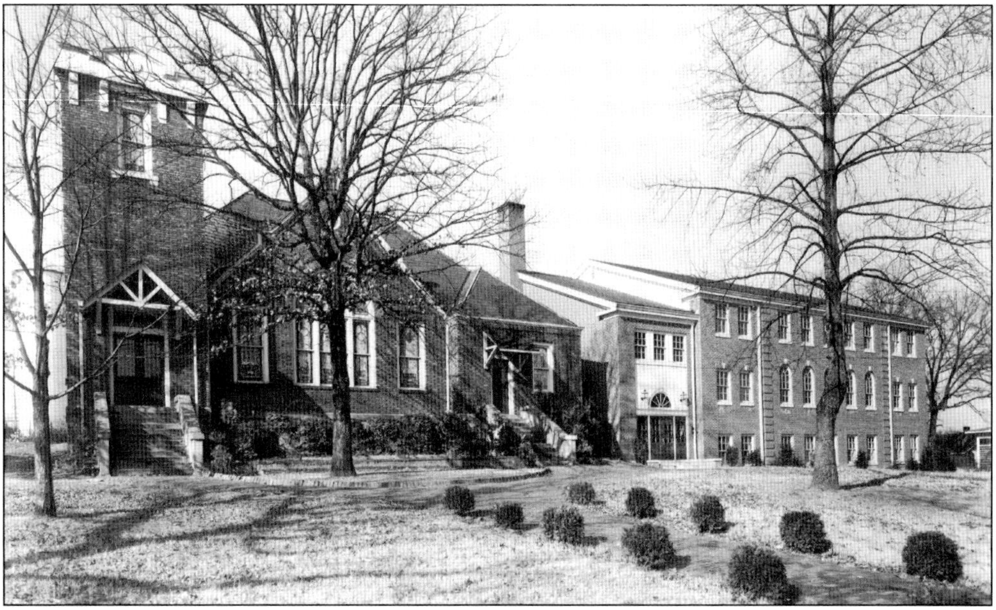

FIRST BAPTIST CHURCH. This church was established in 1874 as the Fellowship Baptist Church, whose members originally met in a brush arbor off Prince Street. The first pastor was Rev. D.W. Thomasson. Charter member Sarah Smith donated the land on which the present church rests. In 1912, the name was changed to First Baptist Church. It has been a mother church for six other Baptist churches in the area: East Belmont Baptist Church, Sunset Forest Baptist Church, South Point Baptist Church, Catawba Heights Baptist Church, Alexander Memorial Baptist Church, and Stowe Memorial Baptist Church. (Courtesy of Millican Pictorial History Museum.)

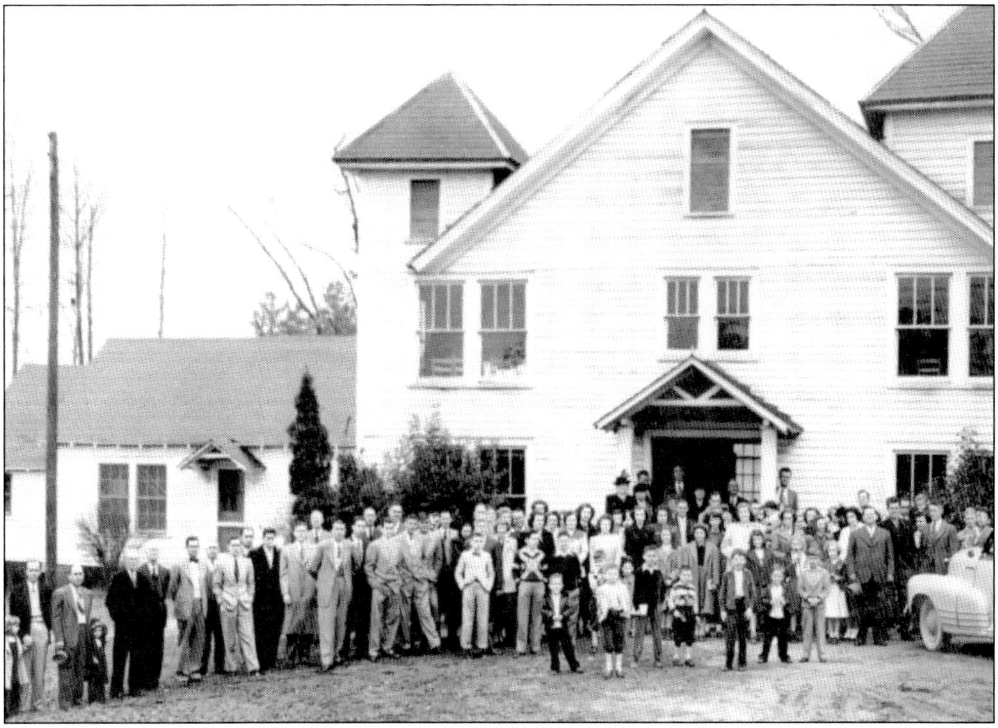

South Point Methodist Church. Established in 1882 and located off the South Point Road, about three miles from Belmont's Central Avenue and Main Street junction, the church served a large portion of South Point residents in its early years. Many fish fries, hosted in the front yard by the men of the church, and quilting activities, held in South Point's women's homes, raised money to build a new modern brick sanctuary. (Courtesy of Millican Pictorial History Museum.)

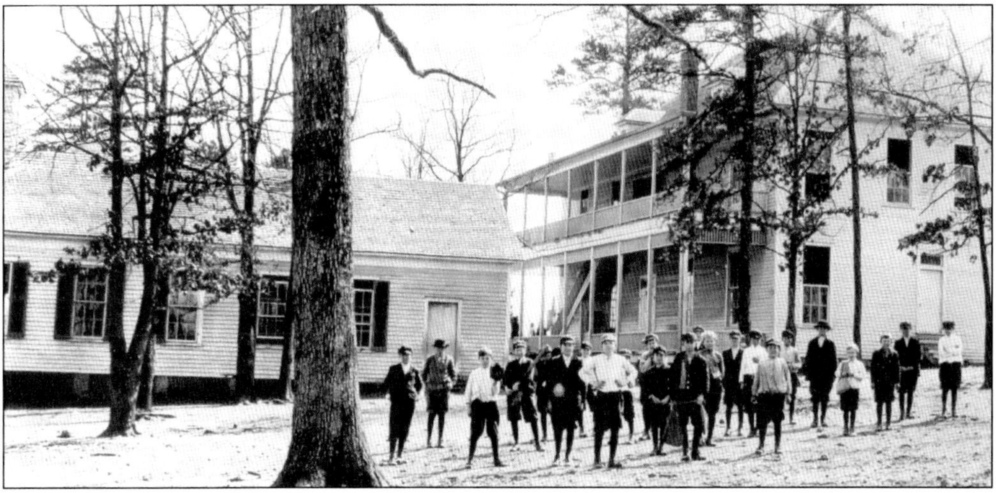

Early Belmont Schools. One of the earliest Belmont schools, built in 1880, was located across Main Street from the entrance to Greenwood Cemetery. Later, under Frank P. Hall, the buildings shown here, which face Central Avenue, were located on the same plot of ground. These buildings were replaced by brick structures, and the first Belmont High School was added to this same property. Later, Hall became a longtime superintendent of Gaston County Schools. (Courtesy of Millican Pictorial History Museum.)

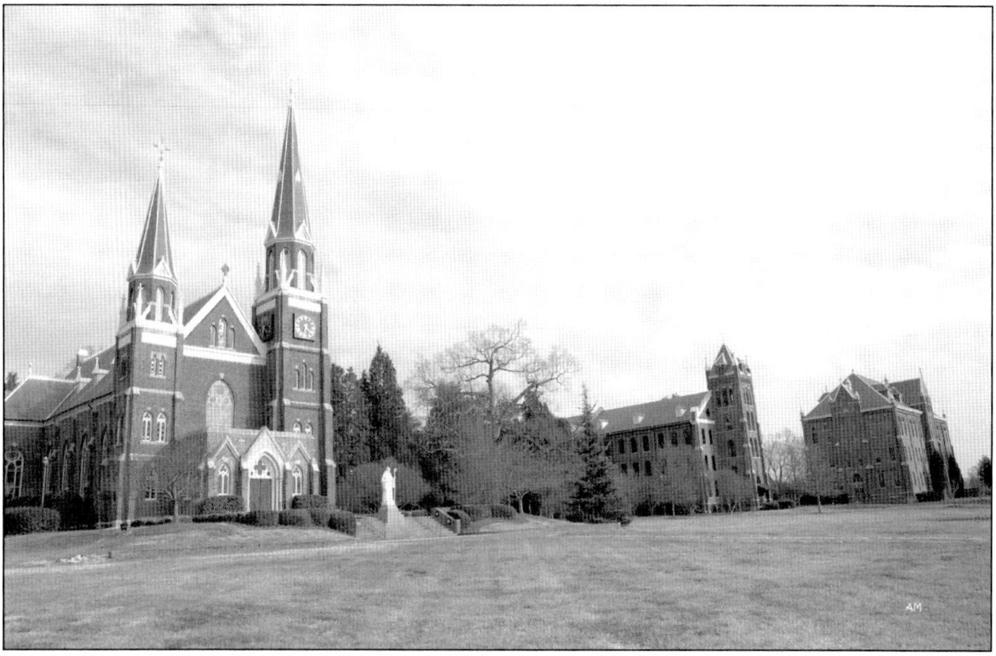

Belmont Abbey College. Built on land known as the Caldwell Estate, which had gone bankrupt during Reconstruction, Belmont Abbey College was founded in 1884. First named Maryhelp Abbey, it was later named Belmont Abbey College. At one time, there was a high school component called Belmont Abbey Preparatory School. Today, Belmont Abbey College has nearly 1,000 students, including day and adult education students. In its early years, "the Abbey" utilized some of its 500 acres as a working farm, whose products and livestock won many blue ribbons at the Gaston County Agricultural Fair. (Courtesy of Millican Pictorial History Museum.)

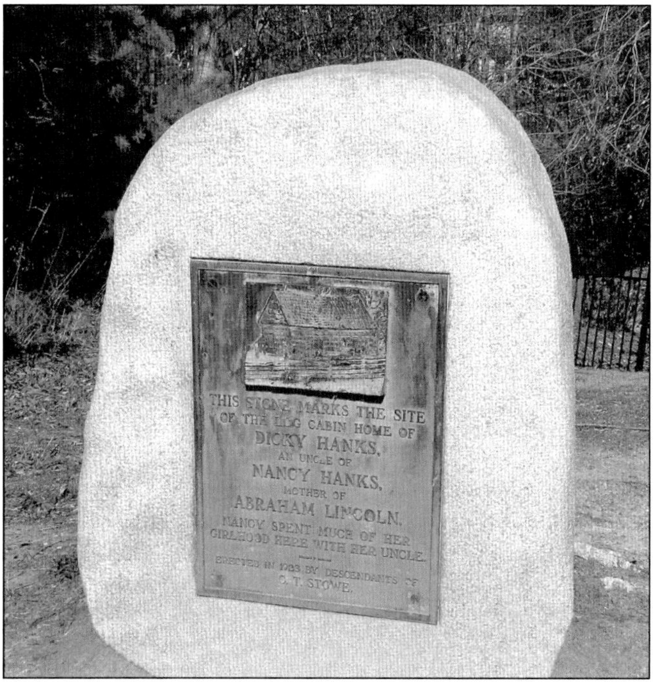

Nancy Hanks Monument. Minnie Stowe Puett strongly believed that Abraham Lincoln's mother, Nancy Hanks, lived with Dickie Hanks, her uncle, for a number of years. Minnie was convinced that this was this same Nancy Hanks who grew up in Dickie Hanks's cabin overlooking the Catawba River. This cabin was located on the property that is now known as Pinsto Forest Housing Development, and the monument still stands in the backyard of one of the residents. This monument was erected by Samuel Pinckney Stowe, son of Charles Theodore Stowe. (Photograph by Jack Page.)

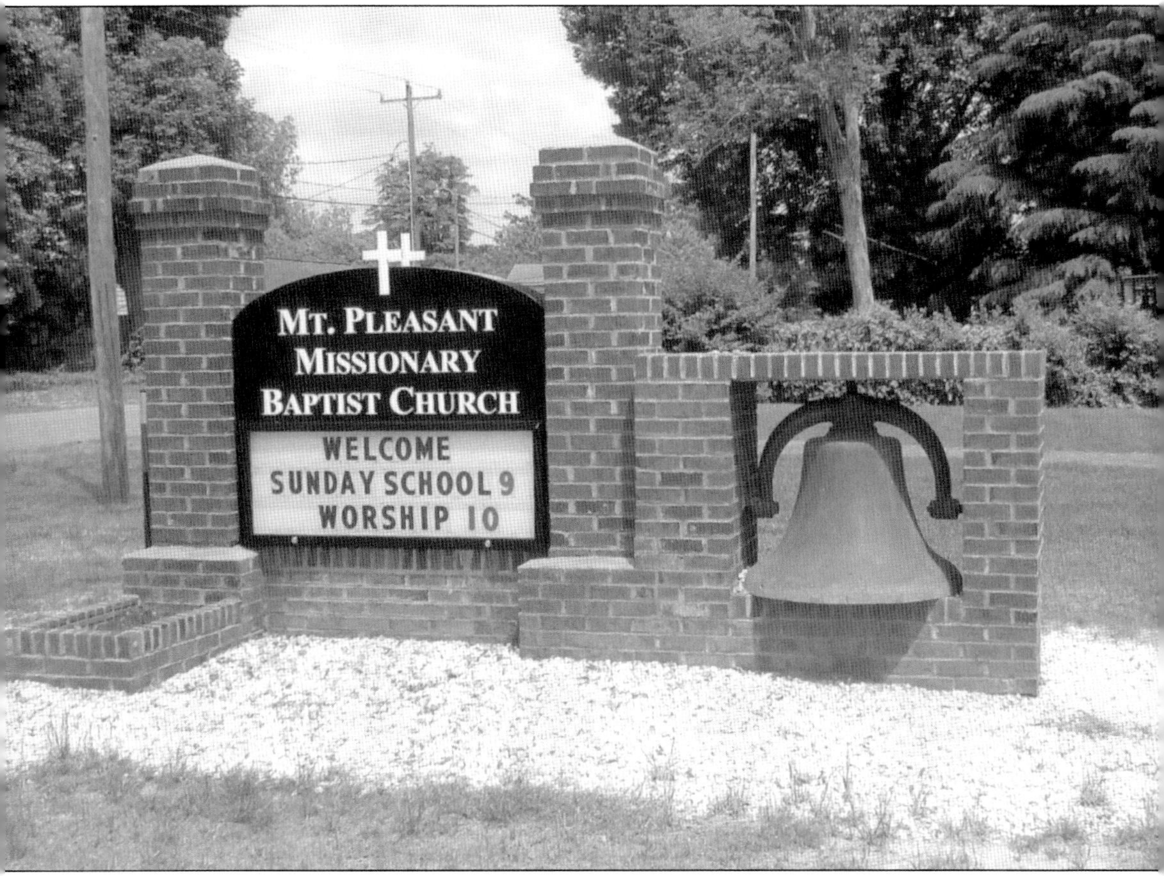

STOWESVILLE MILL BELL AT MT. PLEASANT MISSIONARY BAPTIST CHURCH. Stowe's Factory Cotton Mill was built on the lower South Fork River by the sons of Larkin Stowe in 1848. The product made there, coarse cotton yarn, was vended from the back of a horse-drawn wagon that plied its way throughout the South Point peninsula. Any surplus yarn was sent to Charleston, South Carolina, for shipment overseas. A community developed surrounding this mill whose post office was named Stowesville. The bell seen here is the original bell that called workers when shifts changed. After the Civil War, the factory was sold to Thomas Gaither, a Charlotte merchant whose name was given to the road that led to the mill site. When the mill was dismantled, the bell was given to Mt. Pleasant Missionary Baptist Church, which was located on Gaither Road at that time. (Photograph by Jack Page.)

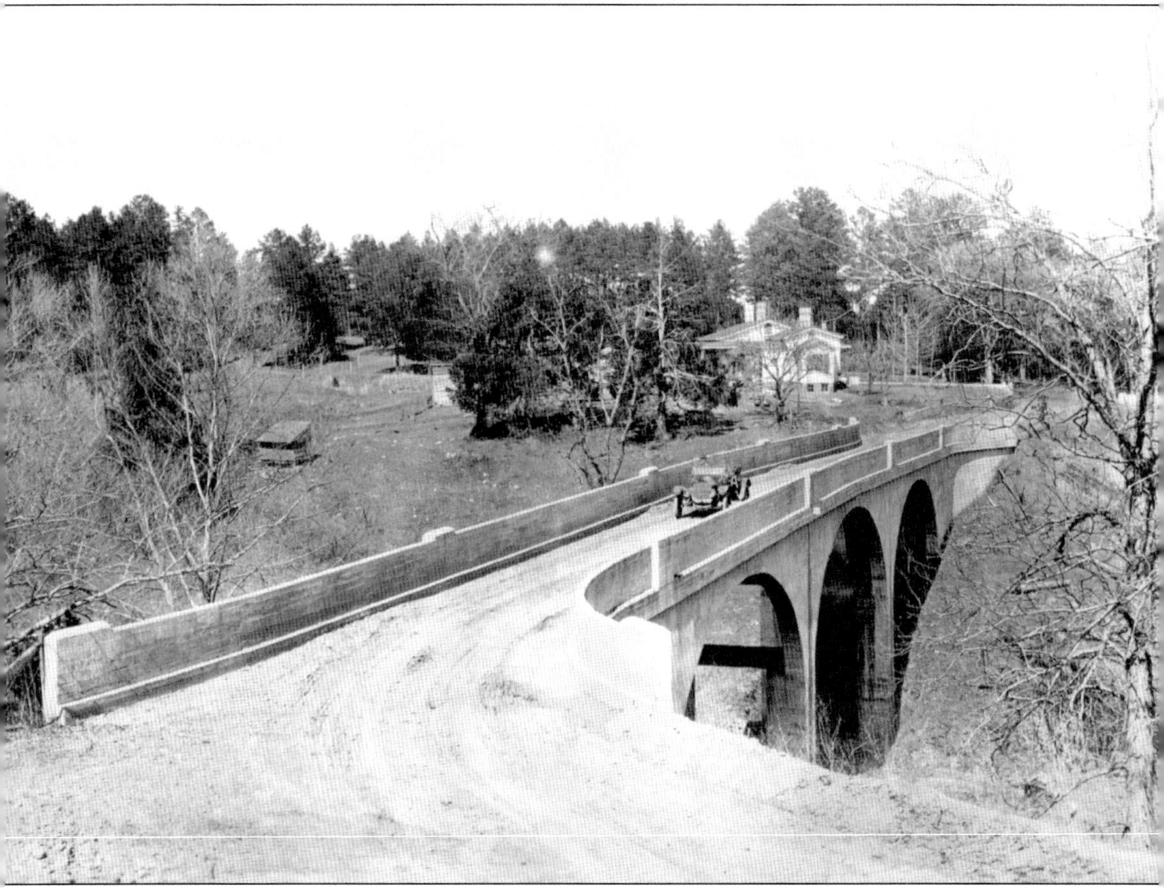

Bridge Connecting Gaston and Mecklenburg Counties. Highway 7 made its way from Gastonia through Lowell and Belmont as it wound through Old Dowd Road and on to Charlotte. Between Belmont and Mecklenburg County, this bridge, built around 1911, spanned the Catawba River. It is on the site of Sloan's Ferry. (Courtesy of Millican Pictorial History Museum.)

Two

TEXTILE ERA
1900–1980s

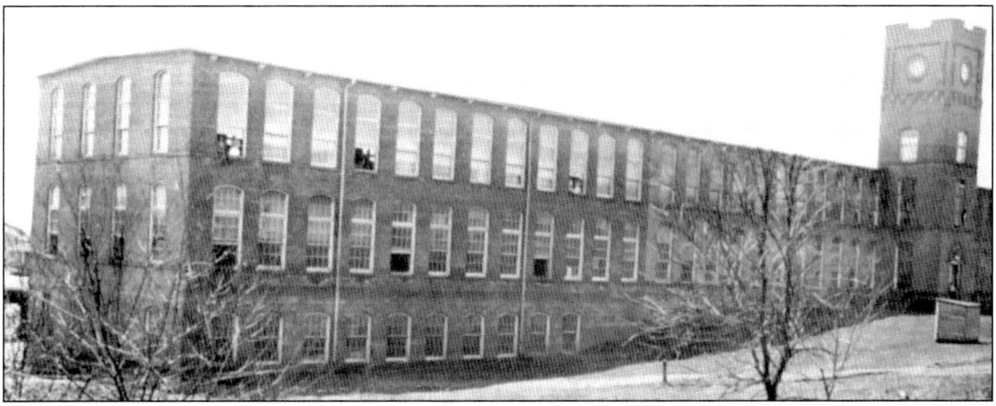

CHRONICLE MILL. The Chronicle Mill, built in 1901 by Robert Lee Stowe Sr., was located on property near the home where Maj. William Chronicle, of Kings Mountain battle fame, was raised. Originally powered by steam, the mill was the first cotton mill in downtown Belmont. Before air-conditioning became available, the mill had dozens of windows to afford ventilation. Later, these windows were bricked over. The mill has been idle for several years. (Courtesy of Millican Pictorial History Museum.)

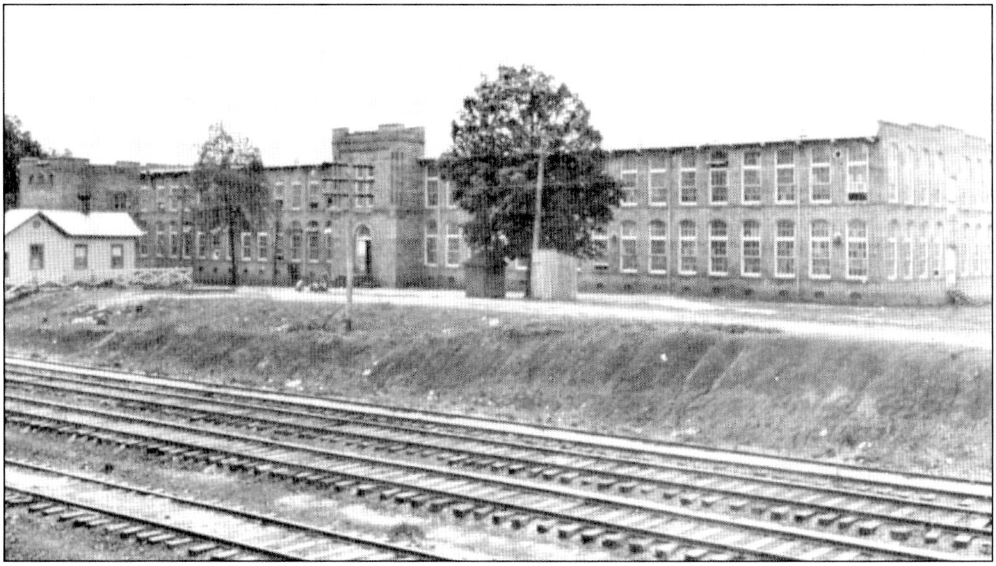

IMPERIAL MILL. The Imperial was the second cotton mill to begin operation in Belmont. Chartered in 1903 with operation beginning in 1905, it enjoyed an upgrade to electricity over steam power, which was used by the Chronicle Mill. This mill was served by the Southern Railway, while most of the other mills in Belmont were served by the Piedmont & Northern Railway. (Courtesy of Millican Pictorial History Museum.)

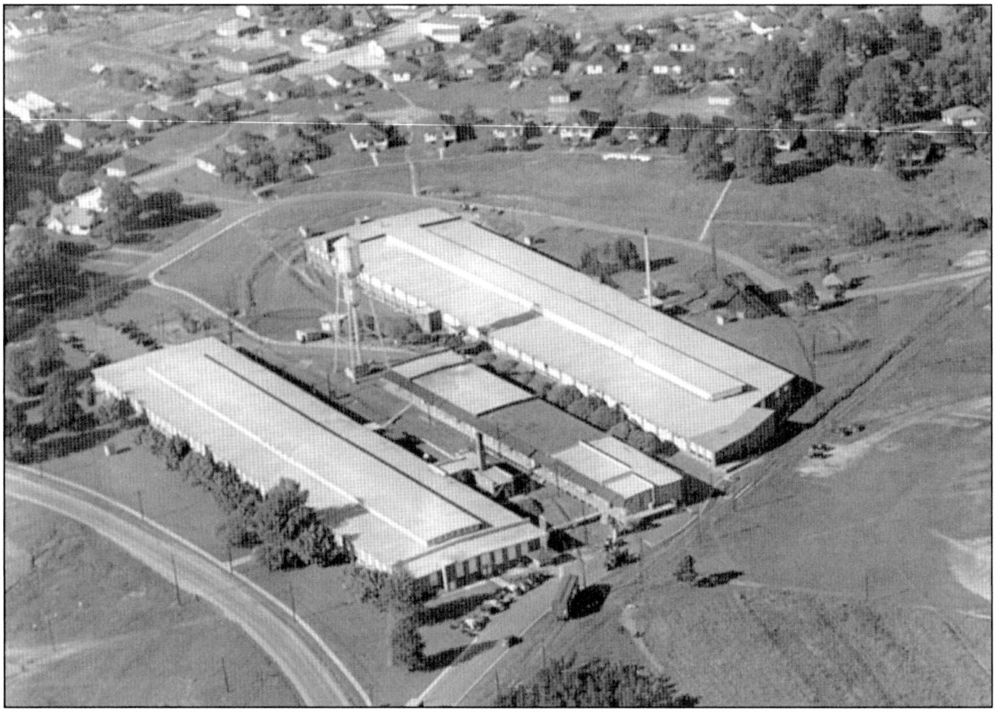

ACME MILLS 1 AND 2. Pictured are the two Acme Mills. This picture is unique in that it depicts most all the components of a typical mill village. Here, in addition to the mills themselves, one can see a water tank, railroad tracks, smokestack, loading dock, parking lot, and a large number of mill houses. (Courtesy of Millican Pictorial History Museum.)

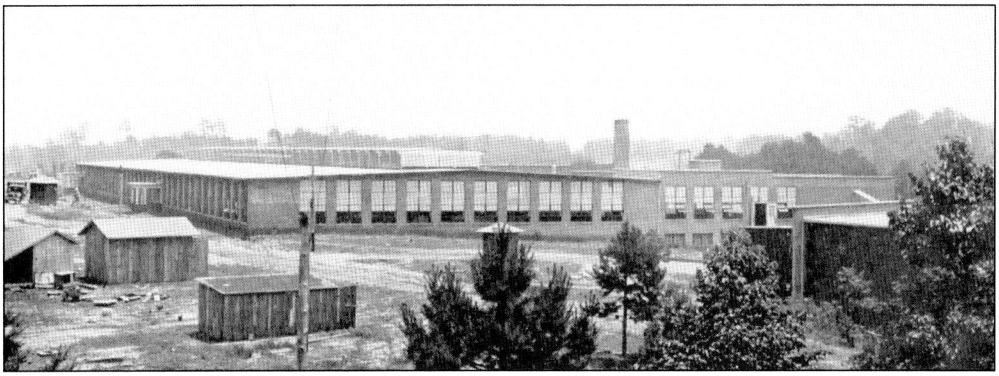

Linford Mills. A.C. Lineberger, J.E. Ford, and Will Puett (brother-in-law of R.L. Stowe) established the Linford Mills in North Belmont. Lineberger and Ford had worked together in the Tuckaseegee Mill in Mount Holly. The Linford Mills, Inc. was one of four cotton textile mills that were built and started operations in 1920. (Courtesy of Millican Pictorial History Museum.)

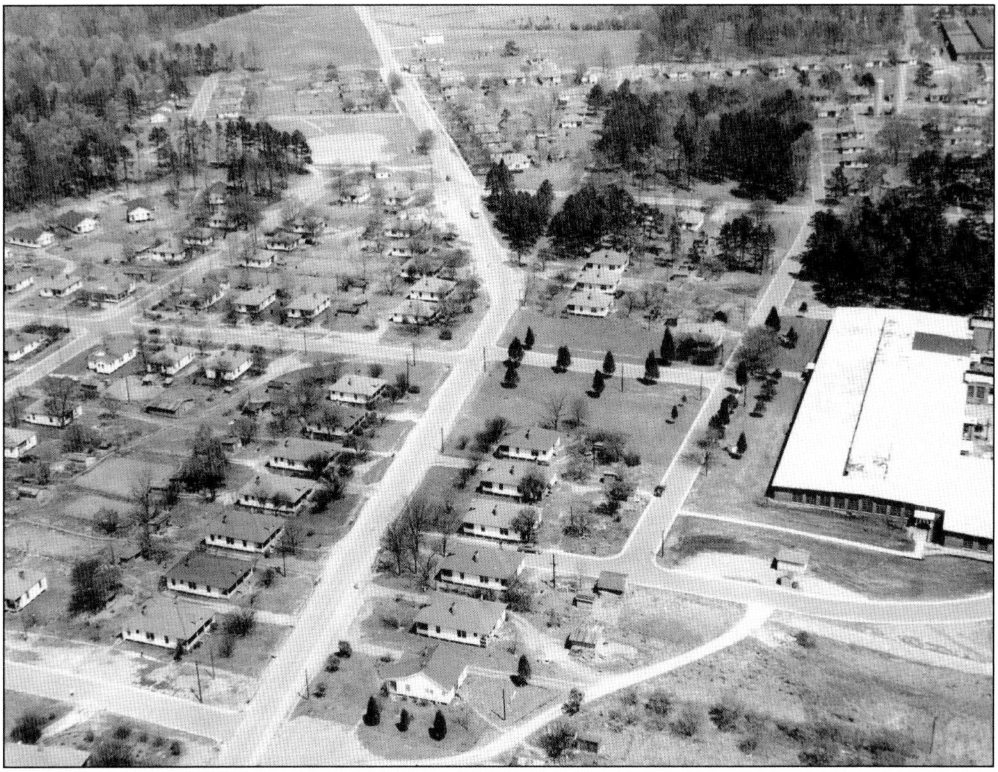

Perfection and Linford Mills Villages. This aerial view illustrates what a mill village looks like. The houses' close proximity to the mills afforded convenient living quarters at a very affordable cost to the workers. A mill whistle summoned the workers to their shifts at 6:00 a.m., 2:00 p.m., and 10:00 p.m. These two mills were organized in the early 1920s. (Courtesy of Millican Pictorial History Museum.)

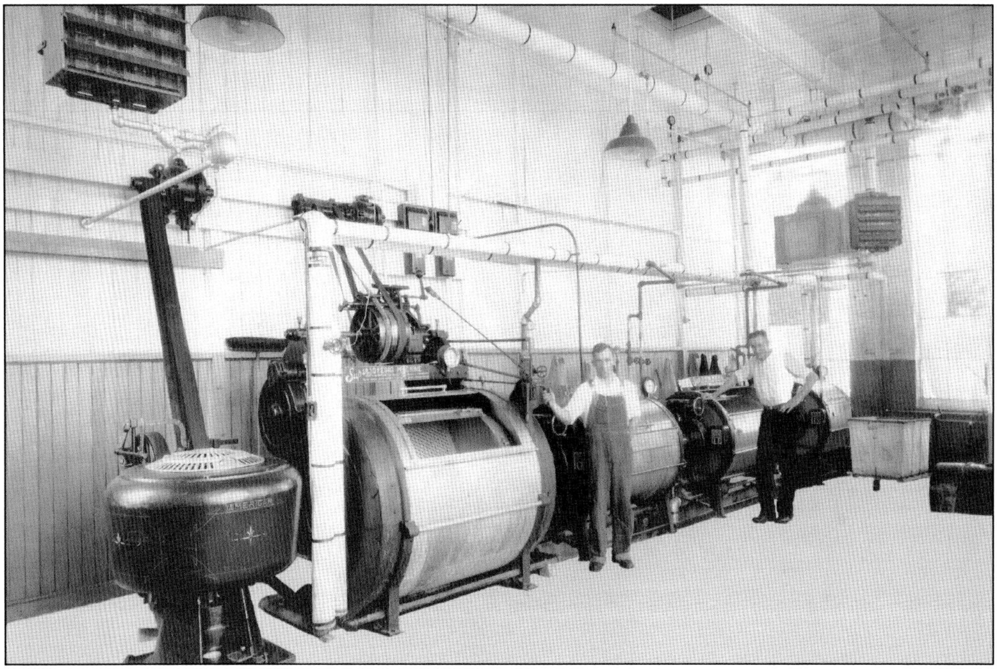

Hatch Hosiery Dye House, 1928. Hatch Hosiery was one of the first departures from strictly cotton spinning mills. This picture depicts the dyeing component of women's hosiery manufacturing. Making full-fashioned hose provided a cleaner work environment for employees, and they had a slight wage advantage over those in the cotton mills. Their directors petitioned the North Carolina General Assembly to allow Belmont to extend its city limits to include Hatch Hosiery and the South Fork Manufacturing Company. This action allowed Belmont to pave streets as well as provide a sewage system and police protection. It also allowed Belmont to extend its tax base. (Courtesy of Millican Pictorial History Museum.)

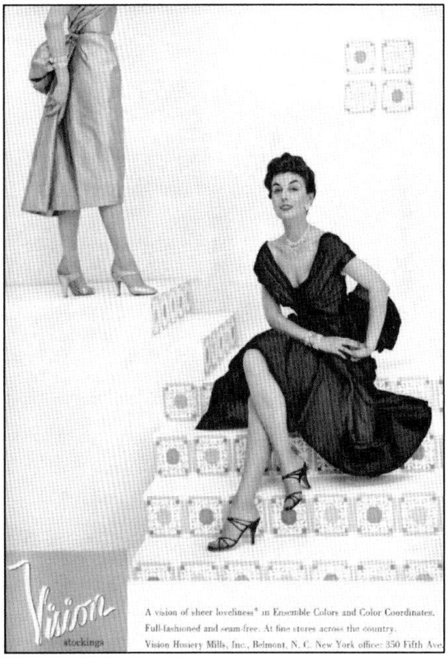

Vision Hosiery Advertisement. Manufacturer of women's seamless hosiery, Vision Hosiery Mills, Inc. produced a product that was popular throughout the United States. The company hired highly skilled workers to work in its plant and paid them higher wages than other local manufacturers. The plants were air-conditioned and offered a cleaner working environment than the cotton mills in the area did. (Courtesy of Millican Pictorial History Museum.)

STOCK CERTIFICATE OF STOWE SPINNING, NORTH BELMONT. This is a blank stock certificate for the Stowe Spinning Company that was valued at $100, a substantial amount of money at the time it was available. The total authorized stock value at this time was $1.8 million. (Courtesy of Millican Pictorial History Museum.)

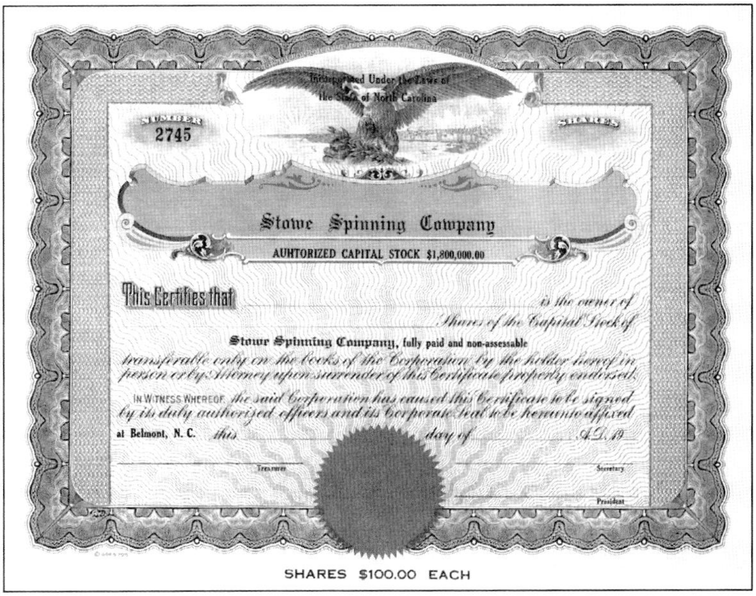

Incorporated Under the Laws of the State of North Carolina

NUMBER 2745 — SHARES

Stowe Spinning Company

AUHTORIZED CAPITAL STOCK $1,800,000.00

This Certifies that ______ is the owner of ______ Shares of the Capital Stock of Stowe Spinning Company, fully paid and non-assessable transferable only on the books of the Corporation by the holder hereof in person or by Attorney upon surrender of this Certificate properly endorsed.

In Witness Whereof the said Corporation has caused this Certificate to be signed by its duly authorized officers and its Corporate Seal to be hereunto affixed at Belmont, N. C. this ______ day of ______ A.D. 19__

Treasurer — Secretary — President

SHARES $100.00 EACH

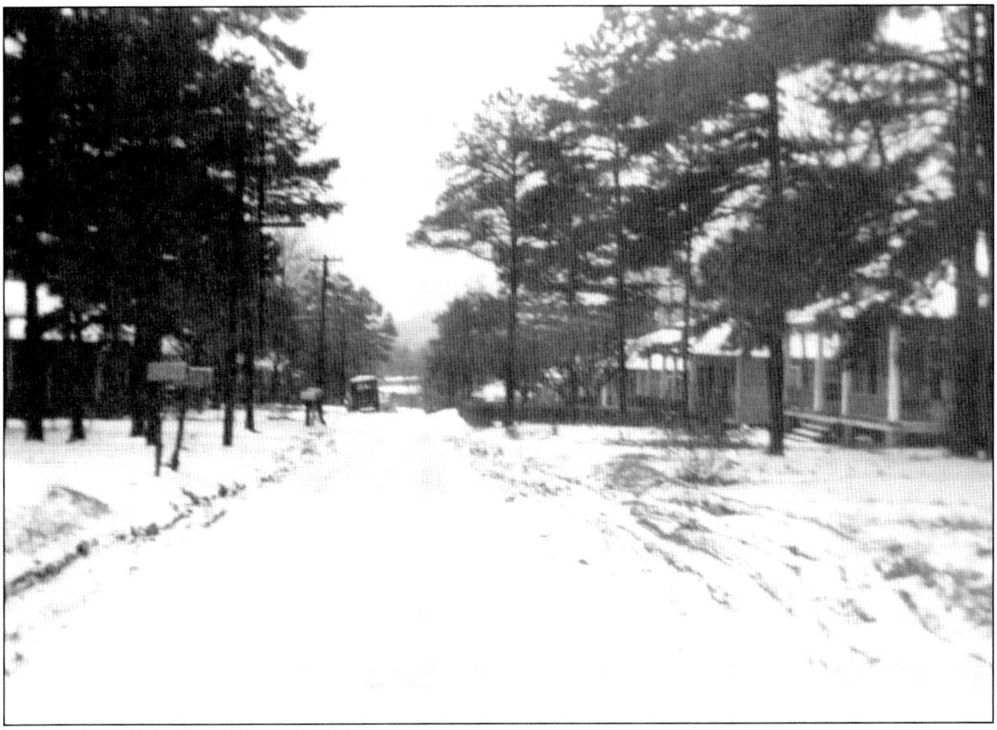

SNOWSTORM, EAGLE VILLAGE, 1938. Mill houses line the road that leads to the Eagle Mill at the foot of the hill. Above the mill on the horizon is the peak of Cramer Mountain (previously called Berry Mountain). When the snow thaws, there will be a muddy mess around the Eagle Mill Village. Most homes did not have grass in the yard or sidewalks, so feet had to be wiped carefully before entering the house. (Courtesy of Millican Pictorial History Museum.)

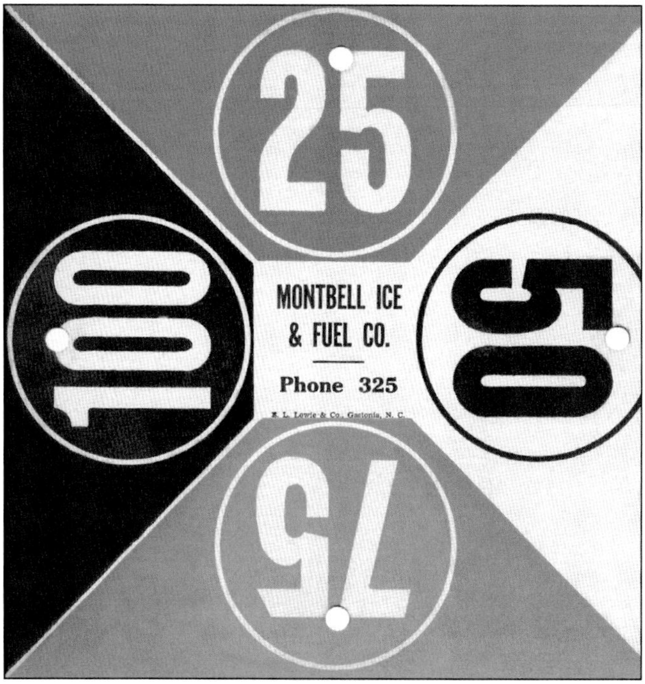

AN ICE CARD. Most mill homes had an icebox during the 1920s and 1930s. The Montbell Ice and Fuel Company provided the ice that was placed in the family icebox. A card like this was hung in a prominent place, usually on a column on the front porch. The amount of ice needed was indicated by the position of the card. In summer, children followed the ice wagon in hopes that they could salvage some ice chips—a free treat. (Courtesy of Millican Pictorial History Museum.)

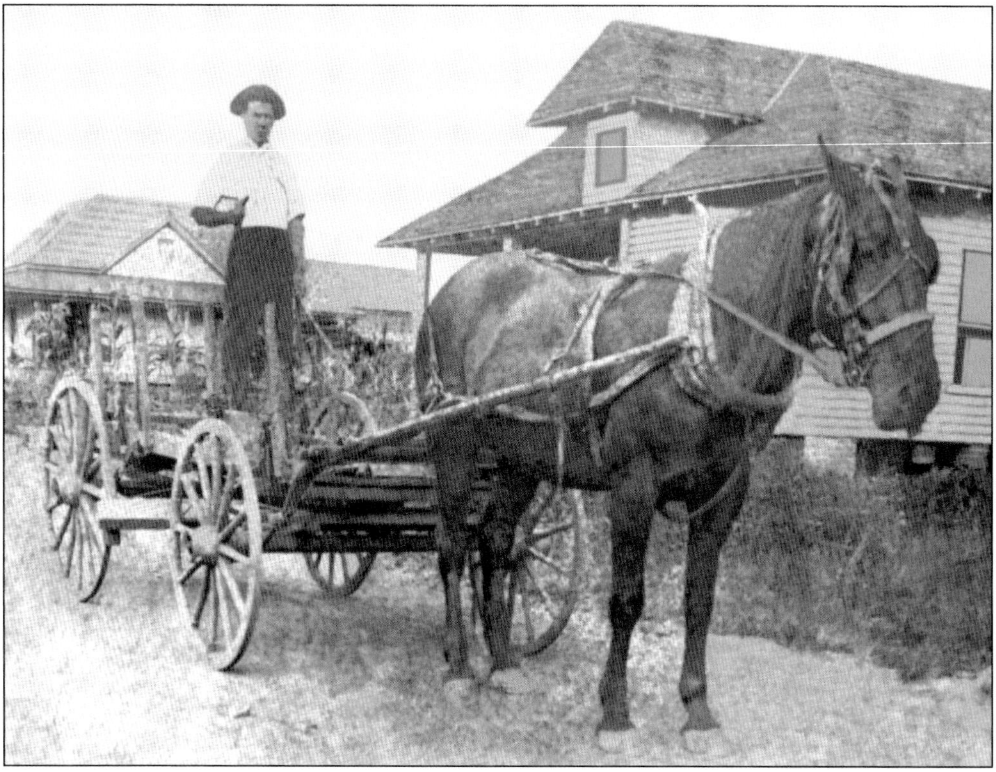

WORKER AT IMPERIAL MILL. A horse and wagon on the streets of Belmont was a common site in the 1920s. Here, William W. Crouse stands ready to haul anything that needs to be moved. He was an employee of the Imperial Mill. (Courtesy of Millican Pictorial History Museum.)

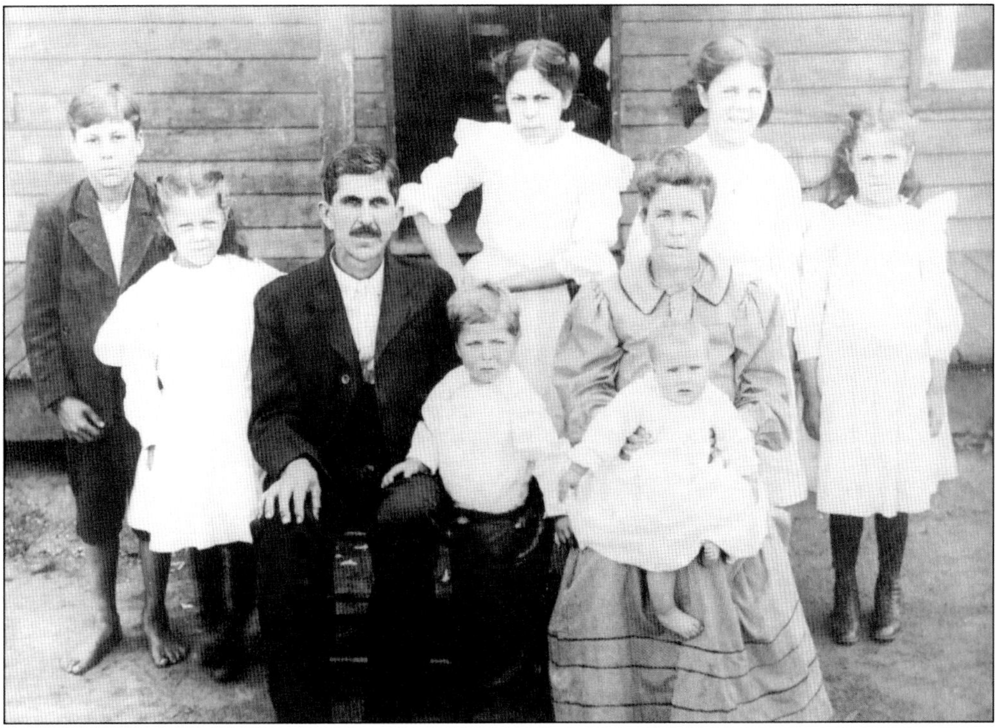

The Long Family, Early 1900s. The Long family looks rather soberly at the camera. Having one's picture taken was a serious affair. Everyone is dressed up in his or her finest, except the lad on the left of the picture, who is barefooted. This may say something about the economic times. (Courtesy of Millican Pictorial History Museum.)

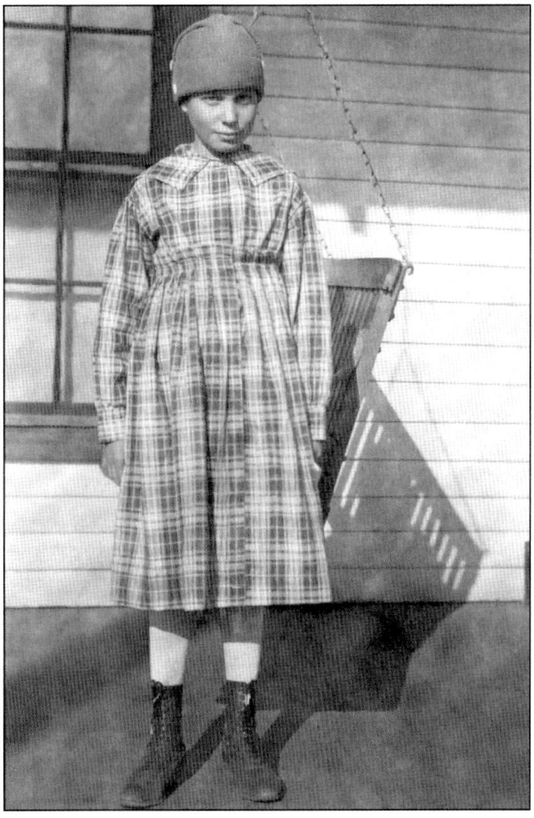

Addie Moore Rogers at the Sterling Mill Village. Standing on her porch at the Sterling Mill Village in the 1920s, Addie Moore Rogers poses in front of the ubiquitous porch swing. A porch swing was for relaxing, cooling off on hot days, and for socializing. Rogers appears to be dressed for cold weather. (Courtesy of Millican Pictorial History Museum.)

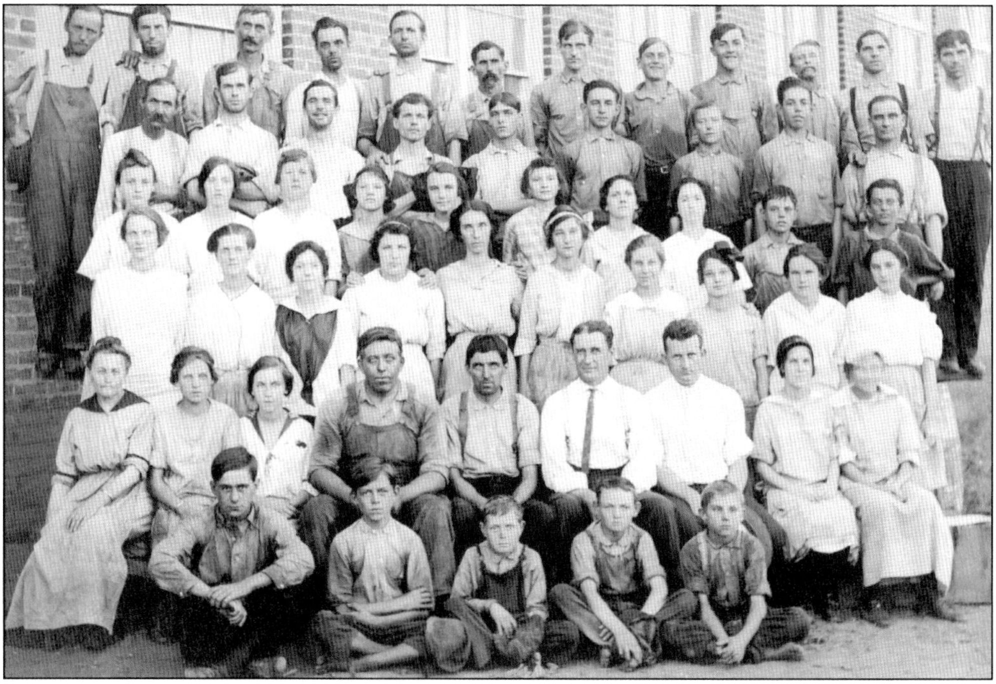

Employees at the National Yarn Mill, 1915. Men in overalls, women in long dresses, and boys in overalls pose for the camera along with the overseer at the National Yarn Mill. Most of the adults are fresh from the mountains of North Carolina, Virginia, Georgia, and Tennessee. They were attracted by recruiters who offered better housing, steady income, nearby churches, a school, and if desired, garden plots. All are seeking a better future for their families. (Courtesy of Millican Pictorial History Museum.)

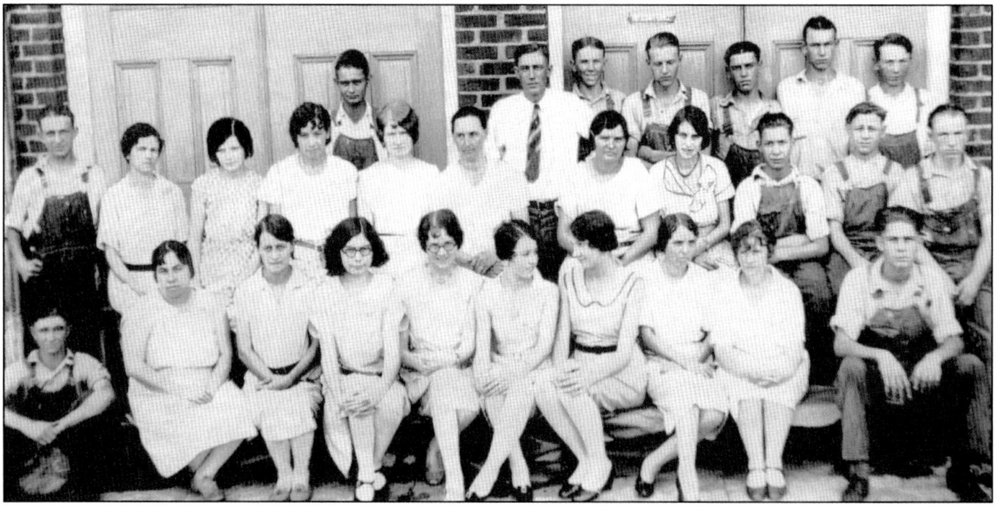

Employees of Majestic Mill. Pictured is a group of employees of the Majestic Mill, the third-oldest mill in Belmont. The building is now used as an antique mall. This is a particularly significant picture because of the dress of these employees. Notice that the women all wear mid-length cotton dresses and the men are all decked out in bib overalls, except for a supervisor, who wears a white shirt and a tie. This picture is from around 1930s. (Courtesy of Millican Pictorial History Museum.)

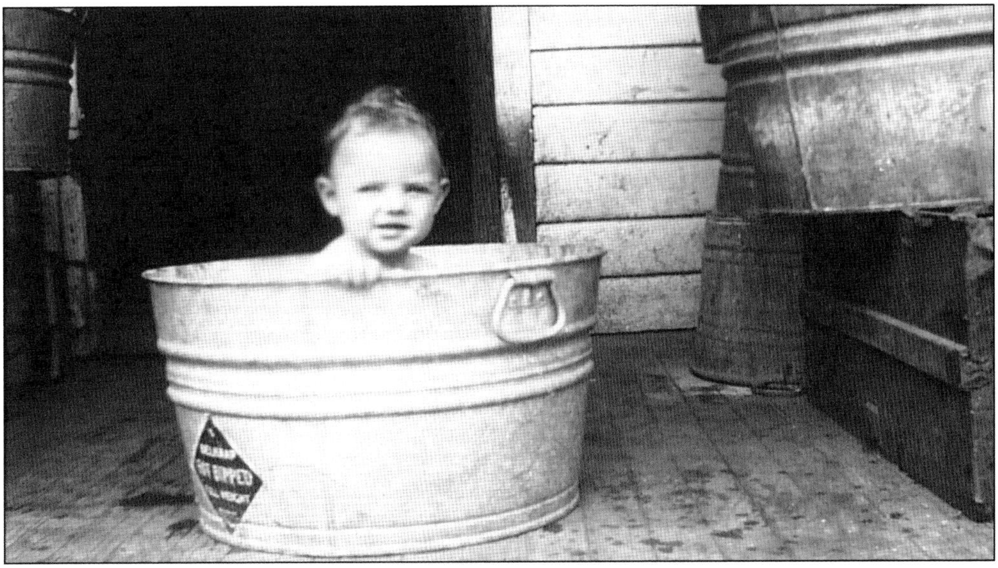

Judy Lane Hagans Taking Bath. Taking a bath in a tin tub on the back porch was a weekly routine. Judy Lane Hagans of 90 1/2 Clayton Street in Acme Village is seen getting her weekly bath. In the winter, this ritual usually took place in the kitchen near the stove, so water could be heated. There appear to be five tubs stacked and ready for Monday's washday chores. (Courtesy of Millican Pictorial History Museum.)

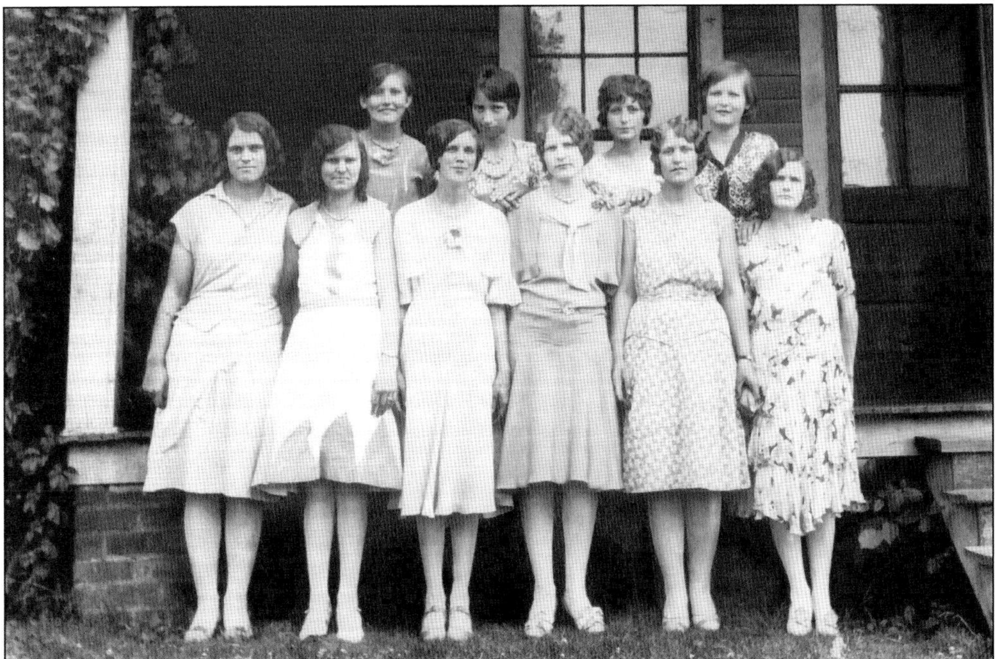

The Climax Mill Village Girl's Club. The young women from the Climax Mill Village formed a social club. They engaged in a variety of fundraisers, put on parties, and played games. They took pride in the community's appearance. This group also pitched in where there was sickness in a family by cooking, cleaning, and doing other household chores. (Courtesy of Millican Pictorial History Museum.)

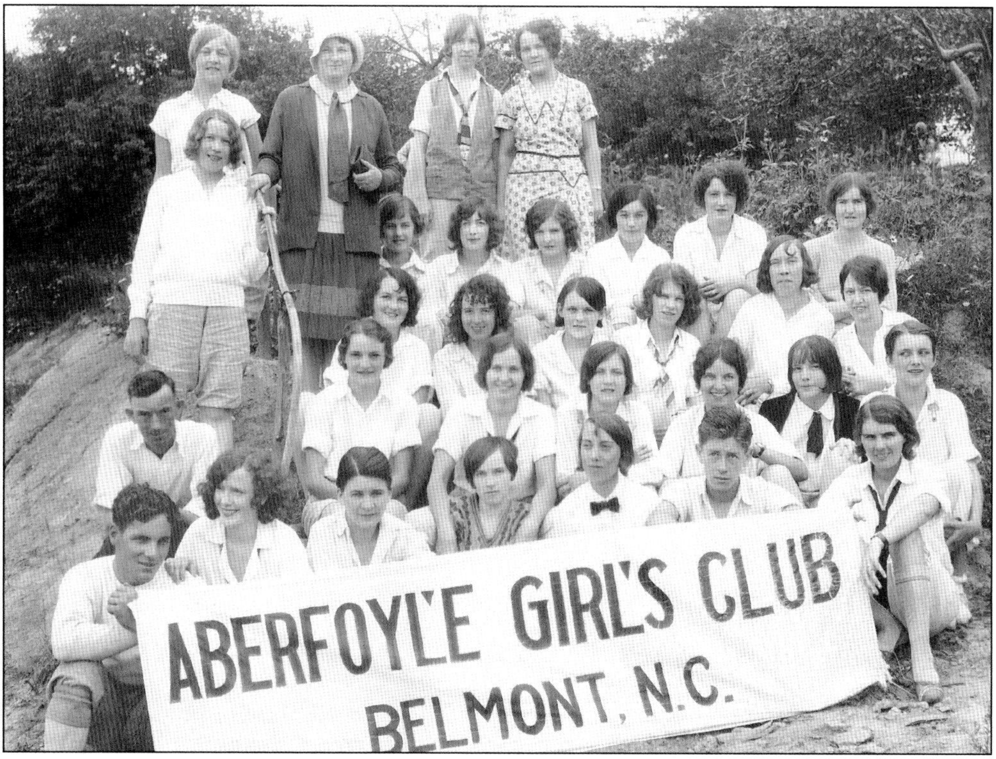

Aberfoyle Mill Girl's Club. One of the advantages of living on a mill hill was the opportunity to enjoy close fellowship with friends and neighbors. These women appear to be happy, well clothed, and likely enjoy various activities such as suppers, sewing, and playing games. Some members collected money to use for community projects and to help others in need. (Courtesy of Millican Pictorial History Museum.)

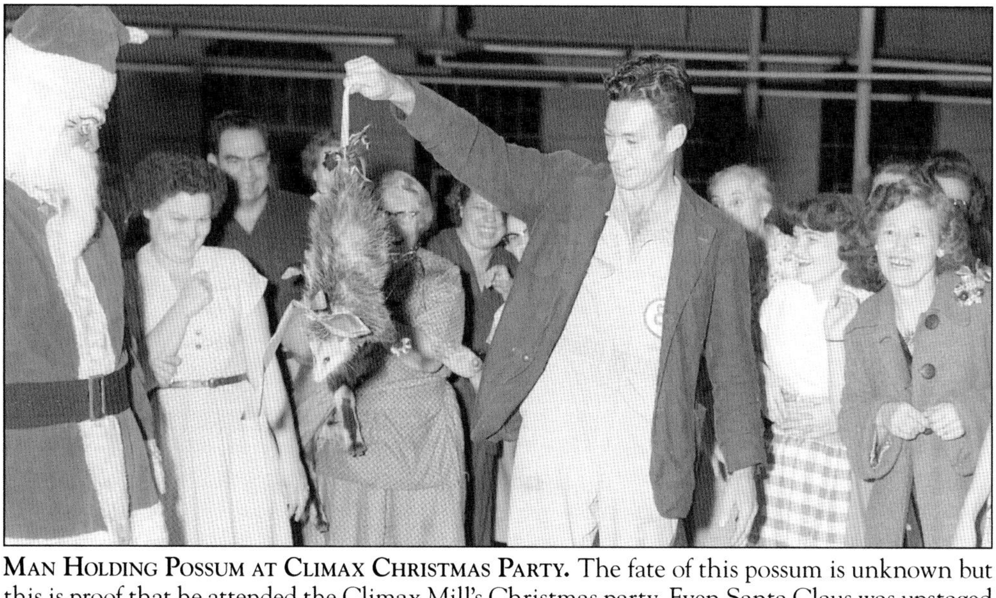

Man Holding Possum at Climax Christmas Party. The fate of this possum is unknown but this is proof that he attended the Climax Mill's Christmas party. Even Santa Claus was upstaged by this critter. (Courtesy of Millican Pictorial History Museum.)

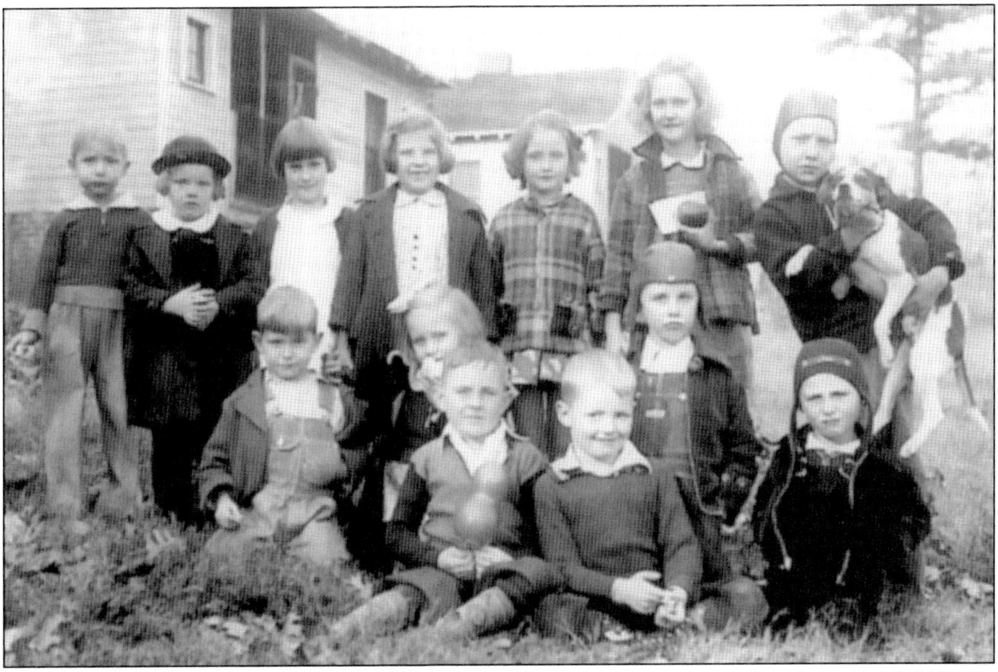

KIDS IN THE ACME MILL VILLAGE. This group of youngsters poses at the Acme Mill Village, probably in the late 1930s. All are well dressed and seem to be proud residents of the Acme Mill Village in North Belmont. Note the three boys on the right who are sporting aviation helmets, a popular choice of headgear for the boys during the days of barnstormers, who flew open-cockpit airplanes. The dog is unidentified. (Courtesy of Millican Pictorial History Museum.)

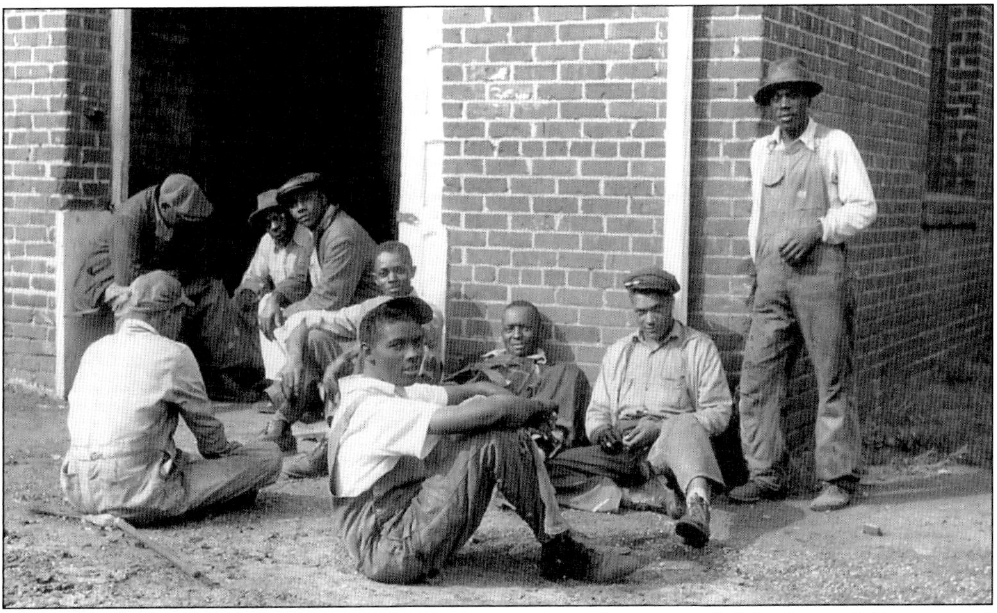

ACME SPINNING MILL WORKERS TAKE A BREAK, 1960S. These men did the heavy lifting around the Acme Spinning Mills. They moved cotton bales from the warehouse into the mill. They also kept the plant clean and orderly and did work around the mill yard. (Courtesy of Millican Pictorial History Museum.)

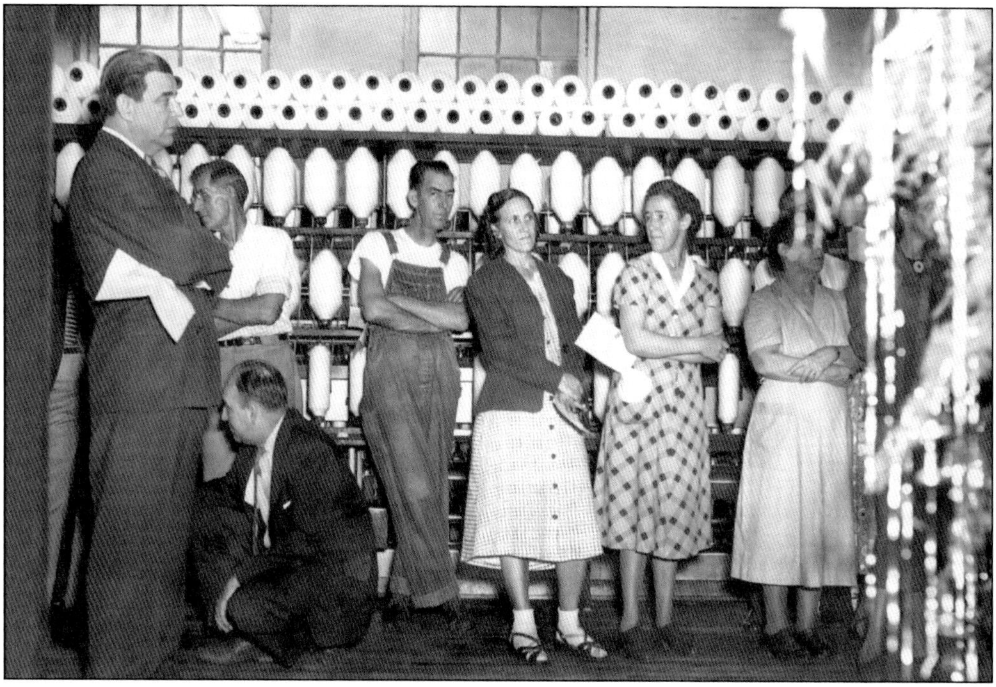

Robert Lee Stowe Jr. Visits Chronicle Mill. Robert Lee Stowe Jr. was a benevolent mill executive, but he was also a strict businessman. In this picture, Stowe tries to engage in conversation with some employees at the Chronicle Mill, but they seem to be intimidated. After all, he had the power to hire and fire. Stowe's actions bear out his reputation of being a fair employer. (Courtesy of Millican Pictorial History Museum.)

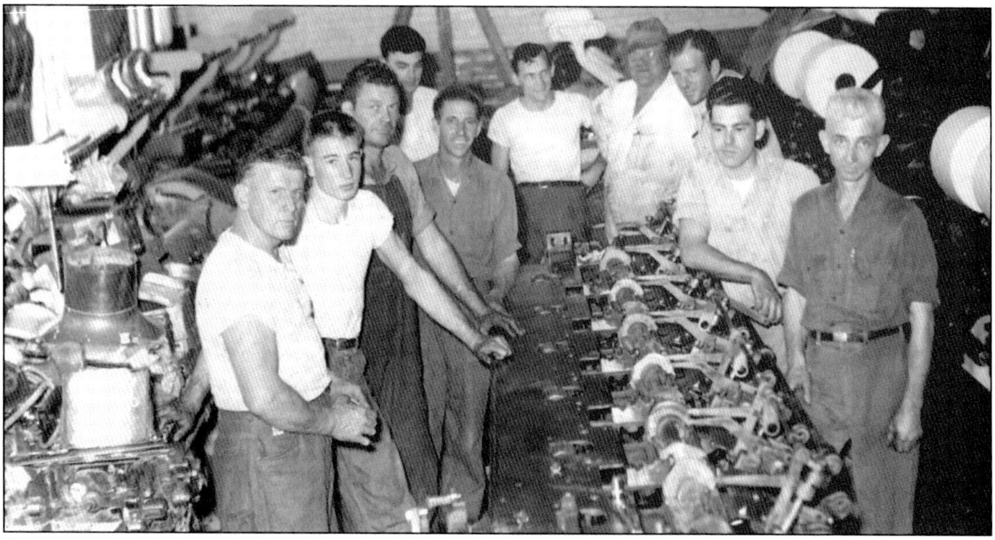

Climax Spinning Employees, 1950. The Lineberger group purchased eight used comber frames with a plan to overhaul them and put them in production. Roy Lawing (first row, far right) supervised this work. The Climax comber hands operated these machines that align cotton fibers and also remove short fibers, which were sold as "waste." Waste was used as padding in upholstery, such as for car seats, cushions of various types, bedding, and anywhere padding was needed. (Courtesy of Millican Pictorial History Museum.)

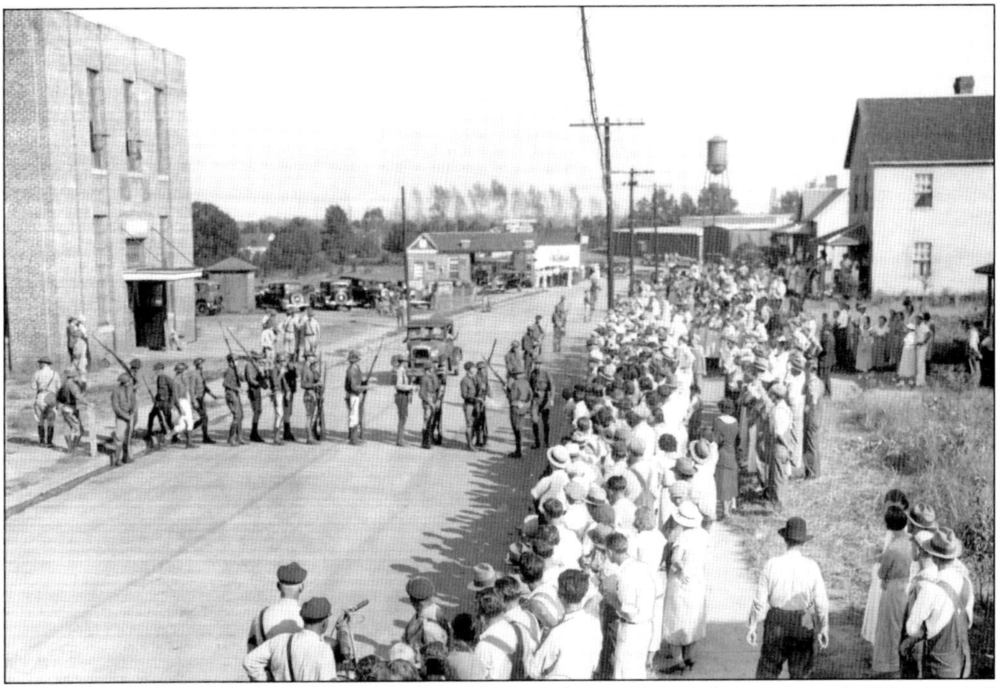

Strike at Knit Products, 1934. Union organizers from industrial centers in the North tried to organize the mill hands in Gaston County. While most of the workers in Belmont wanted no part of a union, there were enough union supporters to cause trouble through threats and actual violence. A group of textile leaders from Belmont and Gaston County went to Raleigh and appealed to Gov. John Christoph Blucher Ehringhaus for National Guard troops to be sent to Belmont to restore order. The National Guard was called out, and under the leadership of Sam Ervin (later "Senator Sam" of Watergate fame), order was restored. There was only one fatality during the course of the National Guard's activities in Belmont. The strikers were reportedly Communist inspired. (Courtesy of Millican Pictorial History Museum.)

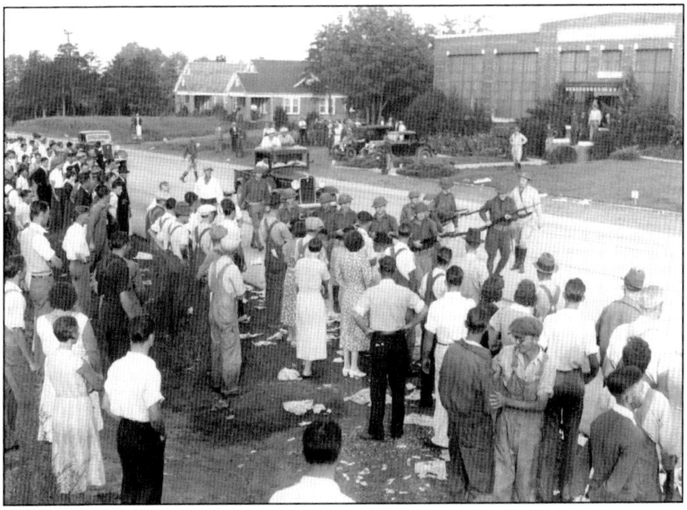

National Guard at Hatch Hosiery. The National Guard was also sent to Hatch Hosiery Mill, where Guardsmen were needed to restore order. Most of the crowd seen here are merely curious bystanders. The mill in the background is Hatch Hosiery and the highway is 29/74. (Courtesy of Millican Pictorial History Museum.)

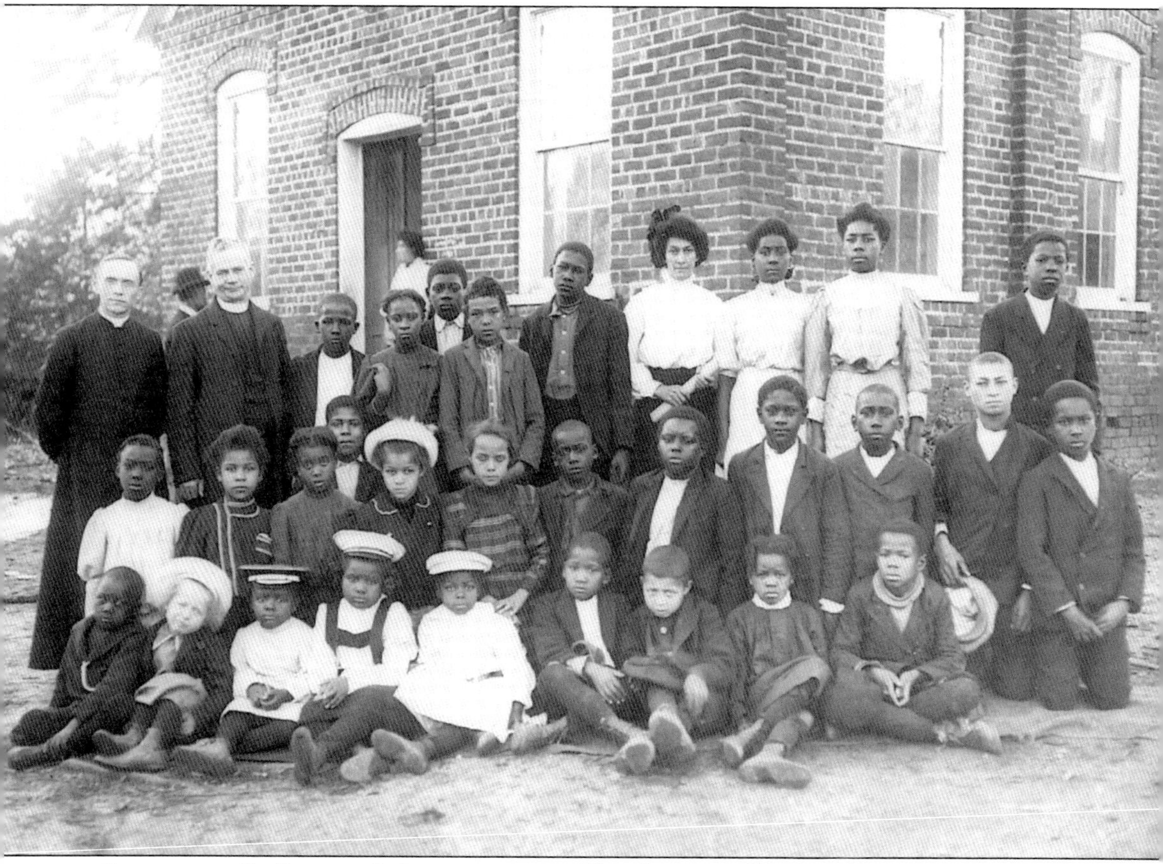

STUDENTS AT ST. BENEDICT'S SCHOOL, C. 1907. The education of black students was not completely neglected in early Belmont. Pictured here are two Benedictine monks and their pupils at St. Benedict's School in 1907. These students were very fortunate to have the educational opportunities offered by the Catholics. Public educational opportunity in North Carolina for African Americans was inferior compared to what white students had at this time. (Courtesy of Millican Pictorial History Museum.)

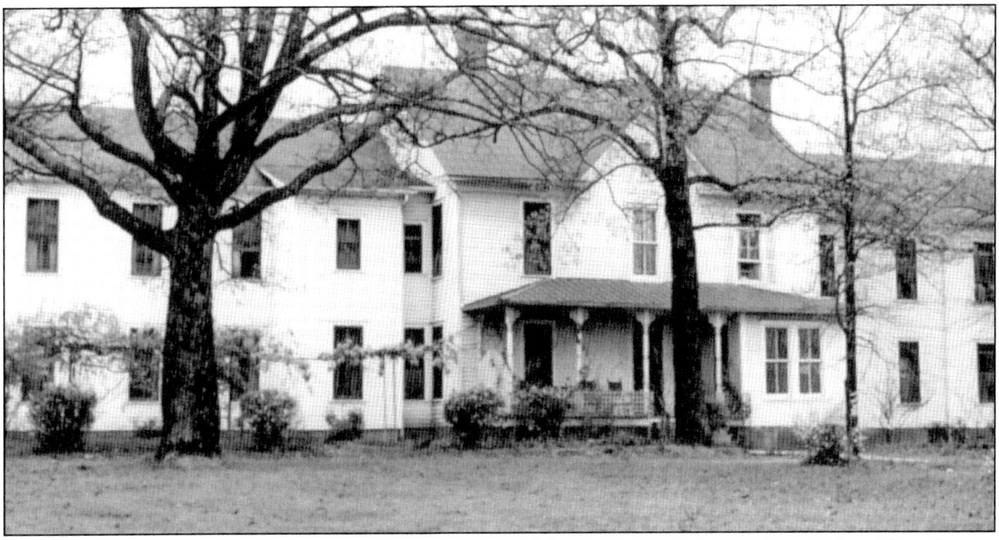

St. Leo's Academy. Standing near the grounds of the present Queen of Apostles Church was St. Leo's Academy, a private military boarding and day school that was begun by Belmont Abbey in 1910. The boys could be seen marching across Main Street to the Sacred Heart Campus for classroom instruction. The academy, which closed in 1962, was attended by boys from many states as well as some local students. (Courtesy of Millican Pictorial History Museum.)

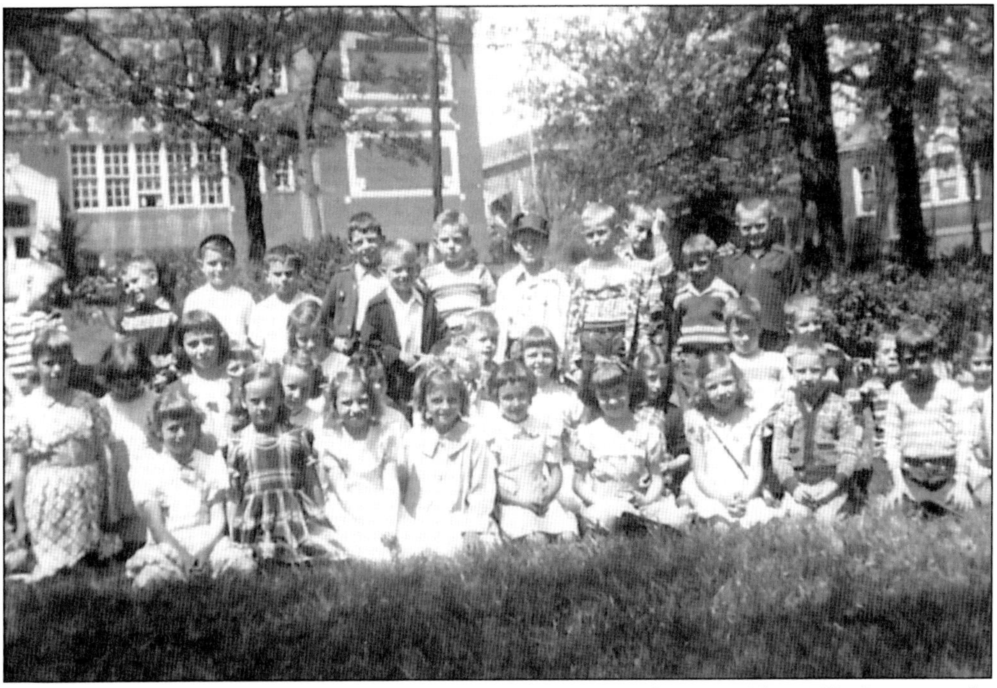

Kathleen Nichols's Second Grade at Belmont Central School. The 1950 class poses for a group picture. Behind the class stand three buildings: Belmont Central School to the left, the old Belmont High School in the center, and Belmont's First Baptist Church is on the right. The old high school building was used as an eighth-grade building for several years after the new high school was built on Central Avenue in 1939. (Courtesy of Millican Pictorial History Museum.)

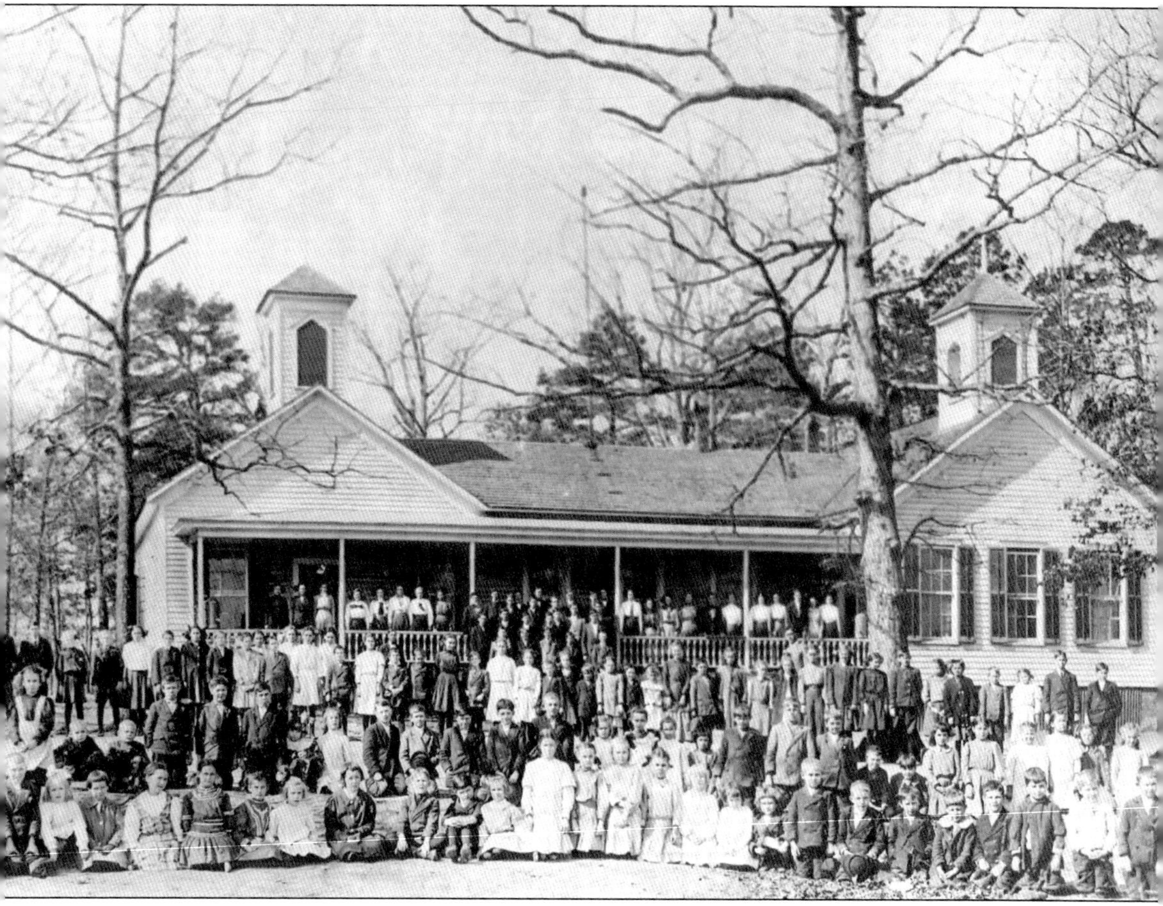

ALL GRADES, BELMONT CENTRAL SCHOOL, 1912. Prior to 1912, there were several small schools that were scattered throughout eastern Gaston County. The Belmont Central student body depicted here drew students from uptown Belmont, East Belmont, the South Point area, and the New Hope area. As time went by and the student body grew, additional buildings were erected to serve an expanded student body. More students were attending school into upper grades whereas previously most dropped out in the middle grades. This structure was replaced by several modern brick buildings. (Courtesy of Millican Pictorial History Museum.)

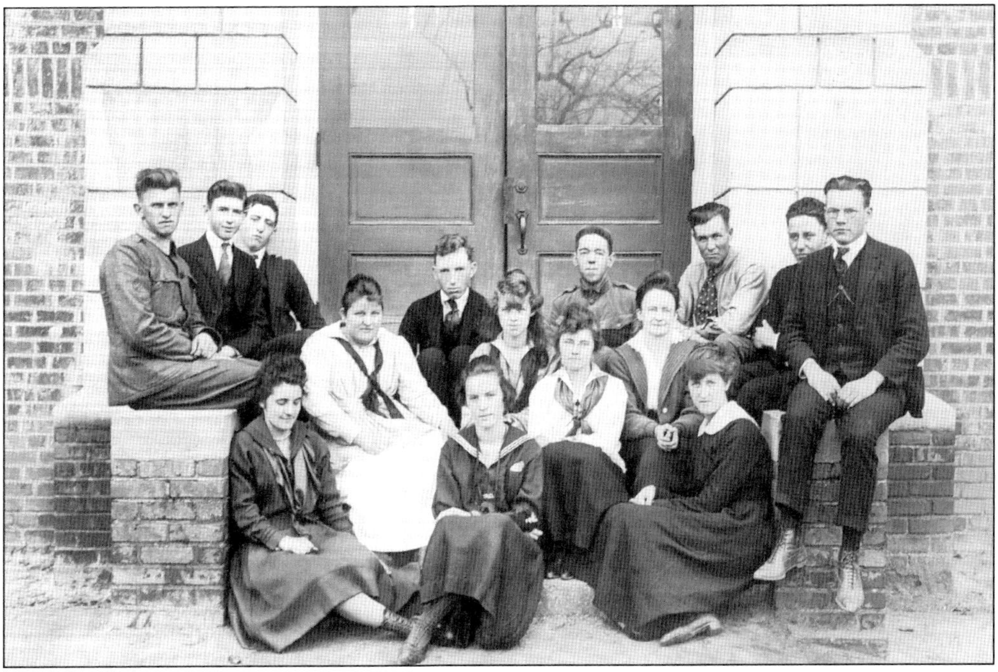

Belmont Central School's Faculty. This picture was taken of the Belmont Central School's faculty during the World War I era. All teachers had to live in private homes, be single, and be certified by the local and state boards of education. In 1926, a teacherage was constructed on the school grounds to accommodate Belmont teachers. (Courtesy of Millican Pictorial History Museum.)

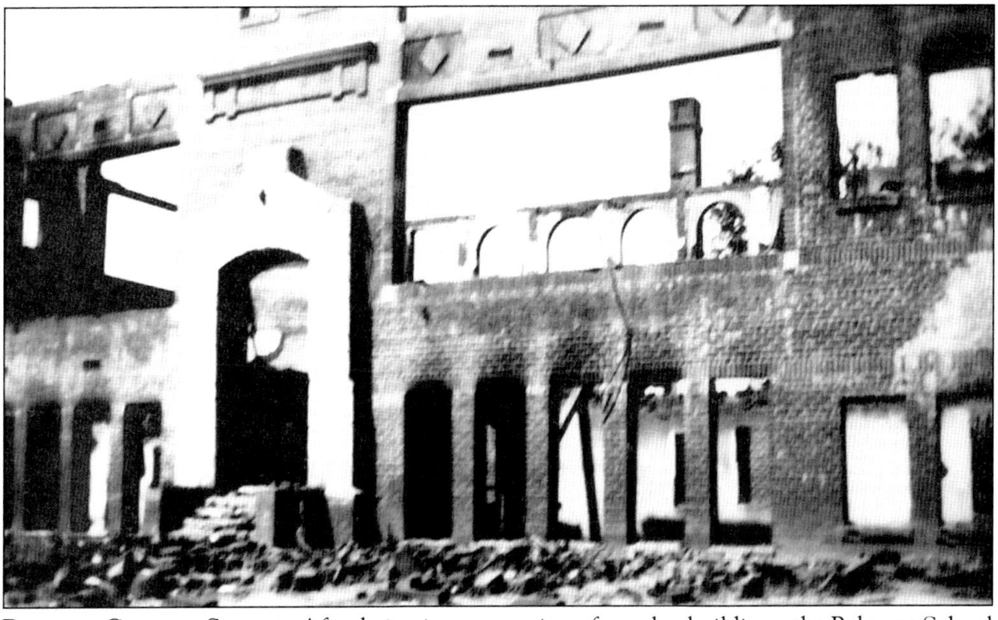

Belmont Central School. After being in a succession of wooden buildings, the Belmont School System was very proud to enter an imposing brick structure in 1921, only to see it burn in 1922. The source of the fire was undetermined. The brick shell seen here was used in the reconstruction. (Courtesy of Millican Pictorial History Museum.)

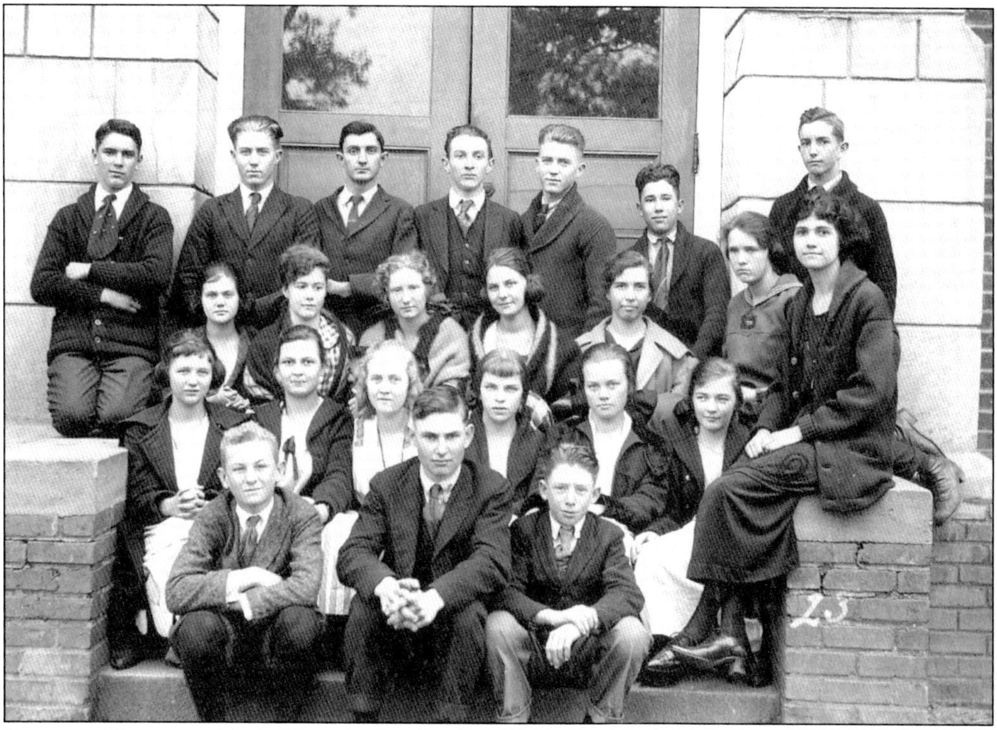

Belmont Central, 1923. These high school students pose on the front steps of Belmont Central School. The high school students shared the building with the elementary students. It would be 16 years before the beautiful Belmont High School (currently Belmont Middle School) was constructed on North Central Avenue. (Courtesy of Millican Pictorial History Museum.)

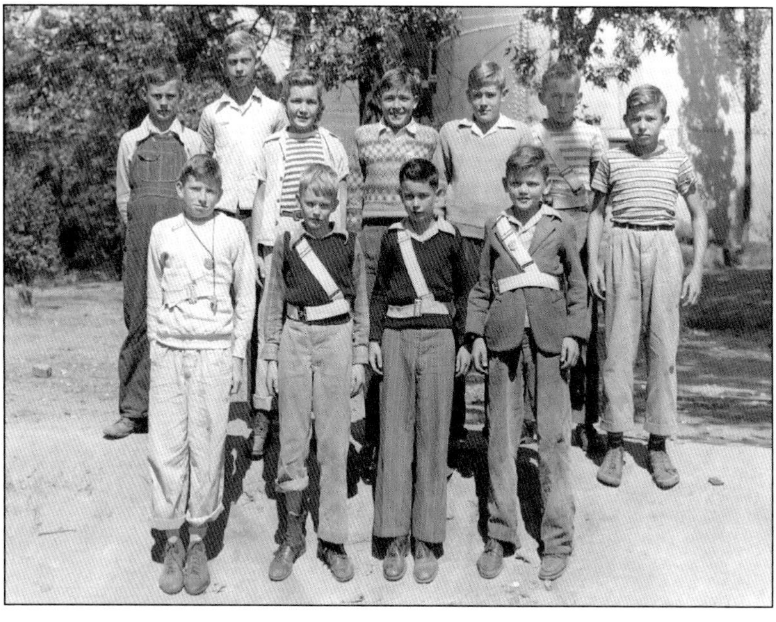

Safety Patrol at Central School in 1946. Being chosen to serve on the safety patrol was quite an honor for a student. Notice the erect posture and sense of pride these boys exhibit. They are serving at Belmont Central School in 1946. (Courtesy of Millican Pictorial History Museum.)

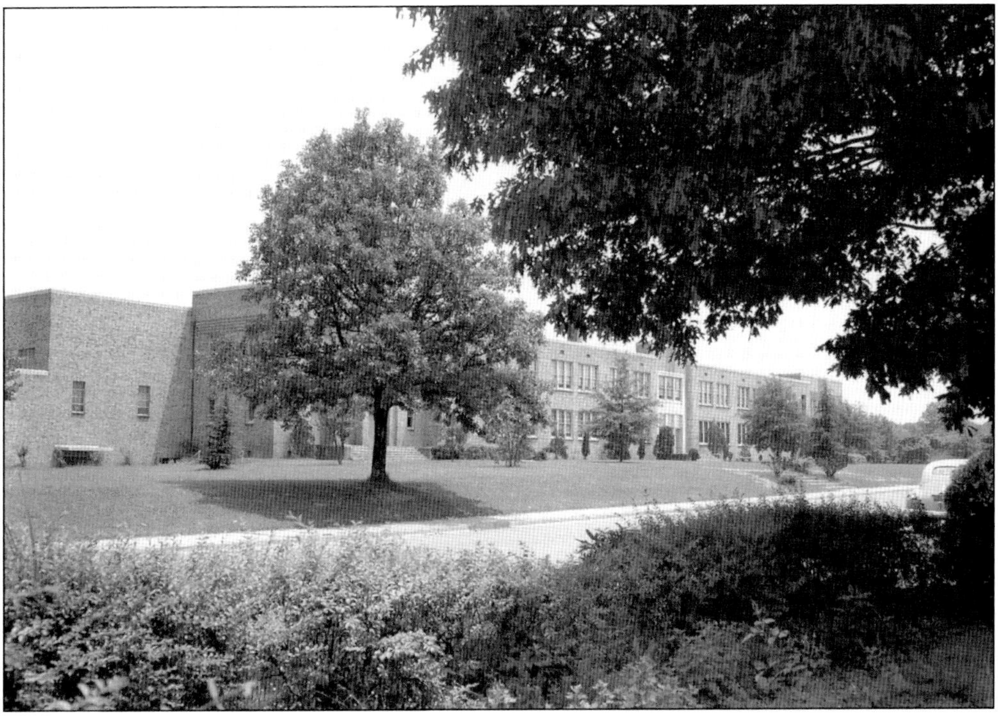

BELMONT HIGH SCHOOL. Built in 1939 by local contractor Will Hand, Belmont High School served all of the surrounding area. It replaced an inadequate building that was on the school property and faced Oak Street. The new building was equipped with a band room, full auditorium, gymnasium, and administrative offices. It also had science laboratories, a home economics lab, typing classes, and looping classes (preparatory for hosiery mill work). With the construction of South Point High in 1964, this building became Belmont Junior High School and later Belmont Middle School. (Courtesy of Millican Pictorial History Museum.)

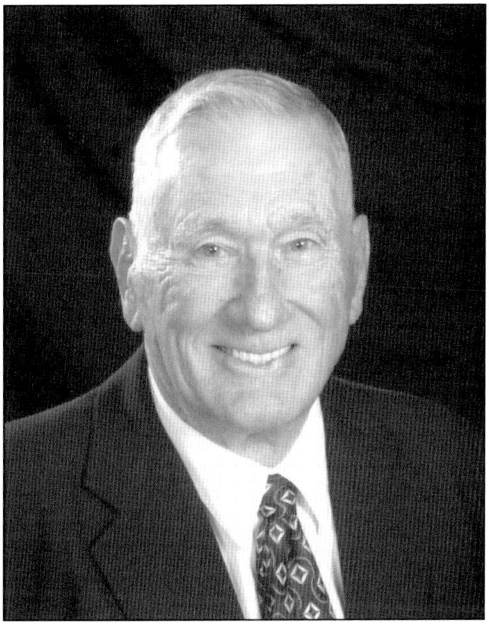

CARROL TRULL. Carrol Trull helped promote the moving of the *Spirit of the Fighting Yank*, which was located on the Belmont High School campus, to the downtown area. Carrol volunteers for the Belmont/Mt. Holly Day Care Center, and he served on the Belmont Historical Society's Board of Directors in its beginning years. He designed and promoted the placement of a monument to honor several important groups of citizens in East Belmont. A group of attractive historic maps of Belmont, East Belmont, and North Belmont was created by Carrol and made available for sale. (Courtesy of Millican Pictorial History Museum.)

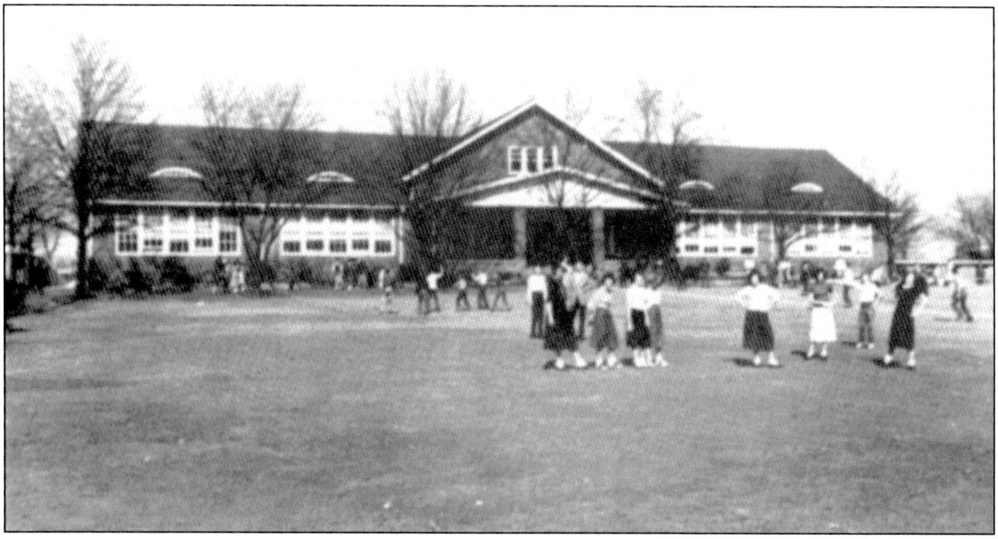

EAST BELMONT SCHOOL. Constructed in 1920, this building replaced a two-room school on the corner of Park Street and Catawba Street that had been open for first and second graders off and on since 1903. The first teacher was Ethel Stowe, daughter of the town's first postmaster, Abram Stowe. In 1909, Andrew A. Armstrong opened the building to teach first and second grades in the daytime and adults at night. Abbie Hall became principal of the newly built and renamed East School. East School had J.B. Page as principal for 18 years, and he was succeeded by Kenneth Rhyne. East Belmont School was built in 1920 to serve the students in the first through the eighth grades who lived in the eastern portion of the community. This building remained in operation until it was replaced in 1973 by a new school located on Ewing Drive named the J.B. Page Elementary School. (Courtesy of Millican Pictorial History Museum.)

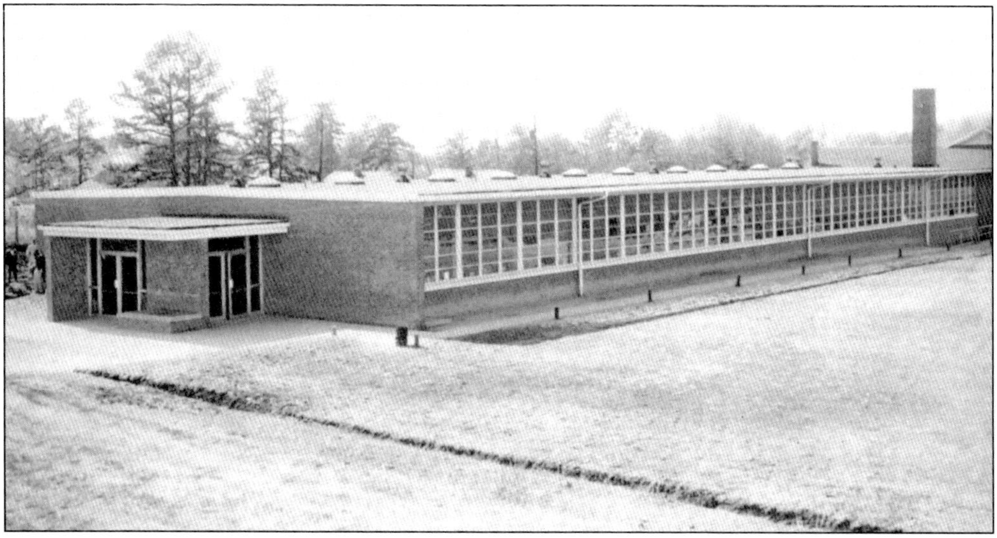

REID SCHOOL. Named for Charles Jesse Bynum Reid, this new school called Reid High School was built in the early 1950s on property traditionally home to a black school. The students in the community took great pride in their new building, which supplemented other structures on the property. When desegregation of the schools took place in 1966, this school was closed, and the students all went to the previously all-white Belmont schools. (Courtesy of Millican Pictorial History Museum.)

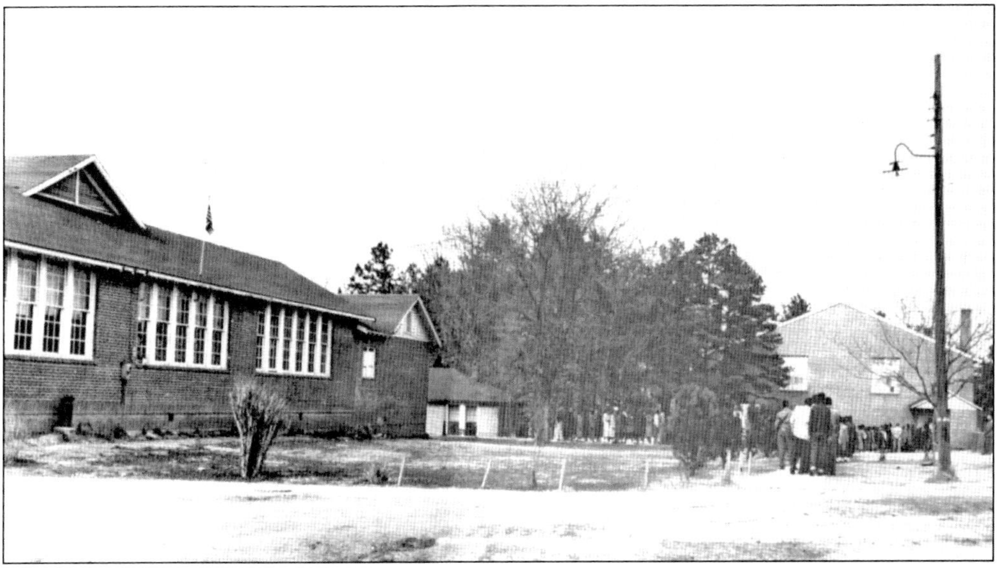

Reid School, Belmont, 1953. Reid School was named for Prof. Charles Jesse Bynum Reid, who was one of the most influential school administrators in Belmont. He came to Belmont around 1921 as a teacher and principal at the school in the black community. In 1932, the school was officially named for Professor Reid, who passed away in 1940. The school was the focal point of the Reid community, which by then also had taken his name. (Courtesy of Millican Pictorial History Museum.)

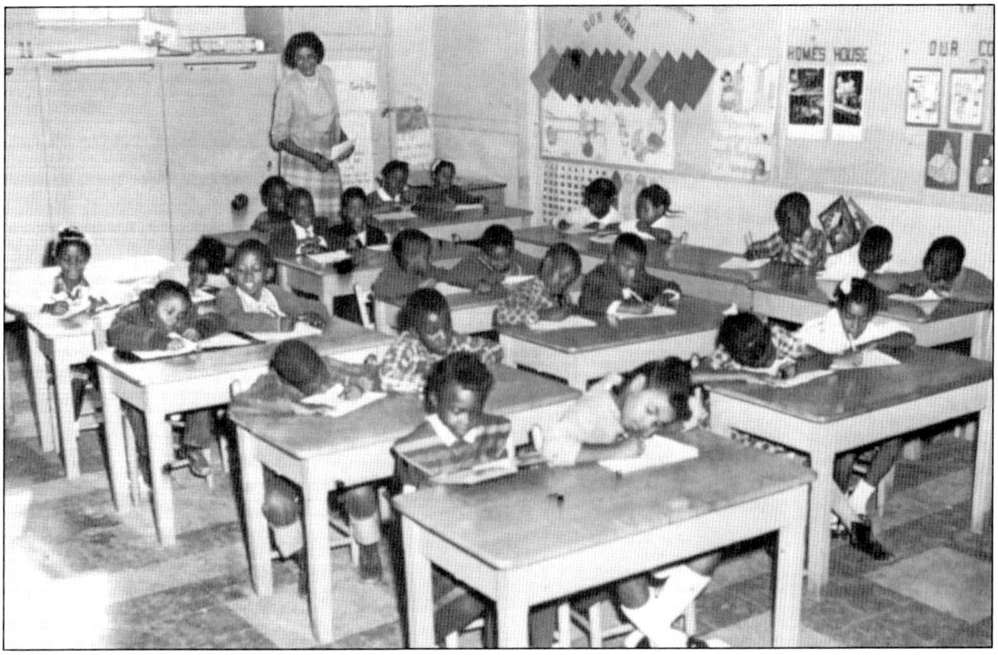

Reid School, 1963. Under the watchful eye of a teacher, these students at Reid School are diligently working. The furniture is obviously at this time out of date, since it had been discarded by some white school that had received new furniture. After desegregation, these students were integrated with the students at the traditionally white schools. (Courtesy of Millican Pictorial History Museum.)

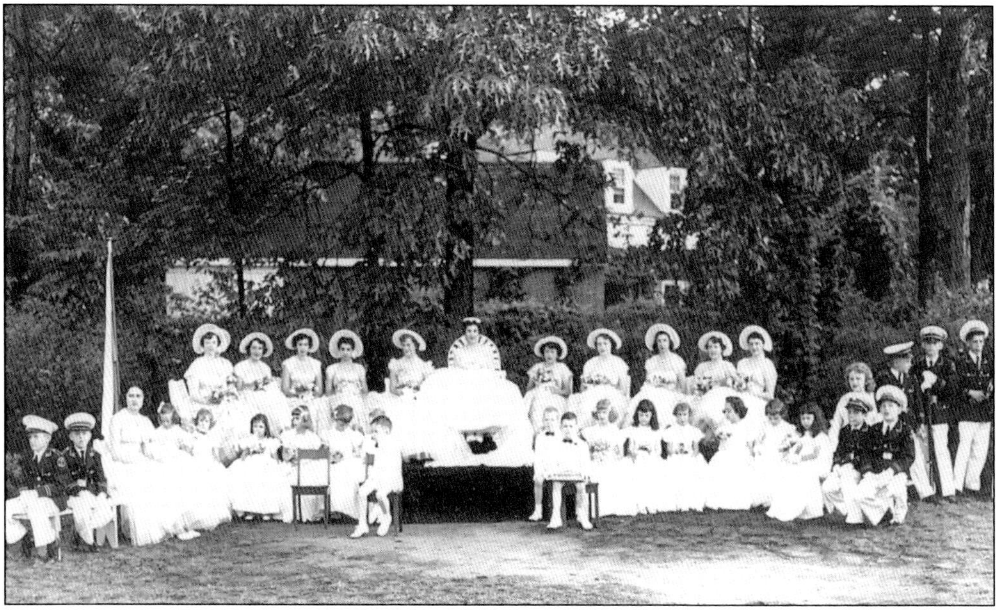

MAY DAY CELEBRATIONS AT SACRED HEART. The Sacred Heart May Day Queen is surrounded by her attendants, and they are about to begin ceremonies that will culminate with a dance around the maypole. Also included in the picture are cadets from St. Leo's Military School dressed in their uniforms. This was an annual ceremony for many years. (Courtesy of Millican Pictorial History Museum.)

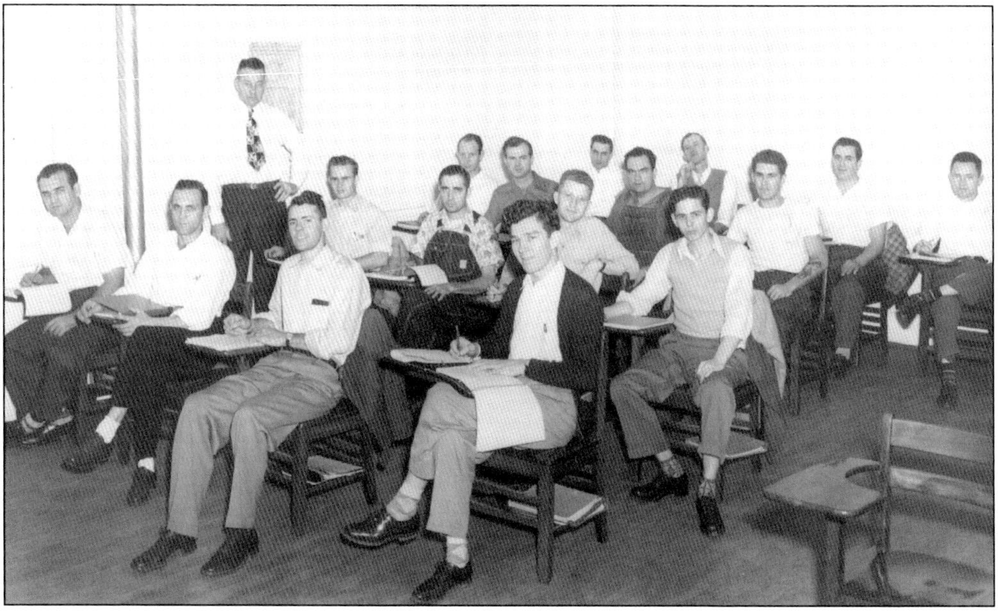

NORTH CAROLINA VOCATIONAL TEXTILE SCHOOL. In order to upgrade employees' textile skills, the State of North Carolina offered classes in cotton mill mathematics, mechanics, human relations, writing skills, and other skills applicable to textile management. Courses in textile skills were also offered to local high school students. The school is presently the East Campus of Gaston College and has a building named in honor of Duke Kimbrell, CEO of Parkdale Mills, one of the world's largest cotton-manufacturing facilities. (Courtesy of Millican Pictorial History Museum.)

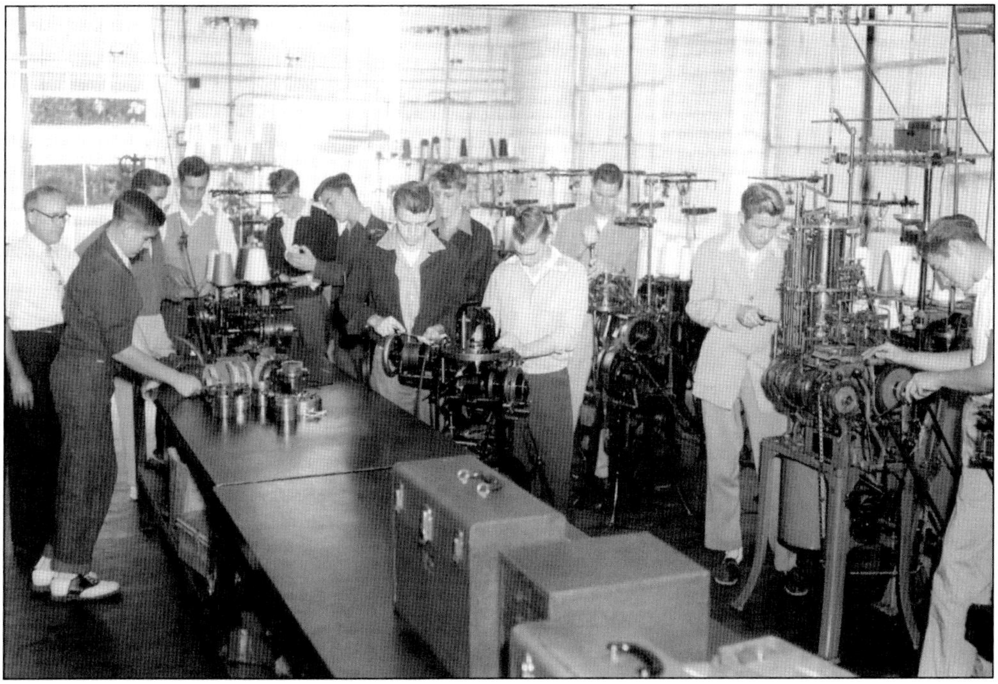

Textile Students at North Carolina Vocational Textile School, 1953. Students from the North Carolina Vocational Textile School came from two sources. One group of students was selected from textile plants by their overseers to attend school to become skilled in special areas for which they had a need. The second group of students was sent from the local high schools as a part of their course load. These students took a general survey of textile manufacturing. The building, the instructor, and machinery were funded by the state. At present, a building has been added, courses have been changed to meet today's needs, and the school is now a part of Gaston College, known as the Duke Kimbrell campus. (Courtesy of Millican Pictorial History Museum.)

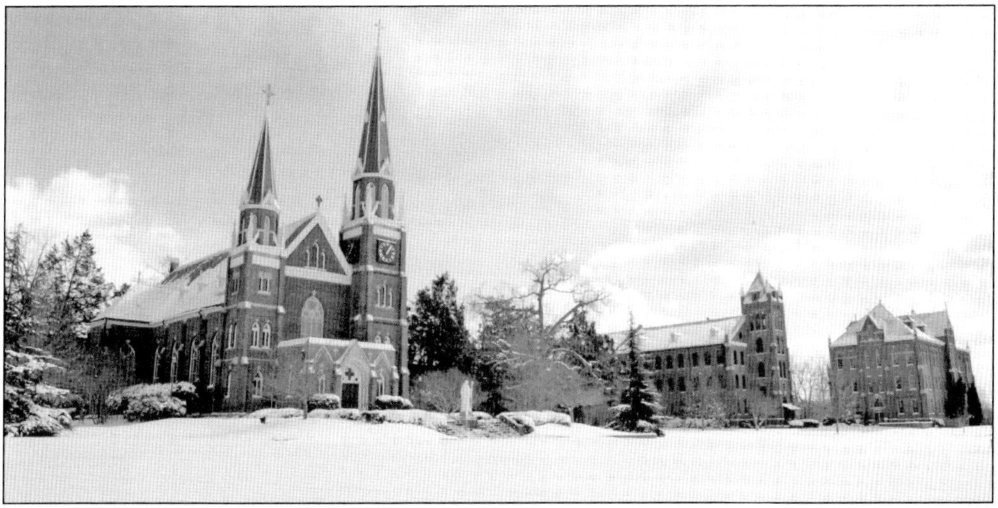

Snowstorm at Belmont Abbey. A recent snowfall on the campus of Belmont Abbey College magnifies its beauty. The buildings are, from left to right, Belmont Abbey Cathedral, the Monastery, and the Robert Lee Stowe Hall, which houses the administrative offices. (Courtesy of Millican Pictorial History Museum.)

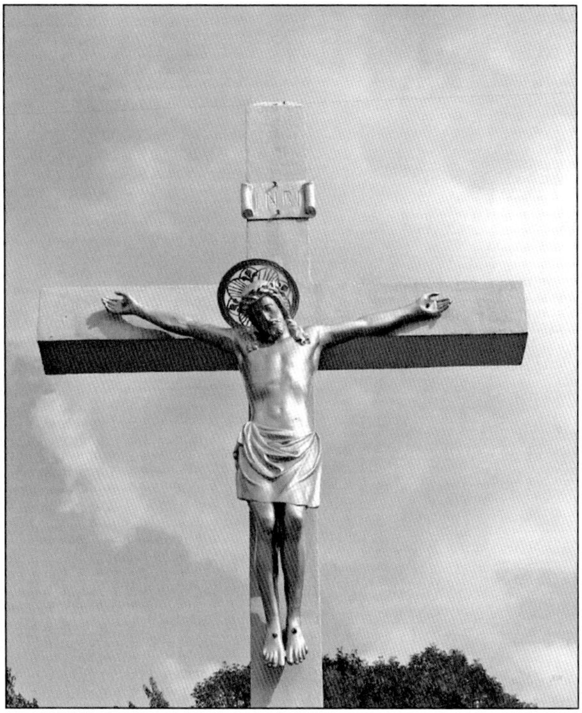

Jesus on the Cross. Belmont Abbey College emphasizes its mission to impart Christian values and ideals to its students. It does also, however, offer a broad survey of other major religions throughout the world for students who are interested. (Courtesy of Millican Pictorial History Museum.)

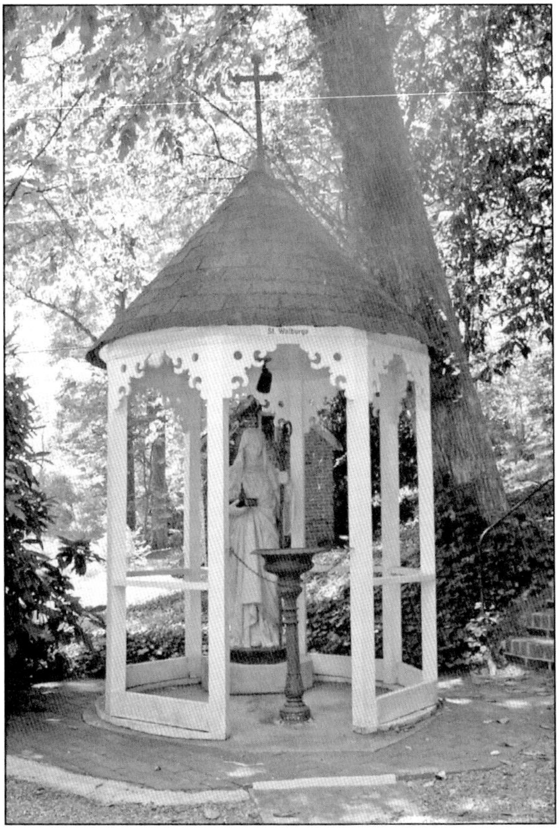

St. Walburga at Belmont Abbey. St. Walburga Fountain is one of the many sacred spots students can enjoy on the Belmont Abbey College campus. (Courtesy of Millican Pictorial History Museum.)

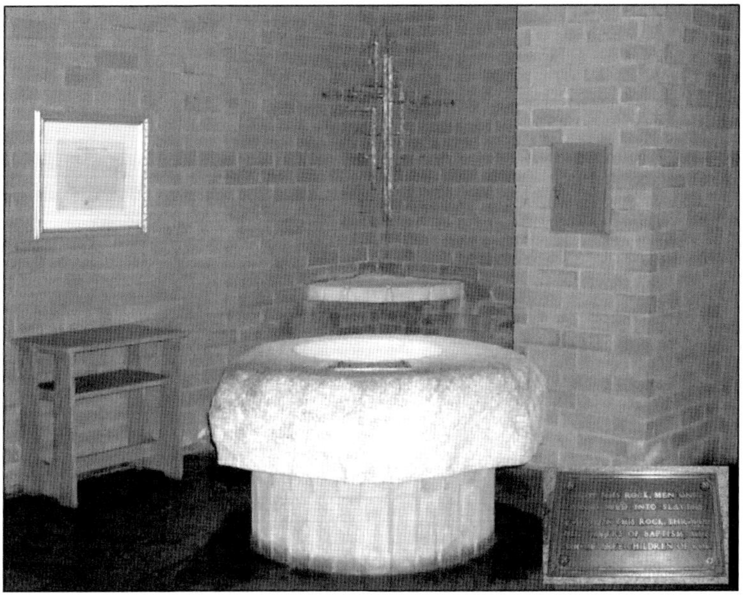

GRANITE BLOCK, NOW A CAMPUS LANDMARK. This plaque reads, "Upon this rock, men once were sold into slavery. Now upon this rock, through the waters of Baptism, men become free children of God." This stone, which stands in the foyer of Belmont Abbey Cathedral, is now used as a baptismal font and has become a campus landmark. (Courtesy of Millican Pictorial History Museum.)

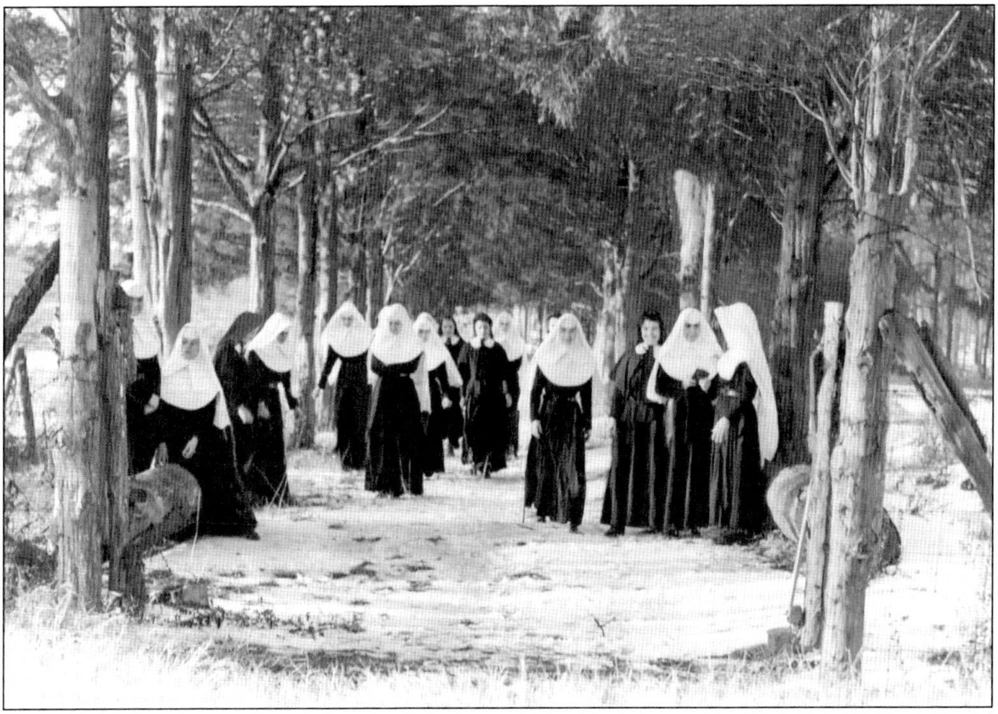

SISTERS OF MERCY. Smiling, the Sisters of Mercy of Sacred Heart enjoy a wintertime stroll and camaraderie. They are dressed in their traditional habits, which will soon be modernized. The sisters performed many duties, including nursing, teaching, private tutoring, caring for less fortunate people, and private music lessons. Some years later, this order sold the Mercy Hospital in Charlotte and invested the proceeds in many worthwhile endeavors. (Courtesy of Millican Pictorial History Museum.)

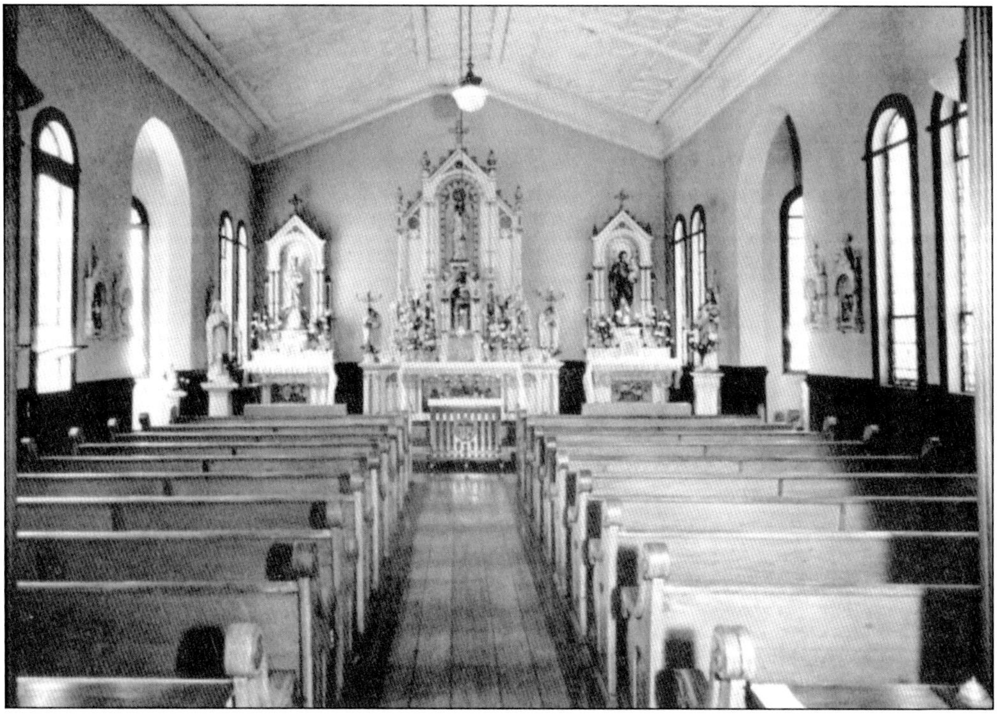

Sacred Heart Sanctuary, 1943. This Sacred Heart sanctuary provided a spiritual respite from the academic studies for the girls attending school there. The décor engendered an atmosphere conducive to meditation and worship. (Courtesy of Millican Pictorial History Museum.)

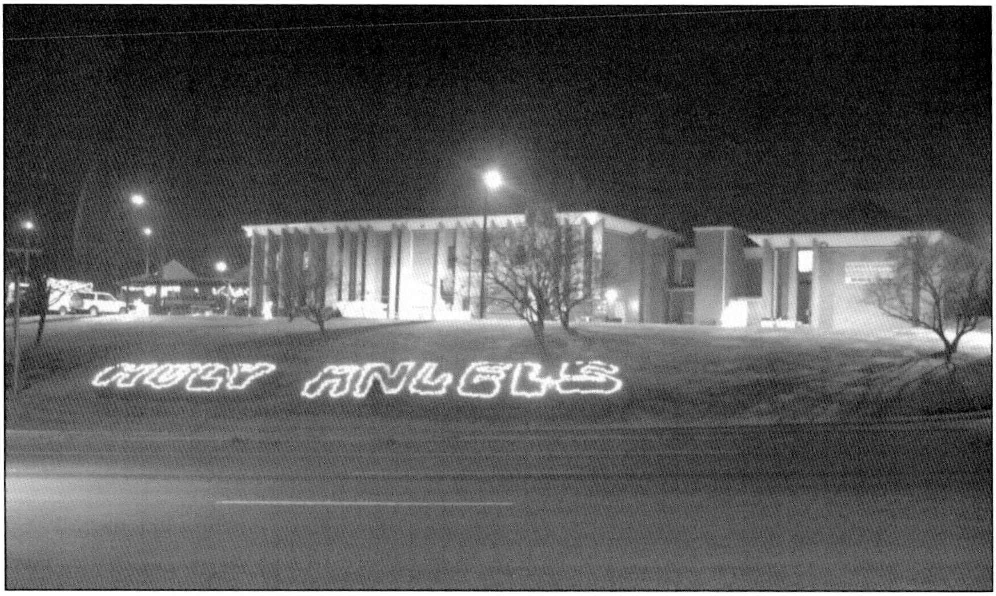

Holy Angels. Holy Angels got its start in the 1950s and became a residential center for the health-care treatment and development for severe mentally and physically handicapped children. The first child enrolled became the inspiration for the Maria Morrow Center, a treatment and educational program begun and run by the Sisters of Mercy. (Courtesy of Millican Pictorial History Museum.)

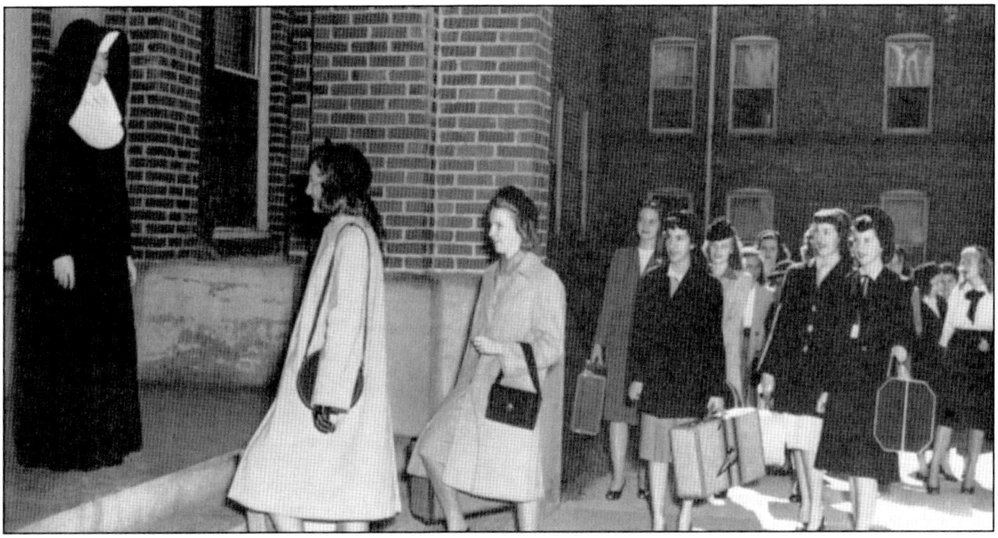

FIRST DAY AT SACRED HEART JUNIOR COLLEGE. These women being greeted by a nun on the front steps of Sacred Heart College will shortly be registering for courses, greeting new roommates, and receiving an orientation. Sacred Heart College and the convent were established in 1892 by the Sisters of Mercy. This college was an important addition to the educational opportunities for students in Belmont and surrounding areas. Students from up and down the Eastern Seaboard and from Latin American countries came to Belmont for their college education. (Courtesy of Millican Pictorial History Museum.)

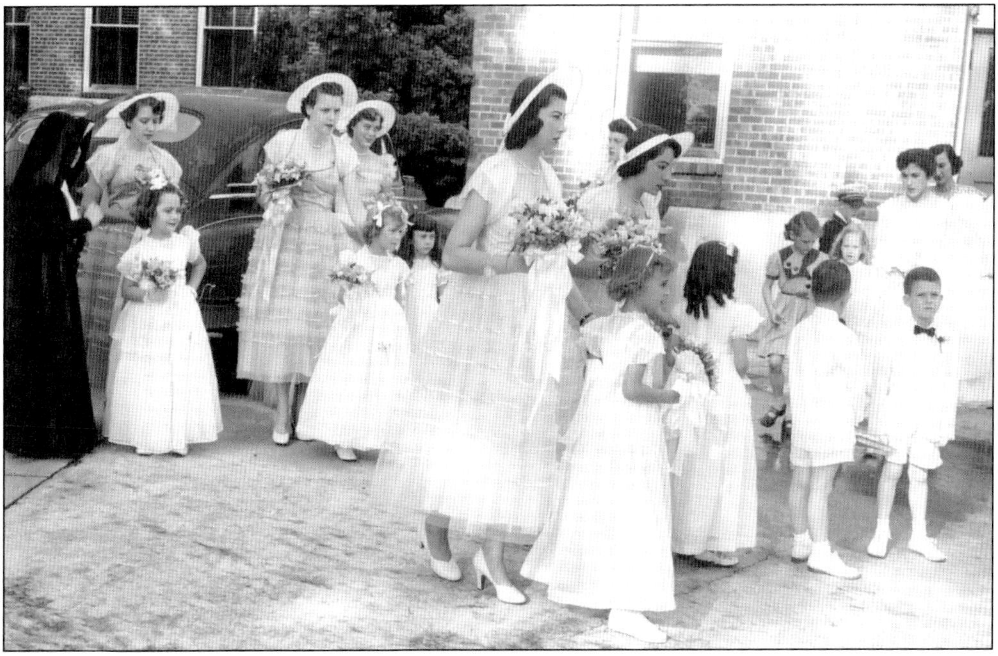

MAY DAY AT SACRED HEART COLLEGE. The May Day activities at Sacred Heart College were quite formal. These activities included awards ceremonies, a live band performance, and speeches by local notables and were culminated by a dance around the maypole. Included were students from both the college and the elementary school component. (Courtesy of Millican Pictorial History Museum.)

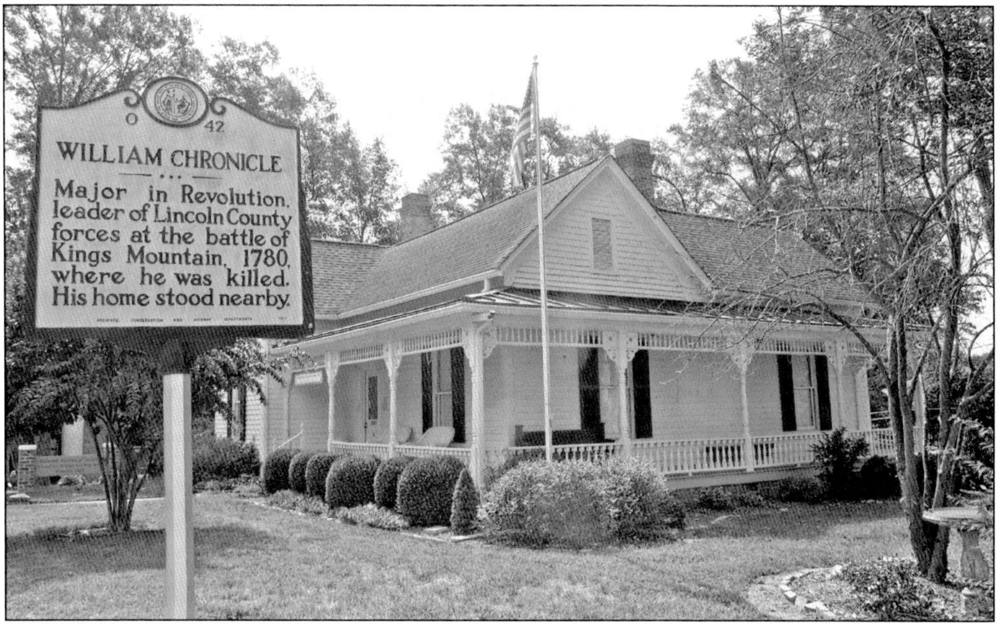

Belmont Historical Society. This home was built in 1899 by Robert Lee Stowe Sr. The property was deeded to the Belmont Historical Society, Inc. in 2006 and has been developed into a historical museum. This museum has an astonishing array of permanent and rotating displays and covers the history of the geographical area from South Point, New Hope, North Belmont, East Belmont, and the city of Belmont. The house itself sits on land that was once part of the plantation belonging to Maj. William Chronicle's family. The Chronicle Mill, begun by R.L. Stowe Sr., was located one block eastward down Catawba Street. This property also contains a freestanding 1899 kitchen building and a mill house that once was a part of the Acme Mill Village. (Courtesy of Millican Pictorial History Museum.)

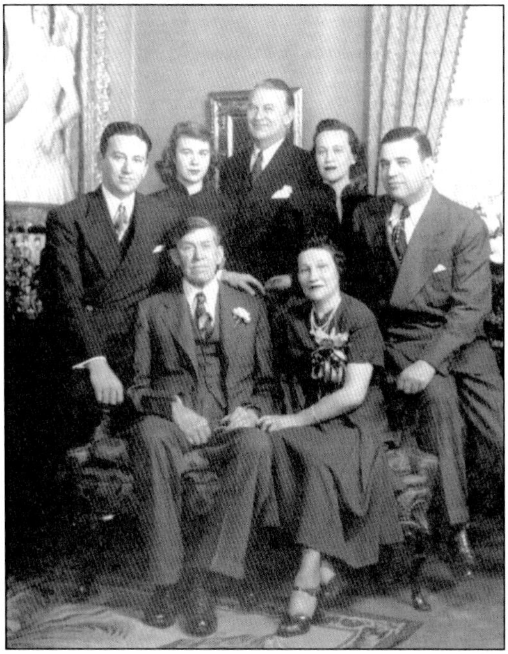

The Stowe Family. Posing for a family portrait are, from left to right, (seated) Robert Lee Stowe Sr. and his wife, Nellie Rhyne Stowe; (standing) son Daniel J. Stowe, granddaughter Catherine Ann Pharr, son-in law Bill Pharr, daughter Catherine Stowe Pharr, and son Robert Lee Stowe Jr. (Courtesy of Millican Pictorial History Museum.)

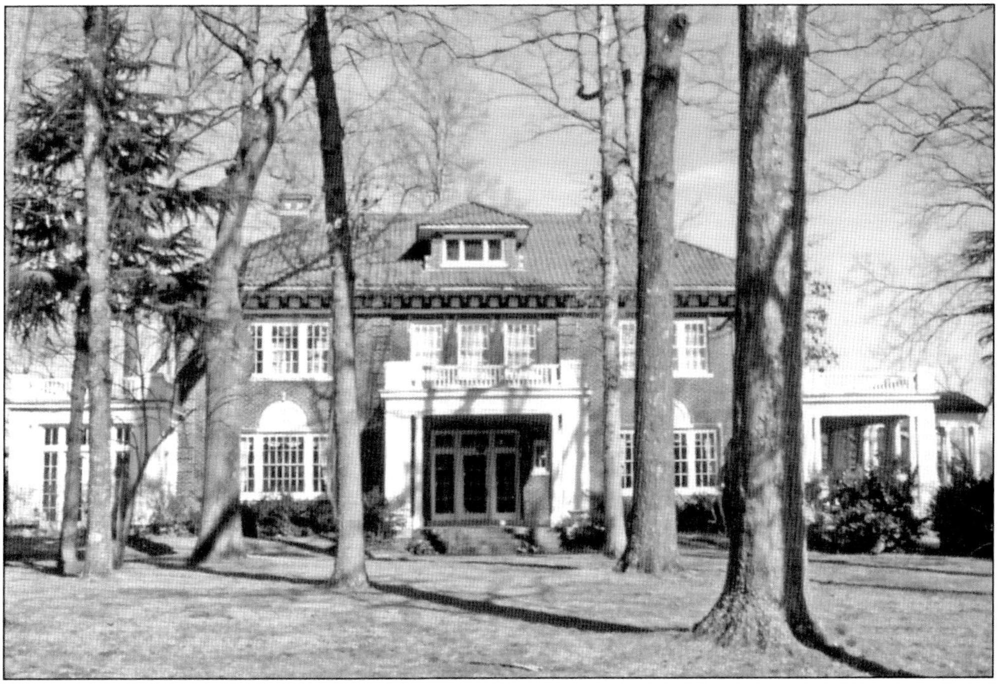

Samuel Pinckney Stowe House. Shortly after the Stowe mansion was completed on South Central Avenue, it was destroyed by fire. In 1924, the house was rebuilt and was the home to the Stowe family for many years. After three generations of Stowes lived here, the home stood empty until it was refurbished and called Stowe Manor. Today, it is a popular place for special events like weddings, receptions, reunions, and other functions. (Courtesy of Millican Pictorial History Museum.)

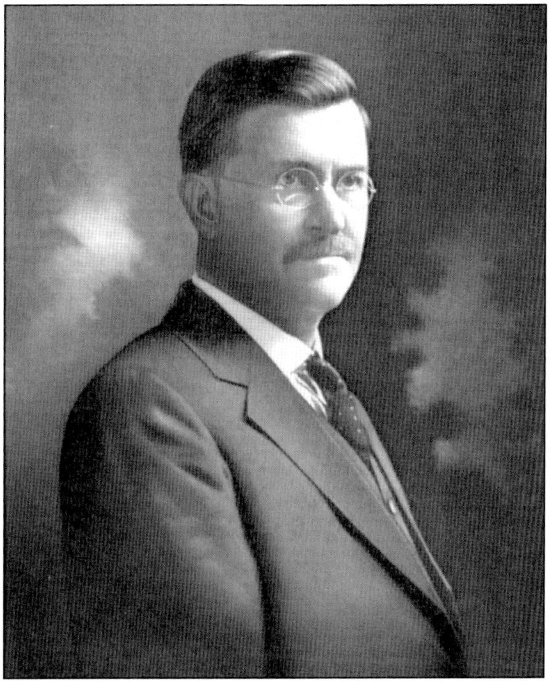

Samuel Pinckney Stowe Sr. Samuel Pinckney "S.P." Stowe Sr., along with his brother R.L. Stowe Sr., was one of Belmont's textile pioneers. After helping with the organization of the Chronicle Mill, he then moved on to be instrumental in the organization of the Majestic Mill, Belmont's third cotton textile mill. Encouraged by his sister Minnie Stowe Puett, S.P. Stowe Sr. erected a monument to Nancy Hanks's memory. In 1940, Belmont Hosiery Mill was on the verge of insolvency, but Stowe came through with an infusion of cash that put the mill on a sound economic footing. His home on the corner of Central Avenue and Keener Boulevard (formerly Pine Street), known as Stowe Manor, is used today for special occasions like weddings, receptions, and so forth. (Courtesy of Millican Pictorial History Museum.)

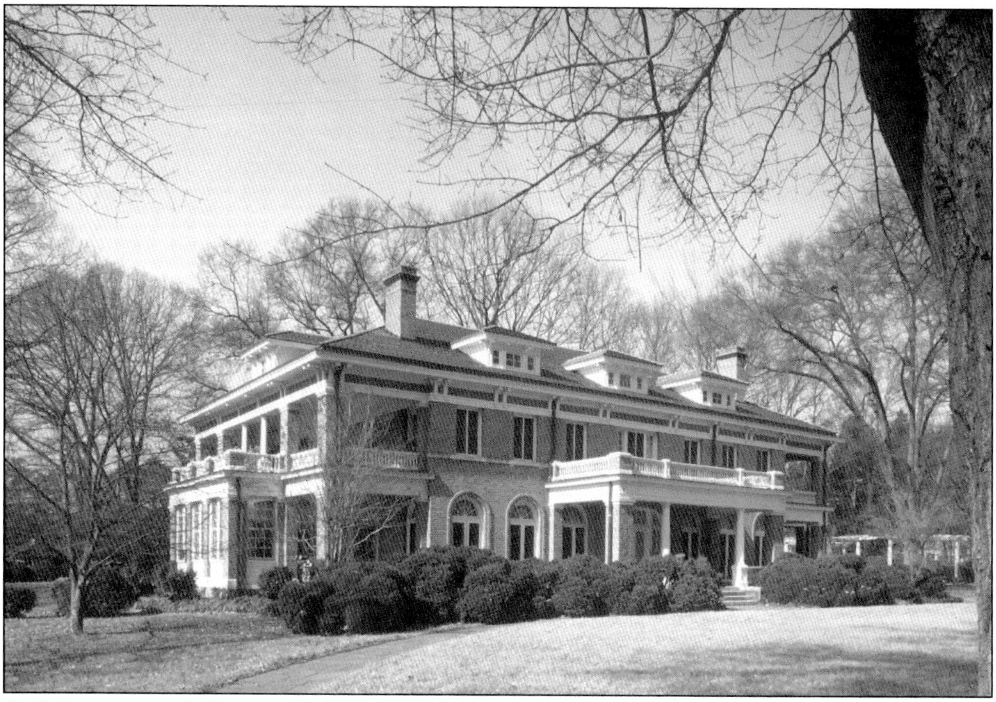

A.C. LINEBERGER'S HOME ON NORTH MAIN STREET. Pictured here is the second Belmont home of Abel Caleb Lineberger. The house was purported at one time to be the largest home in Gaston County. After having grown up working at his father's Woodlawn Mill, also known as the Pinhook Mill, Lineberger moved to Mount Holly to help with a mill in that location. After Stowe's mills got underway, Lineberger was enticed to move to Belmont. He commuted from Mount Holly to Belmont for six years by horse and buggy. His first Belmont home was located on the corner of Main Street and Woodrow Avenue. Due to the need to entertain business associates in the cotton industry, a more lavish home was required. This home was erected at the intersection of North Main Street and Central Avenue. (Courtesy of Millican Pictorial History Museum.)

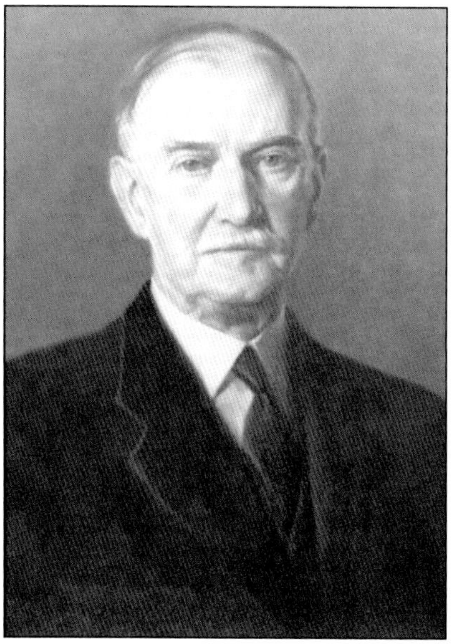

ABEL CALEB "A.C." LINEBERGER. A.C. Lineberger, son of the farmer who started the Pinhook Mill, got his textile basic training at the Pinhook and his formal education at Bryan and Stratton Business School. He was called upon to come to Belmont when a substantial stockholder, Dan Rhyne, insisted that he be put in charge of the management of the Chronicle Mill. Lineberger moved his family from Mount Holly where he worked at the Tuckaseege Mill to Belmont to take the assignment at the Chronicle Mill in 1910. He was instrumental in the formation of the second mill in Belmont, the Imperial Mill. The Lineberger Foundation, noted for its philanthropy, established the Lineberger Cancer Research Center at the University of North Carolina at Chapel Hill, and the Lineberger Stadium at South Point High School was donated by this foundation. Many other donations have been made. (Courtesy of Millican Pictorial History Museum.)

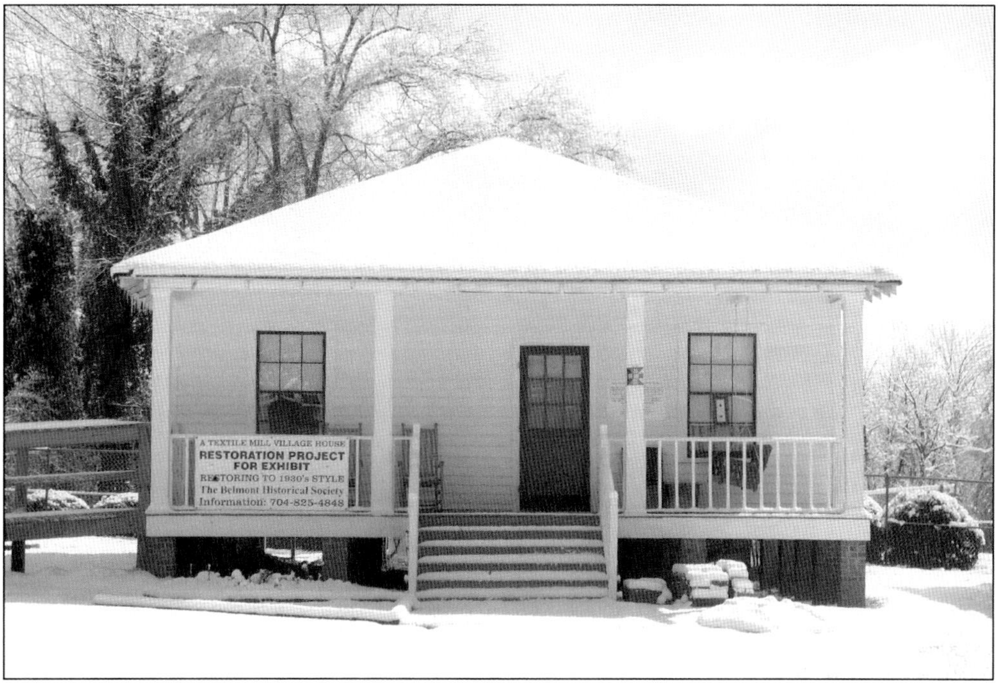

The Belmont Historical Society Mill House. This mill house once stood in the Acme Mill Village in North Belmont. It was moved to the Belmont Historical Society property at the request of Yates Abernethy, one of the founders of the society, who had secured the house from Parkdale Mills. He approached A.C. Lineberger III to ask for money to relocate the house for the purpose of demonstrating a typical 1920s/1930s mill house. The request was granted, and the house was moved; it has been outfitted with period furnishings and has become an educational attraction for the general public. (Courtesy of Millican Pictorial History Museum.)

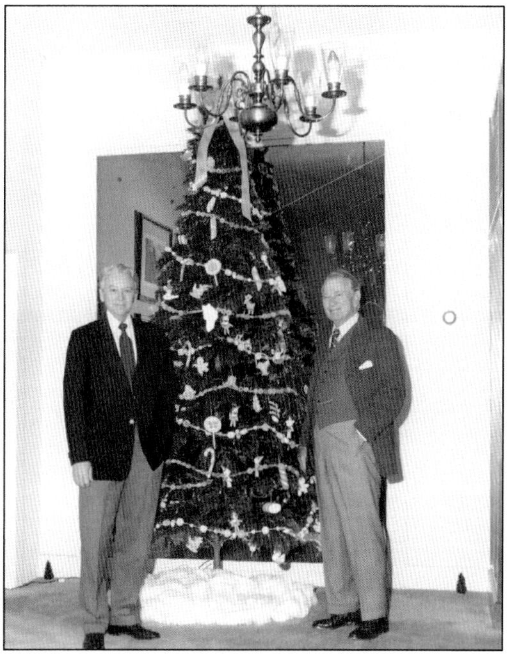

Dan Stowe and Bill Pharr. The Stowe/Pharr team had a deep love and sentiment for Christmas. The team ran the Pharr Yarns Mills in McAdenville. Bill Pharr and his wife, Catherine Stowe Pharr, began the tradition of decorating Christmas trees with beautiful lights all over McAdenville. The Stowe/Pharr Mills paid the electric bills for the month of December, and the town became known far and wide as "Christmas Town, USA." The tradition is still carried out today and is kicked off by the Annual Yule Log Parade. Visitors come to McAdenville from a widespread area to drive through and see the beautiful decorations each year. (Courtesy of Millican Pictorial History Museum.)

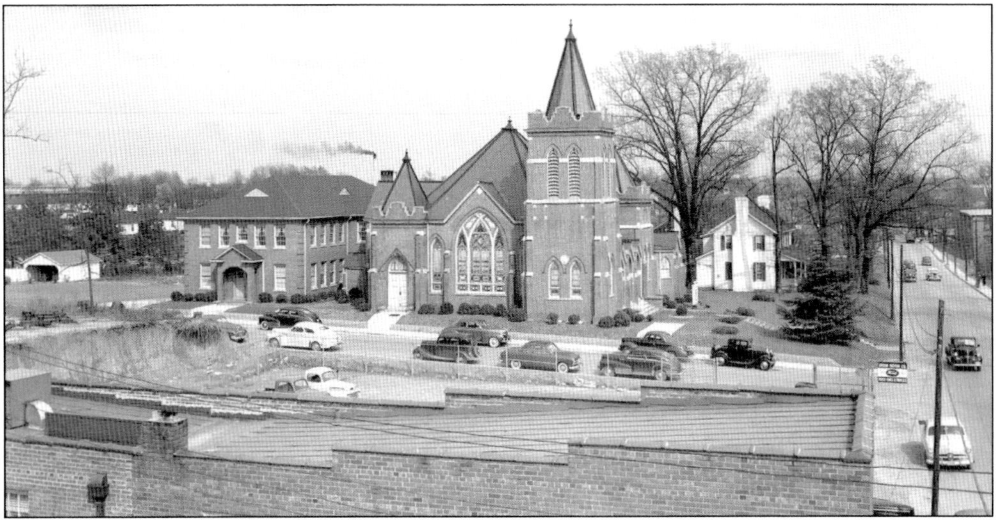

First Presbyterian Church. The First Presbyterian Church is pictured at its second location in Belmont. It was moved to this site from the original lot donated by Dr. W.W. Davis. The original location is where the mill office was constructed. Also seen in this view facing Catawba Street is the Abram Stowe House. The present location of this church is on the southwest corner of Main Street and Central Avenue. (Courtesy of Millican Pictorial History Museum.)

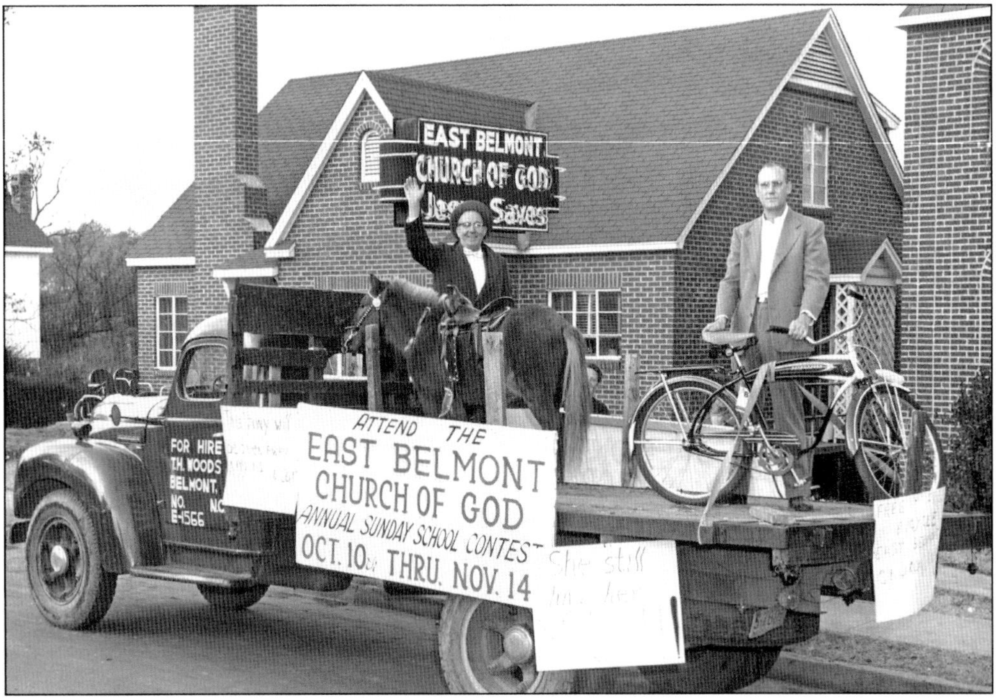

Pastor B.F. Darnell and Floyd Summey. Pastor B.F. Darnell, holding the bicycle, and Floyd Summey, holding a pony (both prizes for Sunday school promotional contests), are ready to ride through town inviting people to come to the East Belmont Church of God on Church Street. Promotional efforts for this church were highly successful, and a new sanctuary was built on Catawba Street. (Courtesy of Millican Pictorial History Museum.)

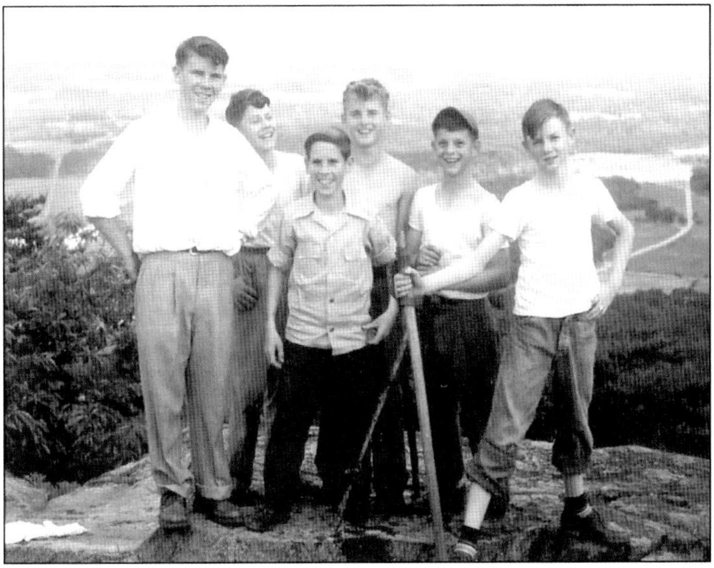

BOYS FROM CENTERVIEW BAPTIST CHURCH. These boys from Centerview Baptist Church in North Belmont have their backs to a panoramic view of Gaston County, as seen from the pinnacle of Crowders Mountain. (Courtesy of Millican Pictorial History Museum.)

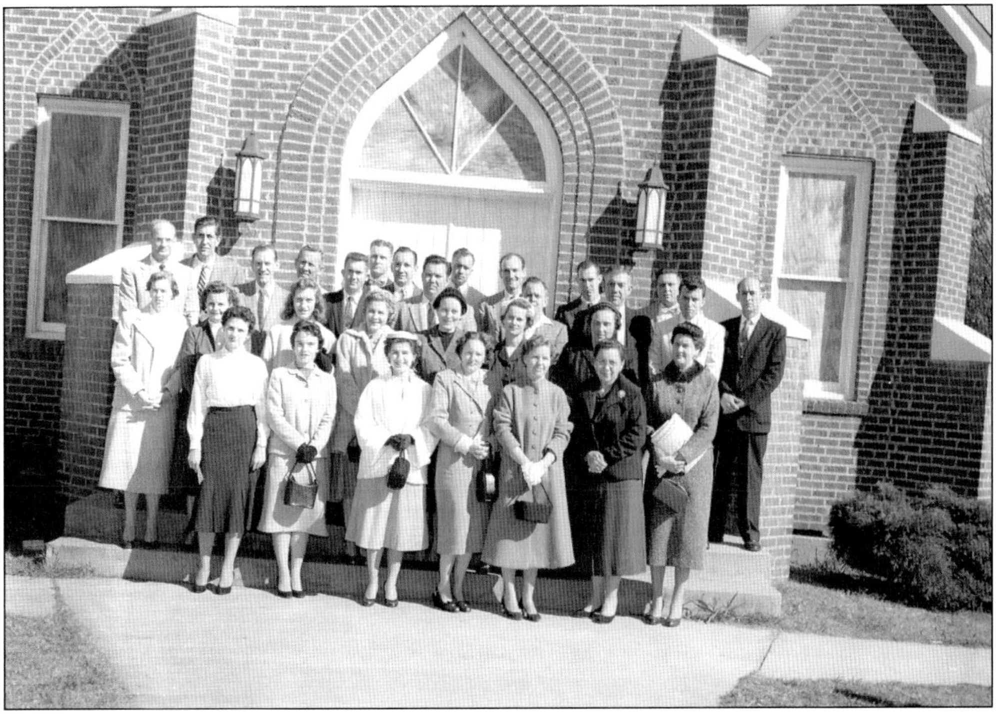

GROUP AT EAST BELMONT PRESBYTERIAN CHURCH, 1950S. The East Belmont Presbyterian Church served the community in East Belmont. The First Presbyterian Church was more than a mile away, so a new Presbyterian church was needed in this area. It is still a viable church on the north side of Catawba Street in East Belmont. (Courtesy of Millican Pictorial History Museum.)

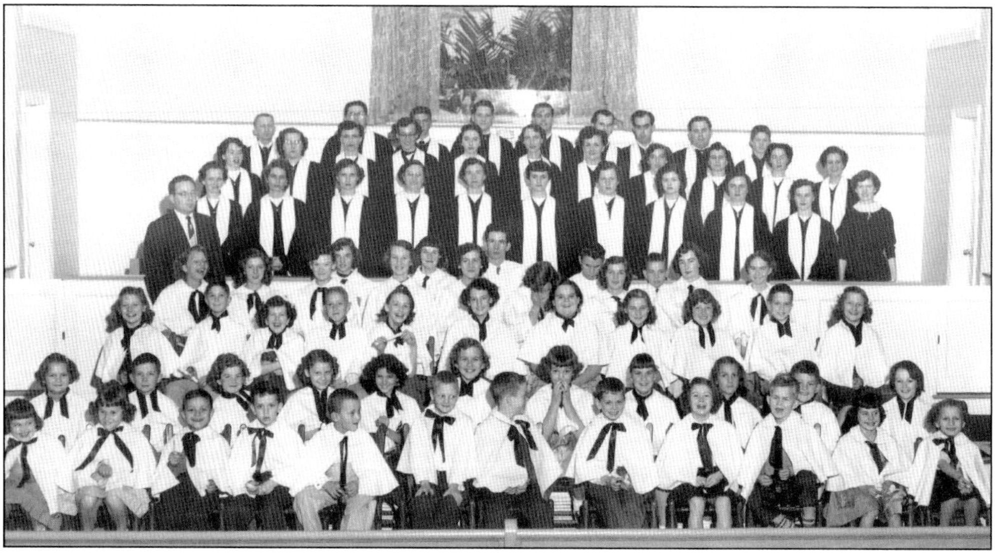

EAST BELMONT BAPTIST CHURCH ADULT AND YOUTH CHOIRS, 1953. Music programs often are the heart of church activities on a regular basis. Week after week, the choirs have practices before participating in the worship service. Such is true of the East Belmont Baptist Church Adult and Youth Choirs, photographed in 1953. The young people gradually matriculate to the adult choir as they become older and more skilled. Seasonal cantatas require a great deal of preparation and dedication, but it seems worthwhile, as it adds to the worship experiences of the church members. Choir members experience spiritual and professional growth through music. (Courtesy of Millican Pictorial History Museum.)

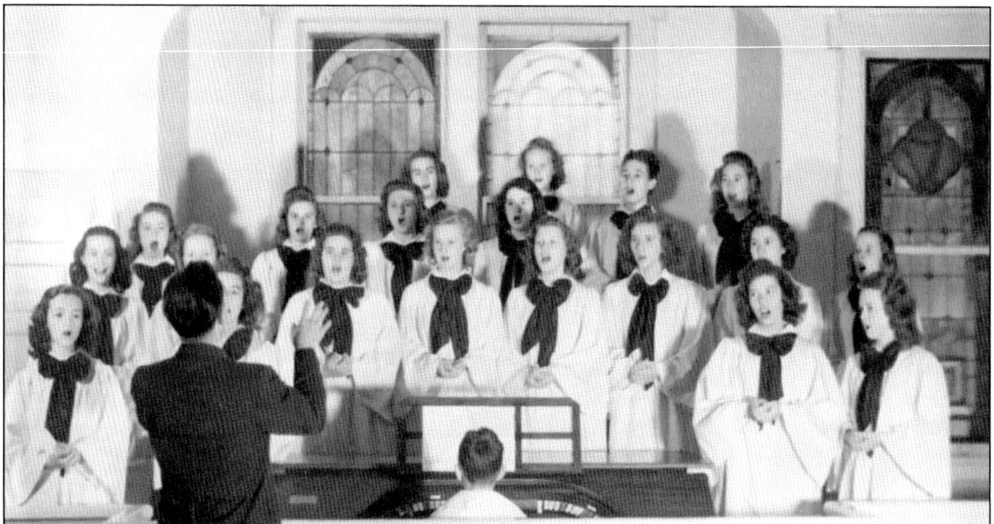

YOUTH CHOIR AT FIRST BAPTIST CHURCH. Under the direction of Newell C. Carter, an unusually talented group of girls, accompanied by Gene Featherstone on the organ, became widely known for its performances. At least three of these became professional musicians: Gene Featherstone, organist; Delores Dellinger, public school music teacher; and Doris Burns, a graduate of Westminster Choir College in Princeton, New Jersey. Burns toured the world as a vocalist and symphony conductor. She retired from her position as head of the vocal and opera department of Yale University. (Courtesy of Millican Pictorial History Museum.)

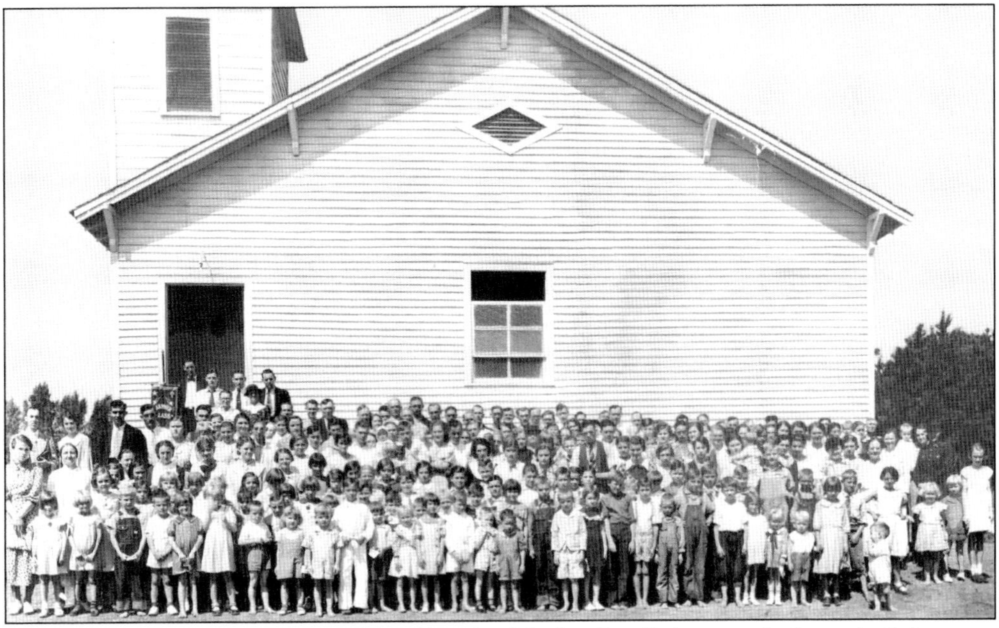

Church of God. This picture is of the Church of God in East Belmont, which was built between 1926 and 1927 on land that was purchased in 1926. The congregation's first services were held in 1927. This view, as seen from Catawba Street, shows the south side of the church. The membership is composed mostly of Stowe Mill employees. (Courtesy of Millican Pictorial History Museum.)

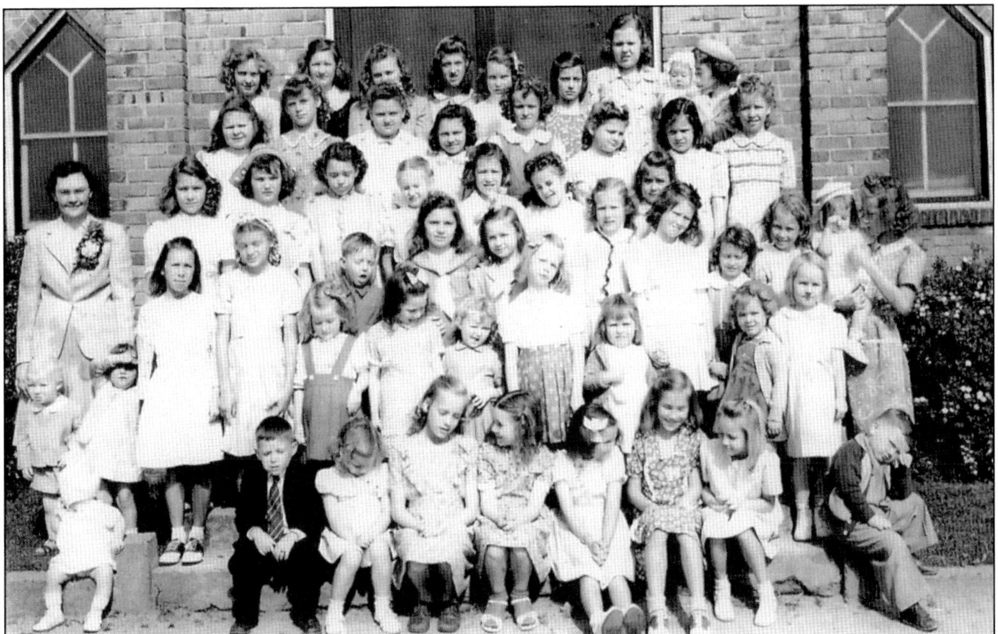

The Church of God Sunday School Classes, 1944. During World War II, there was a strong religious fervor in Belmont's churches. Pictured are girls from Belmont's Church of God. Many of these girls' fathers were in various branches of the military services. The church was a place to worship, socialize, and pray for their loved ones. (Courtesy of Millican Pictorial History Museum.)

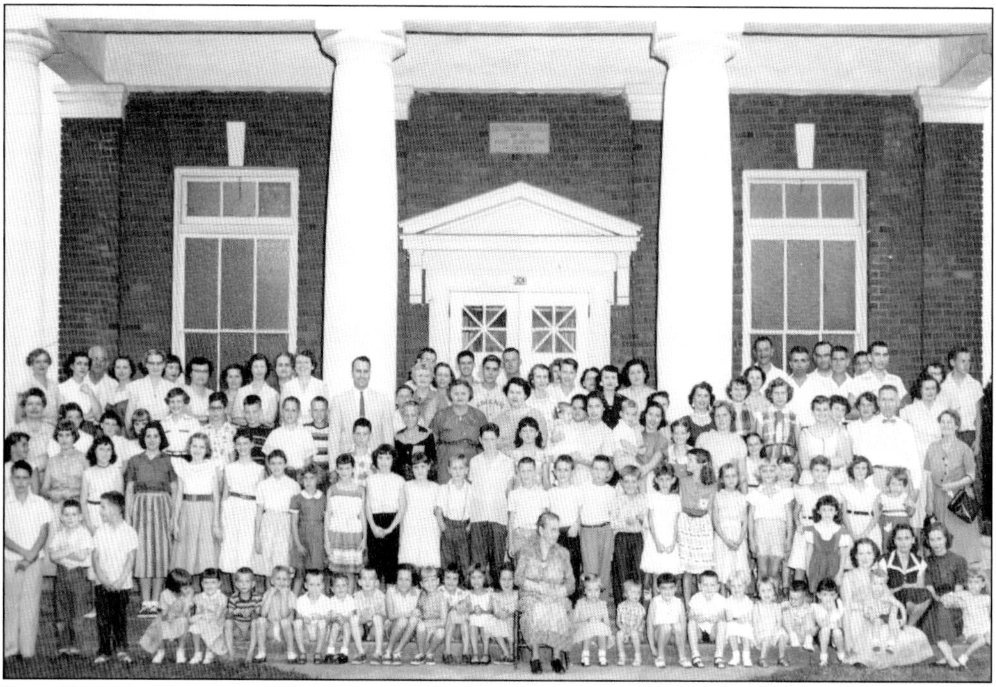

East Belmont Lutheran Church, 1951. The Lutheran church in East Belmont outgrew its facilities during the 1950s, as witnessed by the large group of young people in this congregational picture. The church was relocated to a site on North Main Street. The pastor at this time was Rev. Harry Robinson. (Courtesy of Millican Pictorial History Museum.)

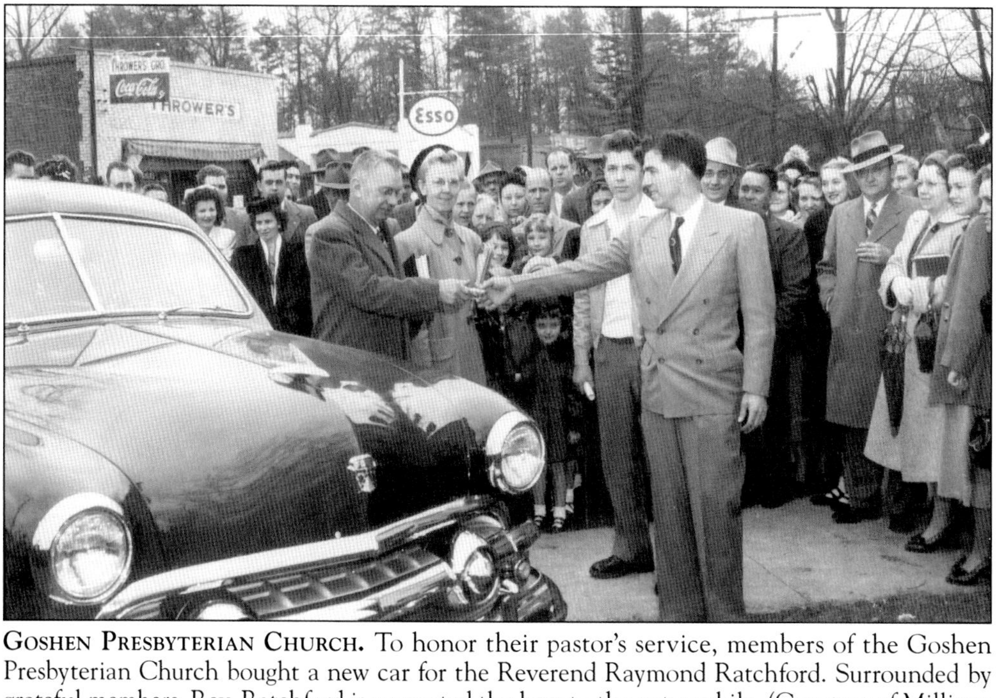

Goshen Presbyterian Church. To honor their pastor's service, members of the Goshen Presbyterian Church bought a new car for the Reverend Raymond Ratchford. Surrounded by grateful members, Rev. Ratchford is presented the keys to the automobile. (Courtesy of Millican Pictorial History Museum.)

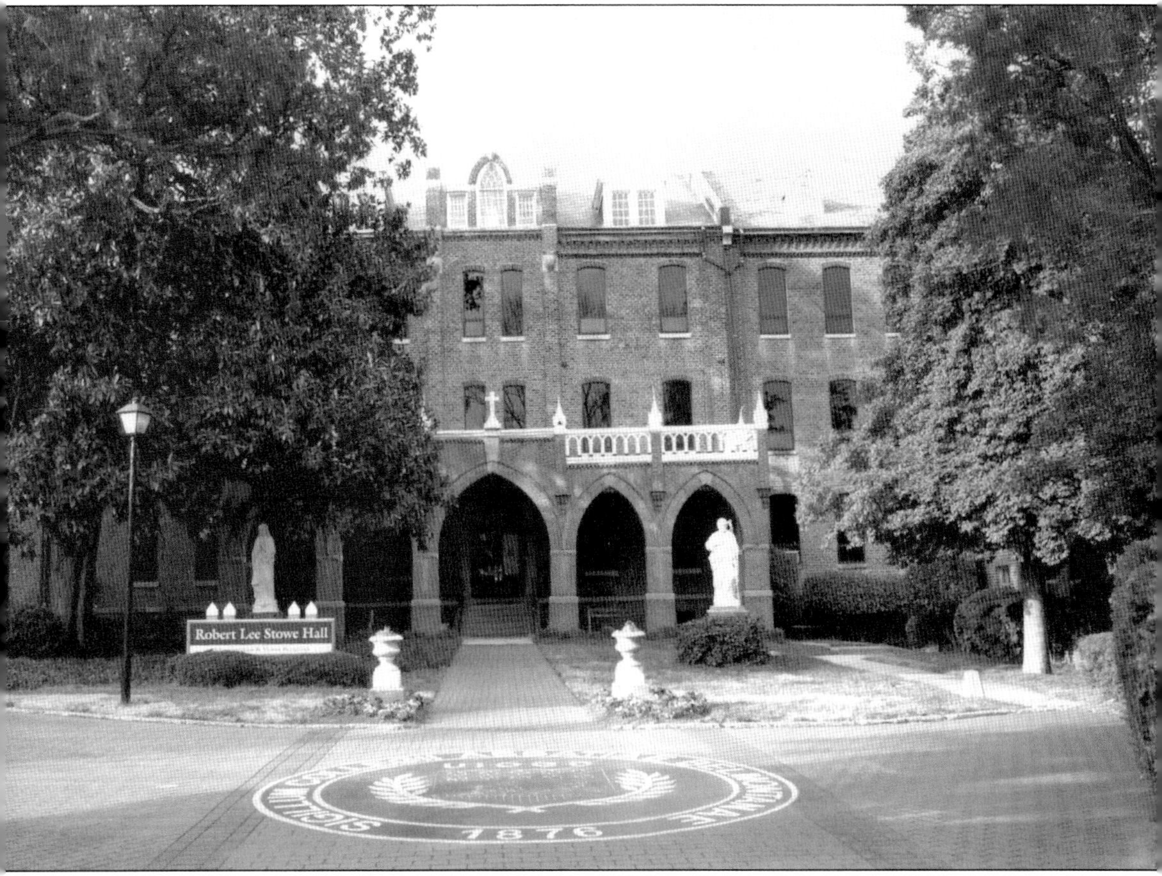

Robert Lee Stowe Hall. Honoring Robert Lee Stowe Sr., who was a staunch supporter of Belmont Abbey College, this building bears his name. In the foreground, the Belmont Abbey seal is embedded in the walkway approaching the building. (Courtesy of Millican Pictorial History Museum.)

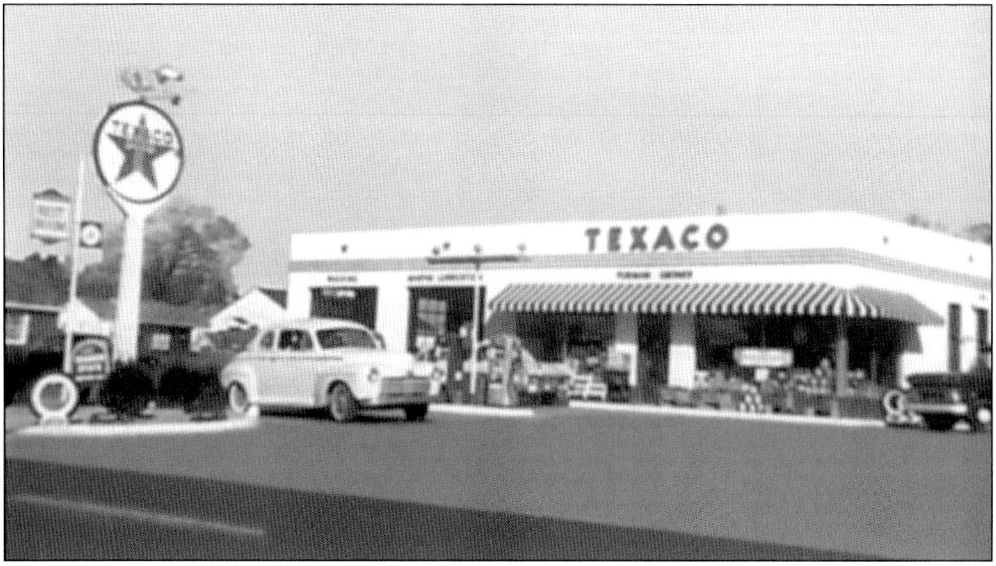

GRONER'S SERVICE STATION ON SOUTH CENTRAL AVENUE. For many years, Furman Groner's Texaco service station served most of the people who traveled South Point Road. Eventually, this business passed into the hands of Furman's son, Jimmy Groner, who was assisted by his mother, Louise Groner. (Courtesy of Millican Pictorial History Museum.)

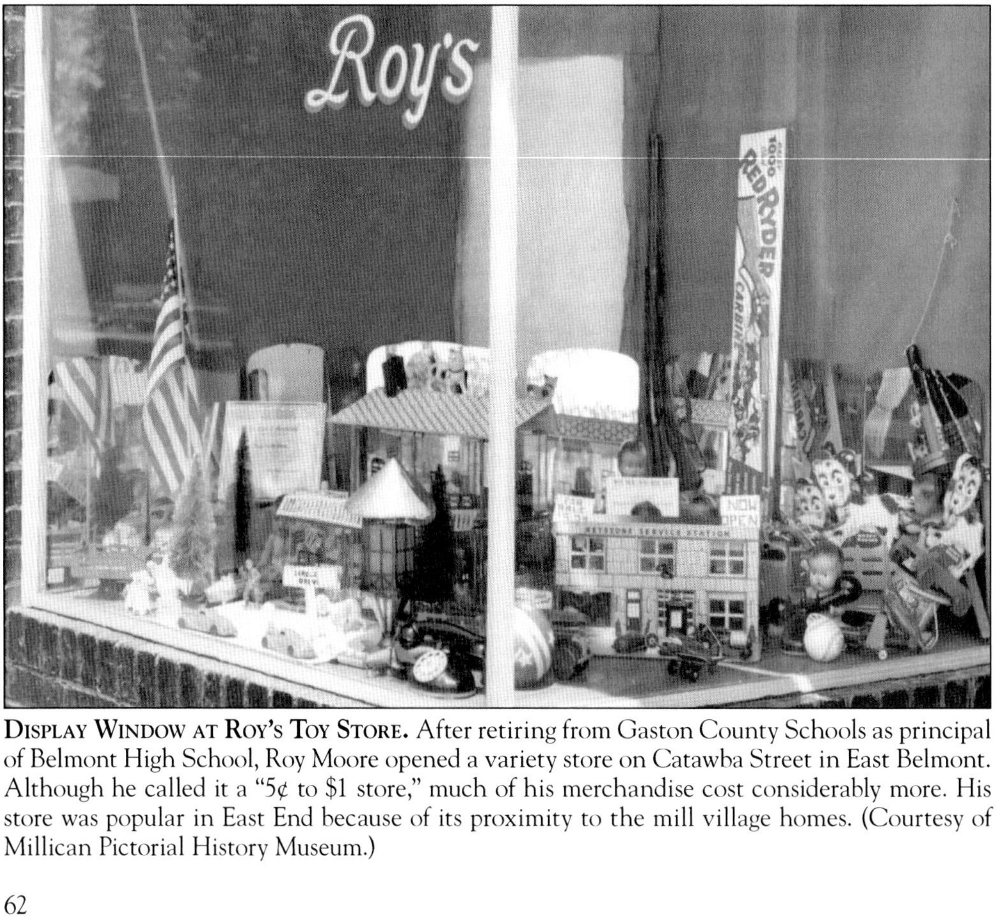

DISPLAY WINDOW AT ROY'S TOY STORE. After retiring from Gaston County Schools as principal of Belmont High School, Roy Moore opened a variety store on Catawba Street in East Belmont. Although he called it a "5¢ to $1 store," much of his merchandise cost considerably more. His store was popular in East End because of its proximity to the mill village homes. (Courtesy of Millican Pictorial History Museum.)

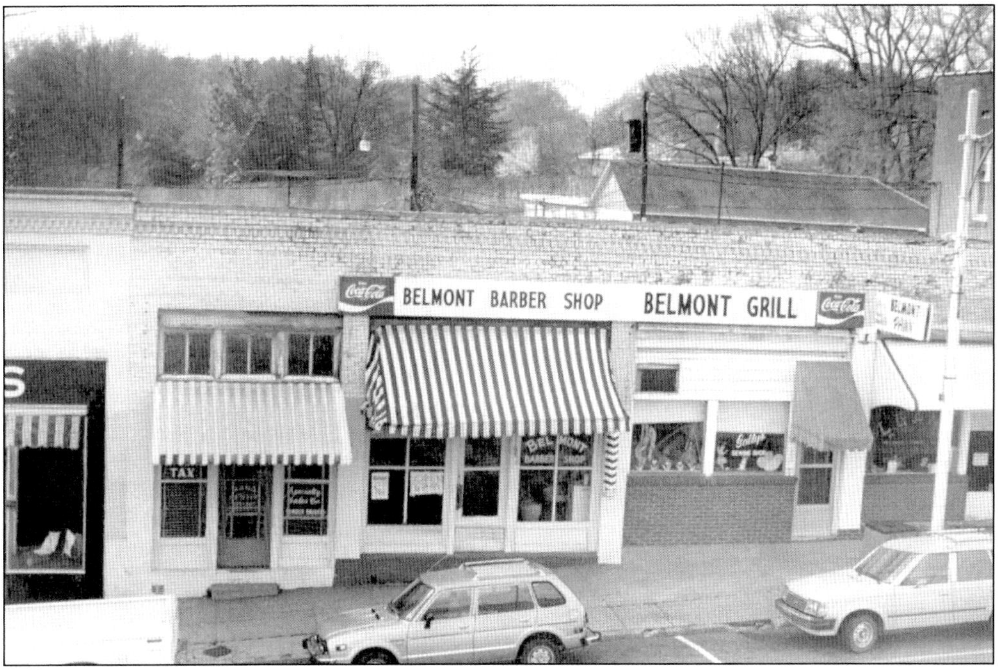

Belmont Shops on Main Street. Eli Cohen's Women's Wear is partially depicted in this snapshot taken from the upstairs of Stowe Mercantile. Others in this line of businesses are Hand's Tax Service, Belmont Barber Shop, Sally's Sewing Shop, and the Belmont Pawn Shop. The sign proclaiming Belmont Grill is out of date; the owner had closed the grill but has not removed his sign. (Courtesy of Millican Pictorial History Museum.)

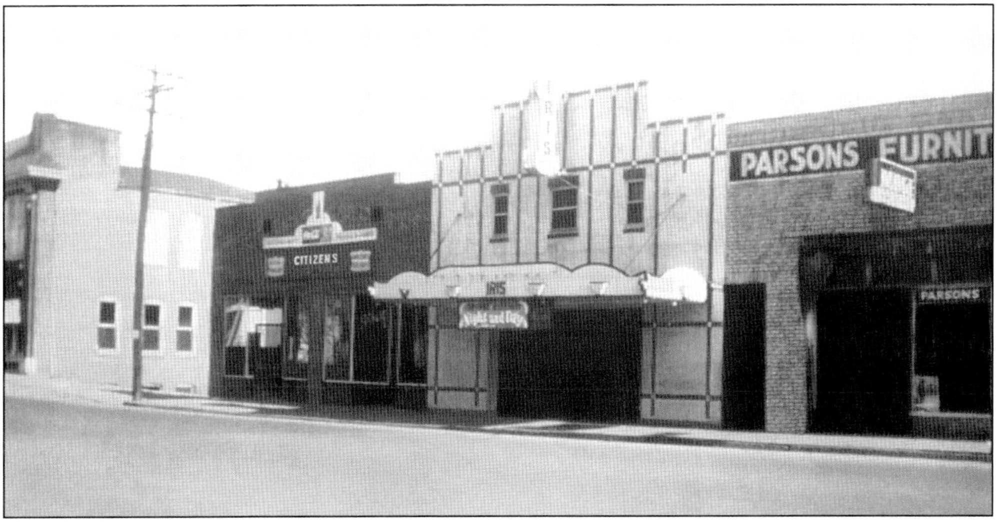

Citizen's Grocery, Iris Theater, and Parson's Furniture. Citizen's Grocery was said to be the first "supermarket" in Belmont. There were many small community groceries scattered over the mill hills. The Iris Theater was one of three of Earnest Wade's theaters in Belmont; this one is located downtown. The Parson brothers Grady and Tom and Chesley Sedberry advertised "Everything for the Home." Theirs was a complete line of furniture, carpets, and linoleum rugs for the kitchen and bathroom. To the far left is Belmont City Hall. There was a recorder's court on the second floor and a city jail in the basement. (Courtesy of Millican Pictorial History Museum.)

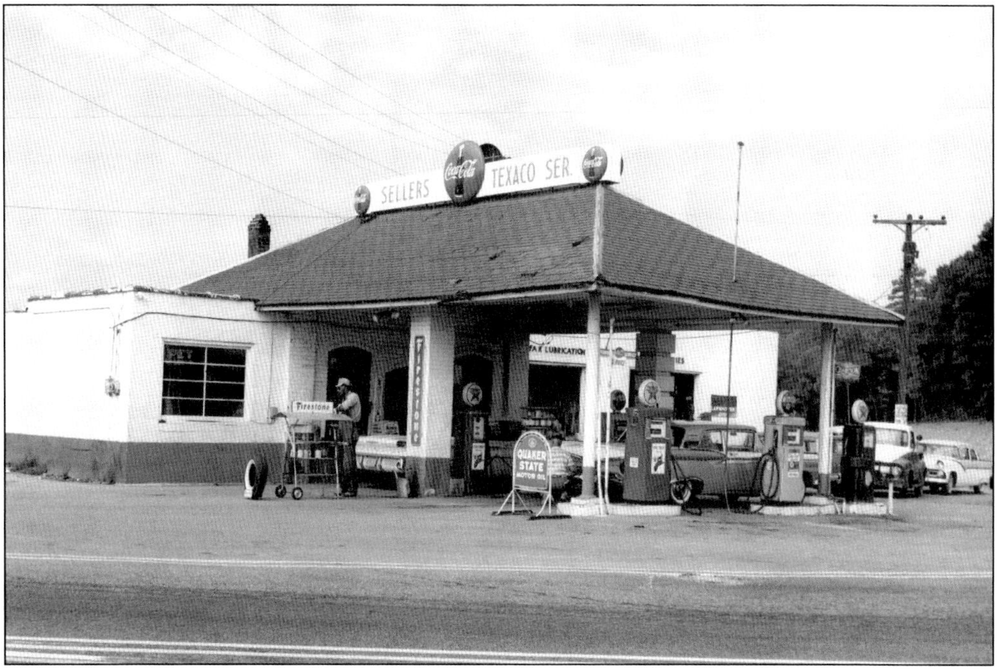

SELLERS TEXACO SERVICE. This service station was run by brothers Russell and Pete Sellers. It was located on the corner of McAdenville Road and the Belmont/Mount Holly Road. Currently, this corner is occupied by the Hawthorne Ford dealership. (Courtesy of Millican Pictorial History Museum.)

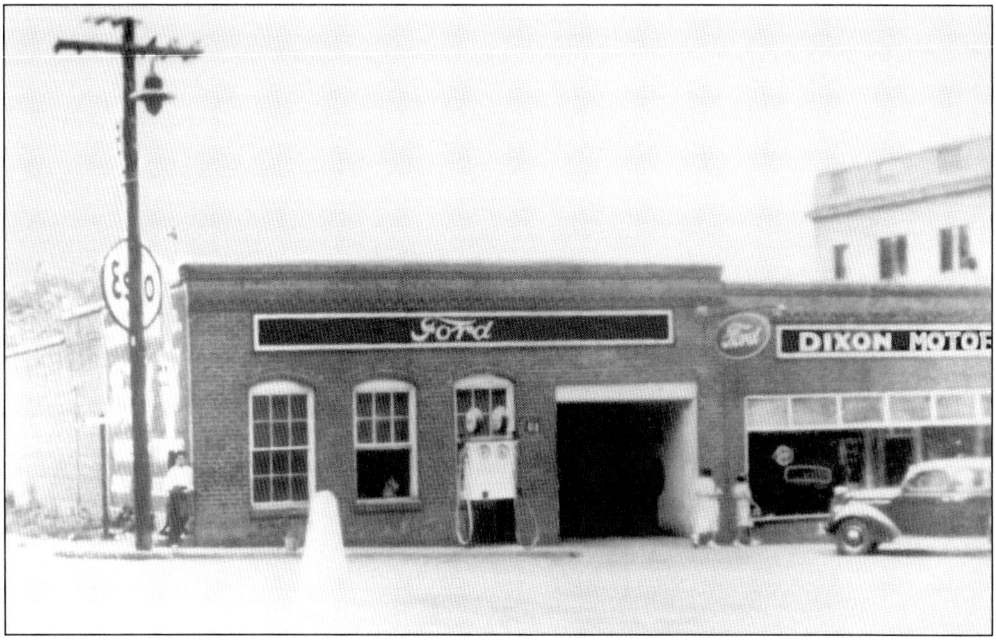

DIXON MOTOR COMPANY. Dixon Motor/Service Station, a full-service station and a Ford automobile dealership, was located on the corner of Main and Catawba Streets. William Dixon, Neely Frank Dixon, and Clarence Dixon were owners and operators of this enterprise. (Courtesy of Millican Pictorial History Museum.)

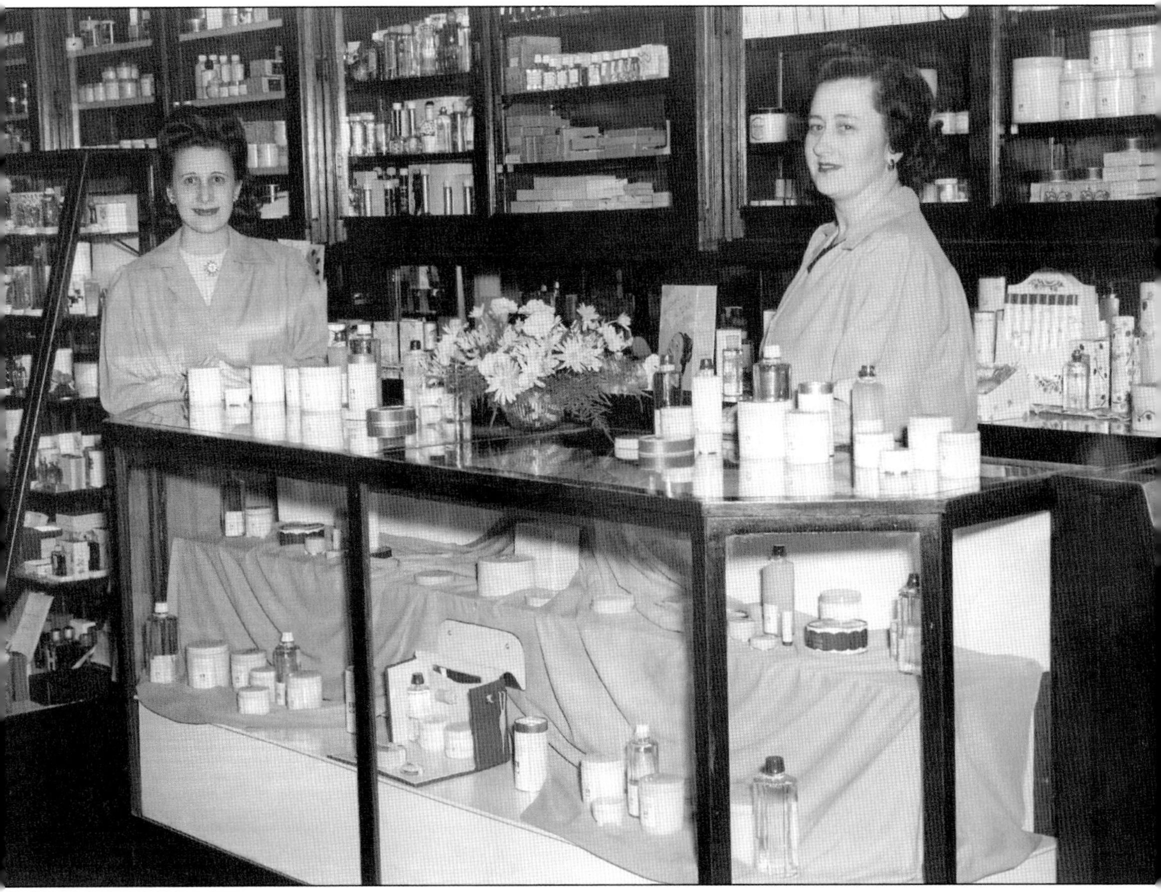

Dollie Ritchey and Grace Sparks in Robinson Drug Store. Ritchey (left) and Sparks are pictured at the cosmetics counter of Robinson's Drug Store in the 1940s. The soda fountain and its chairs and benches were popular hangouts for the teachers from the teacherage as well as for local teenagers. (Courtesy of Millican Pictorial History Museum.)

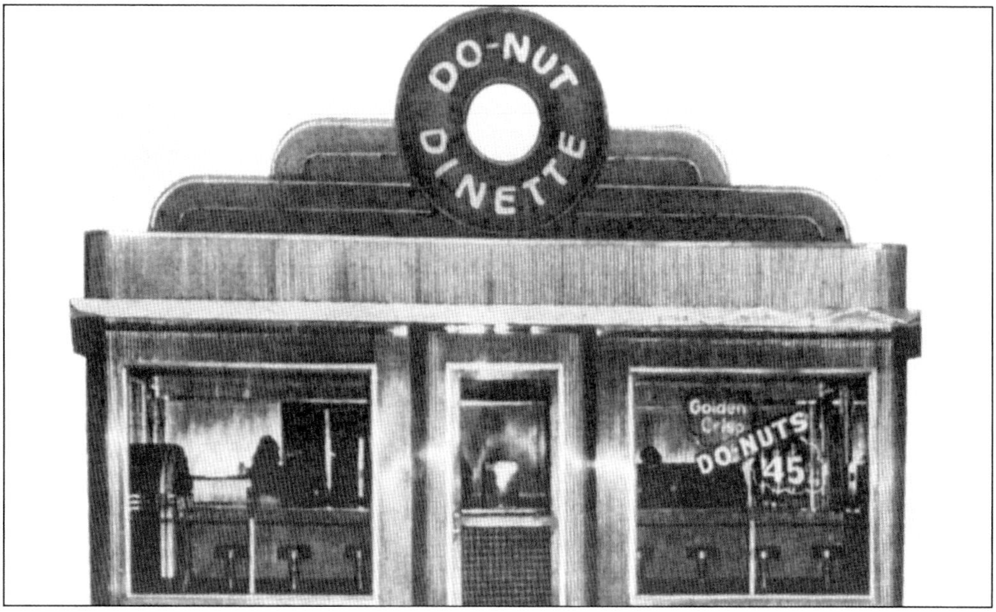

Do-Nut Dinette. On the north side of Wilkinson Boulevard, Alvin "Dub" Rankin and his brother-in-law Clyde Thrower obtained a doughnut franchise and constructed this building. The Do-Nut Dinette stood on property leased from the Sisters of Mercy. The restaurant was on the main line of east-west traffic between Wilmington and Asheville and north-south traffic between Washington and Atlanta, on Highway 29/74. At one time, business was so brisk that Dub and Clyde were frying 500 pounds of flour a week into donuts that were sold for 5¢ each. (Courtesy of Millican Pictorial History Museum.)

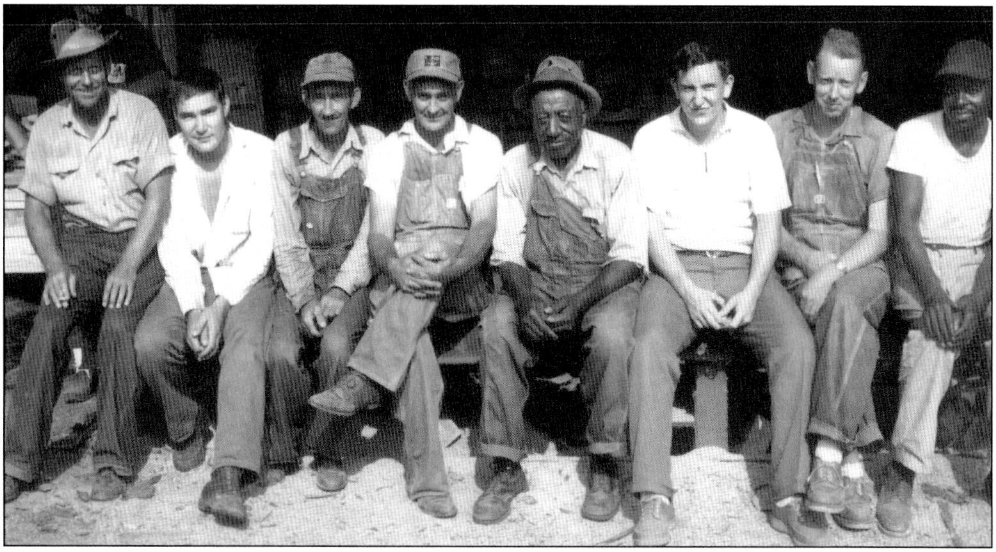

Workers at Belmont Lumber Company. The men pictured are laborers at Belmont Lumber Company. Their duties were to stack lumber and fill orders to required dimensions, and several employees were general carpenters. They are identified as, from left to right, two relatives of Luther White, Luther "Luke" White, Reedy Rhyne, Will Sims, another relative of Luther White, Glen Armstrong, and Robert Crawford. Luther White and his relatives moved to Belmont from Copper Hill, Tennessee, in the early 1960s. (Courtesy of Millican Pictorial History Museum.)

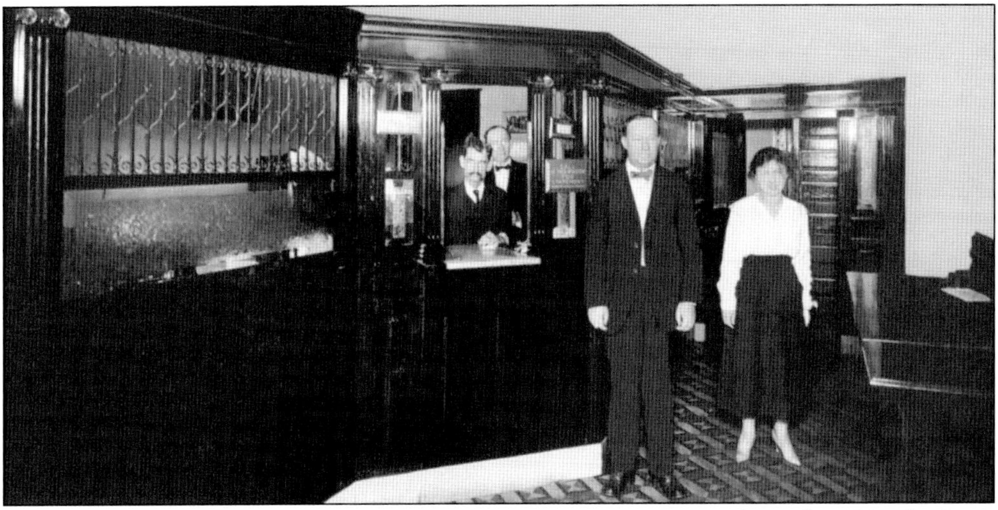

Bank of Belmont in the Hotel Building in the Early 1920s. In the early 1920s, the Bank of Belmont was housed in the front portion of the Belmont Hotel. Will Puett, brother-in-law of Robert Lee Stowe Sr., was cashier. The Bank of Belmont was moved across Main Street to a new three-story building in the mid-1920s. Belmont's first elevator was in this structure. This new building's basement held a shoe shop, a barbershop, and Wilson's Printing Service. The first floor housed the bank, with its walk-in safe and boardrooms in the rear portion. The three upper floors were home to law offices, insurance offices, and offices for textile businesses. (Courtesy of Millican Pictorial History Museum.)

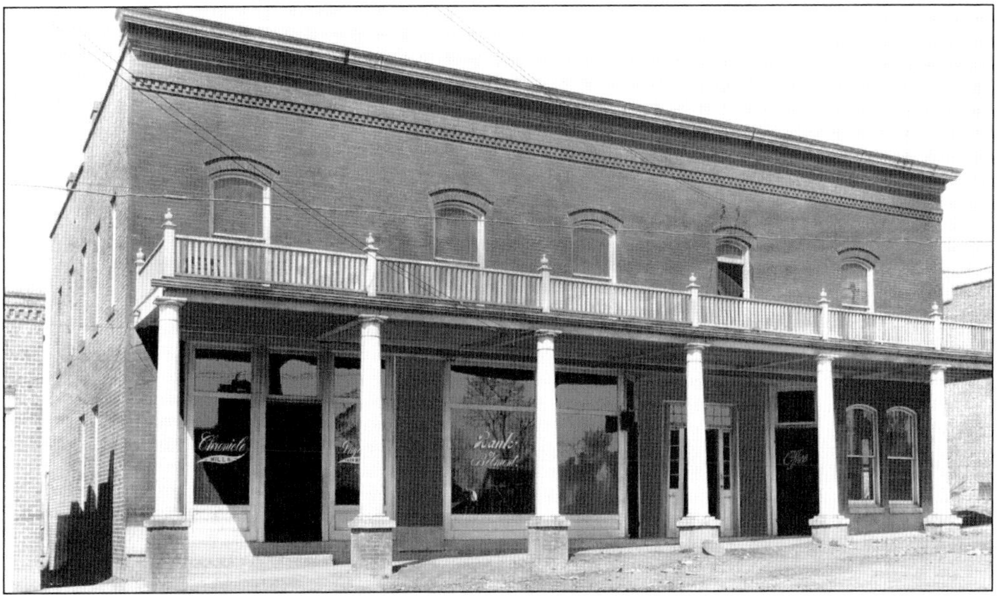

Belmont Hotel (1918) and Chronicle Mill Office. The Gullick Building was constructed in 1918 at the request of many textile executives. The mill business was thriving, and there was a need for accommodations for buyers and sellers of textile products. The hotel was conveniently located only one block from the railroad depot. The second floor was used to house guests, while the ground floor contained mill offices, the telephone office, and the Bank of Belmont. Over the years, many varied businesses have been located in this building. The facade has been gone for many years. (Courtesy of Millican Pictorial History Museum.)

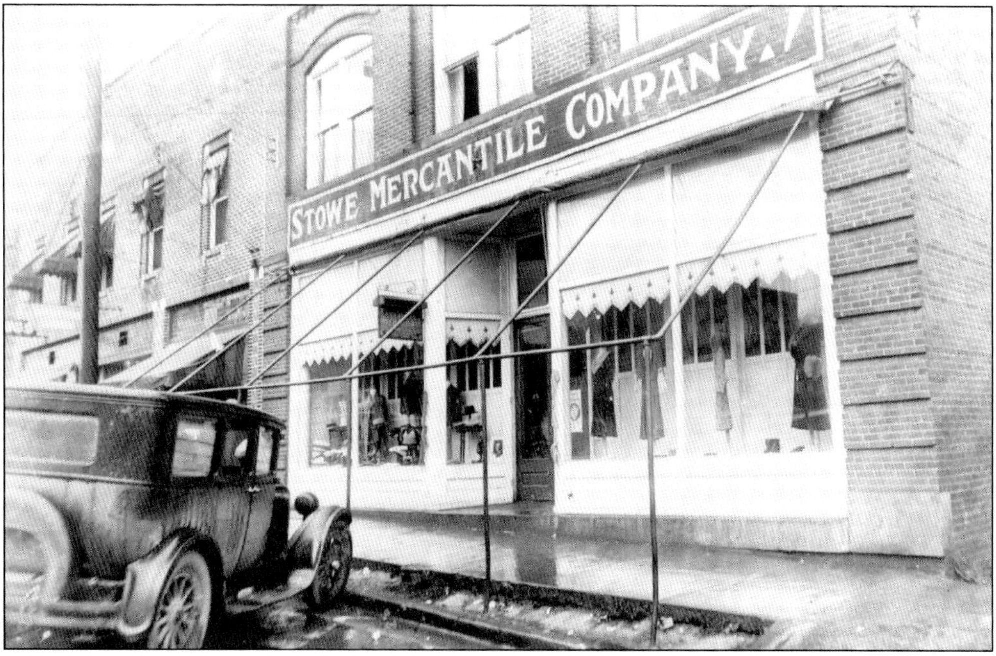

Stowe Mercantile Company. For many years, Stowe Mercantile Company was the anchor of Belmont's retail industry. This store served all of the mill workers and allowed them to charge merchandise. These charges were deducted from the workers' paychecks. A customer could buy any kind of merchandise—from clothes, cloth, groceries, fertilizers, plow chains, to, later, TV sets, furniture, and kitchen appliances. The store has changed owners several times in recent years. (Courtesy of Millican Pictorial History Museum.)

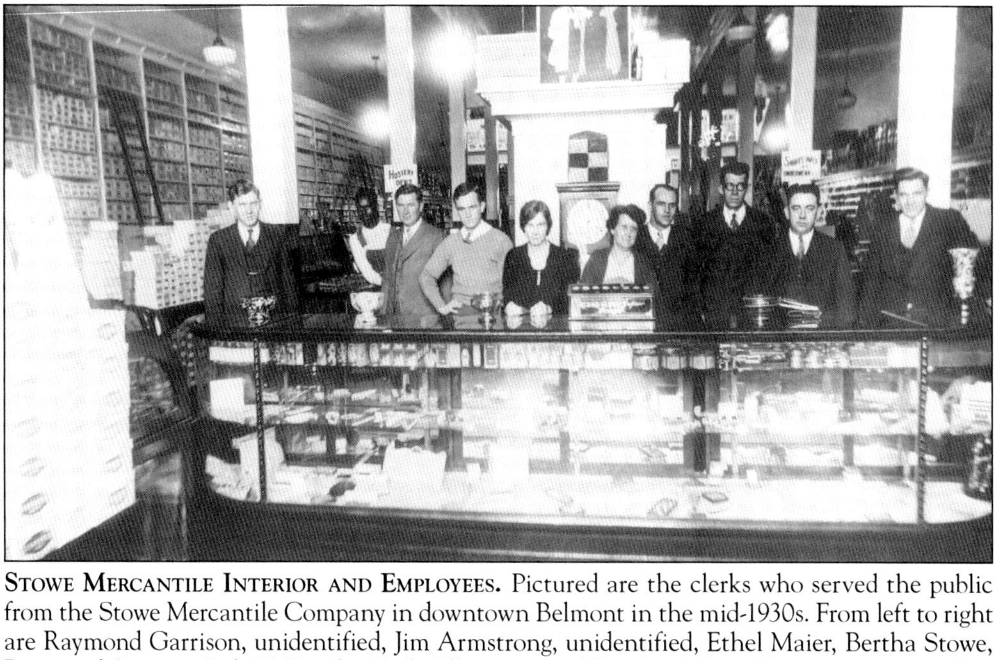

Stowe Mercantile Interior and Employees. Pictured are the clerks who served the public from the Stowe Mercantile Company in downtown Belmont in the mid-1930s. From left to right are Raymond Garrison, unidentified, Jim Armstrong, unidentified, Ethel Maier, Bertha Stowe, Raymond Stewart, Bob McKnight, Early Ellington, and Frank McKee. This picture was taken from the front entrance. (Courtesy of Millican Pictorial History Museum.)

Bank of Belmont. The Bank of Belmont, organized in 1906, was originally housed in the Belmont Hotel. A new building was erected in the mid-1920s. It was very modern for its time, having an elevator to reach to the third floor. In 1928, its assets were $1,546,825.19. It was the only bank in Gaston County to stay open during the Wall Street crash of 1929. (Courtesy of Millican Pictorial History Museum.)

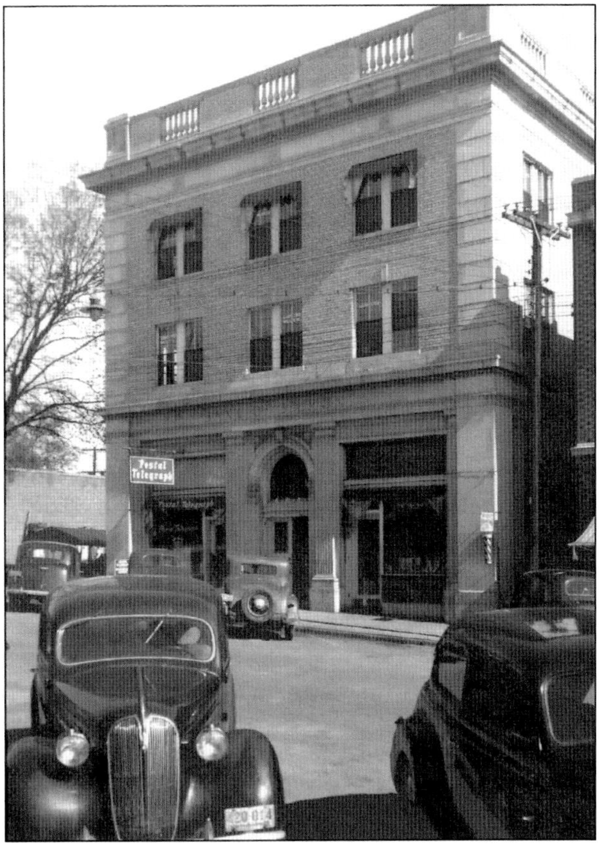

Armstrong-Lewis Grocery, c. 1920–1930. This store, Armstrong-Lewis Grocery, existed in a transitional era for Belmont. The store provided delivery service for regular customers and was known for its quality meats. Also, the company was a vendor for locally grown produce and eggs. G.W. Howe Company had no meat market, and Armstrong-Lewis provided meats for Howe's customers. (Courtesy of Millican Pictorial History Museum.)

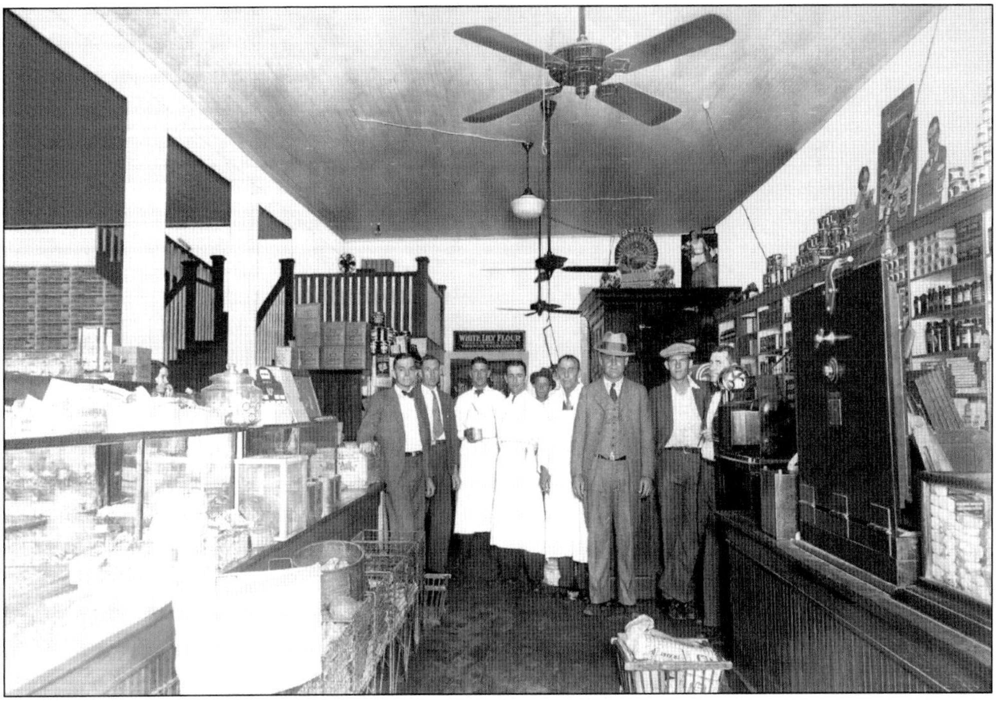

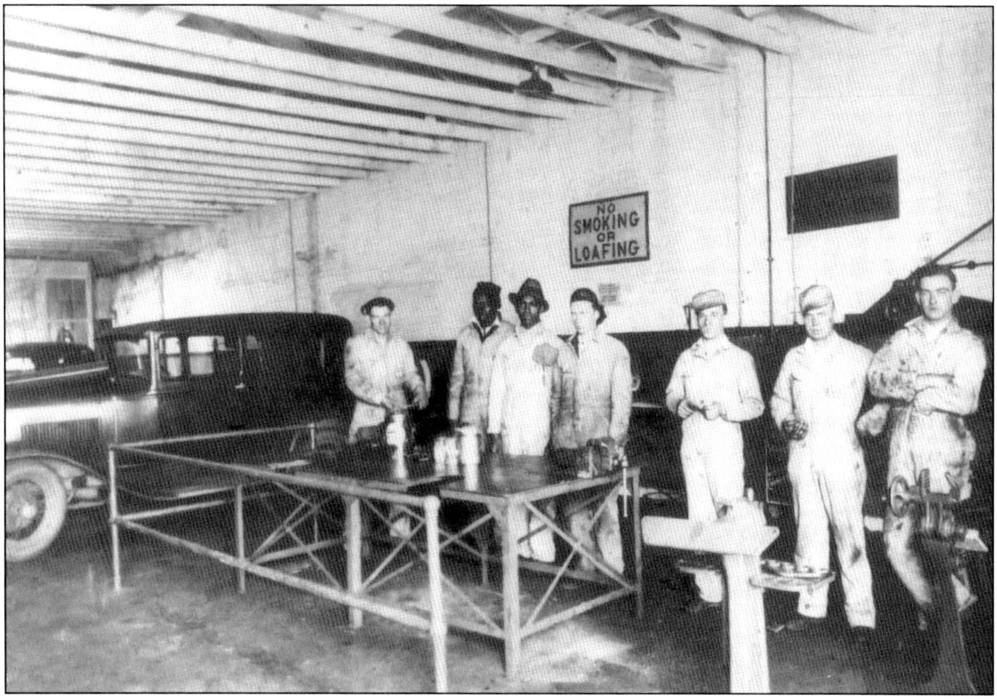

DIXON MOTOR COMPANY WORKERS. Dixon Motor Company's grease monkeys pose for a picture inside the garage. At the time this picture was taken, in the 1930s, this was the largest repair shop in this area. (Courtesy of Millican Pictorial History Museum.)

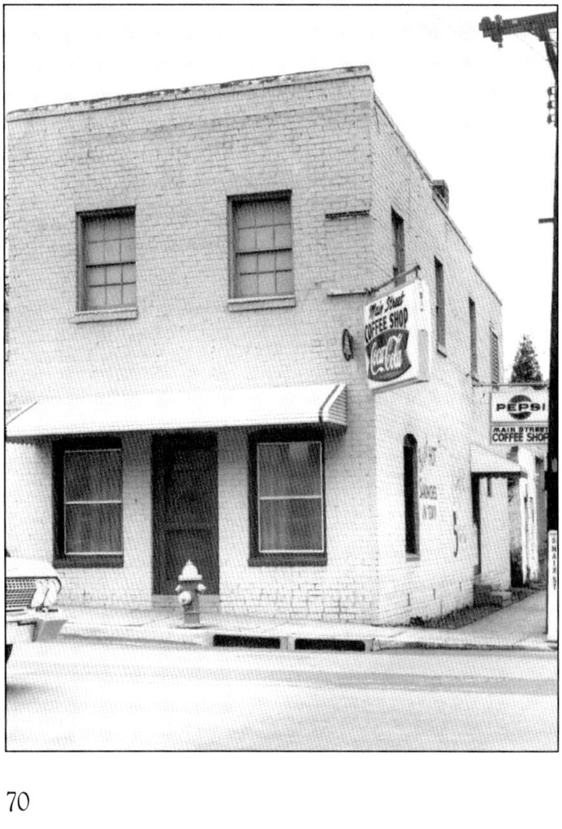

MAIN STREET COFFEE SHOP. Prior to World War II, this building housed Hamp's Café. When the war broke out, this café was flooded with Army personnel from across the Catawba River at Morris Field, an Army Air Forces training field. The soldiers saw this as a popular place to hang out, drink beer, and date Belmont girls. After the war, Sam Hagley's son-in-law opened Mitch's Cafe. When this was closed, Hagley Tailor Shop was set up. Since it closed, the building has been used for many different businesses, such as a real estate office and insurance office. (Courtesy of Millican Pictorial History Museum.)

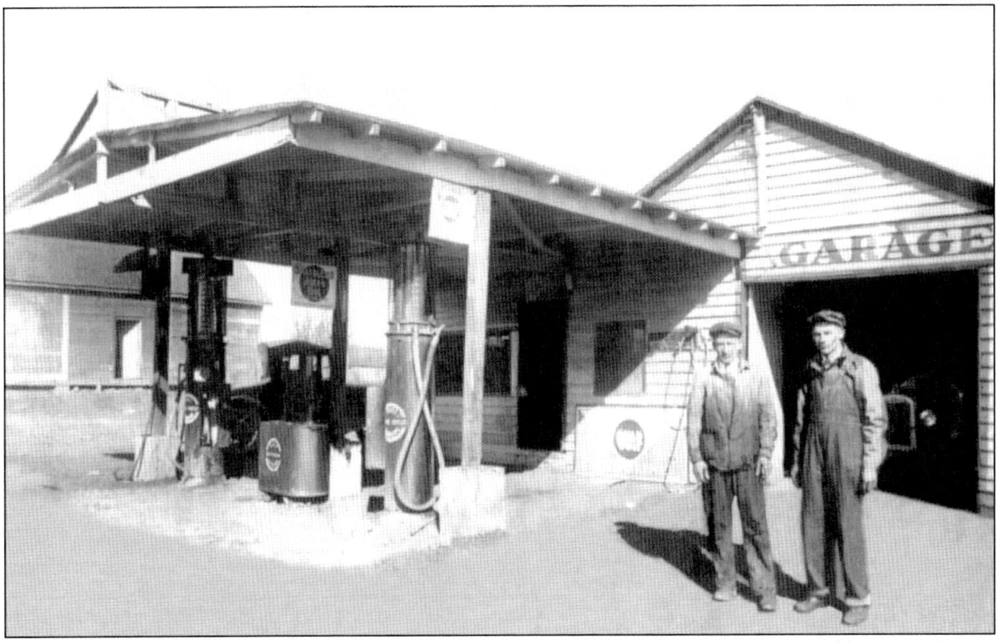

EAST END GARAGE, 1920S. One of Belmont's earliest service stations was operated by Price Ewing Sr. (left) and Hoyle Robinson (right). This 1920s picture features two gravity-fed gasoline pumps with glass containers that measured the gas. A Ford Model T is parked in the background between the two pumps. The apparel worn by Ewing and Robinson indicates that they were hands-on mechanics. (Courtesy of Millican Pictorial History Museum.)

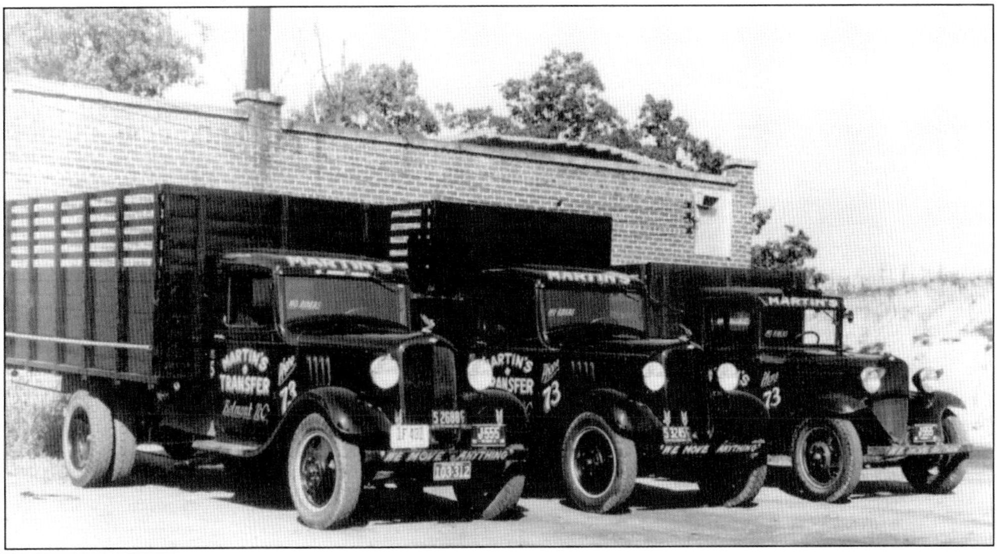

TRUCKS OF MARTIN'S TRANSFER COMPANY, 1935. These three trucks belonging to Martin's Transfer Company are parked and all shined up for this photograph. The building in the background is the original Belmont Chevrolet place, and the graveled bank beyond the third truck was eventually flattened, with its gravelly soil sold for paving driveways. The phone number painted on the trucks, 73, is a clue to the fact that this was a very early business in Belmont. Also, the logo on the bumpers reads, "We Move Anything"—quite a boast to live up to. (Courtesy of Millican Pictorial History Museum.)

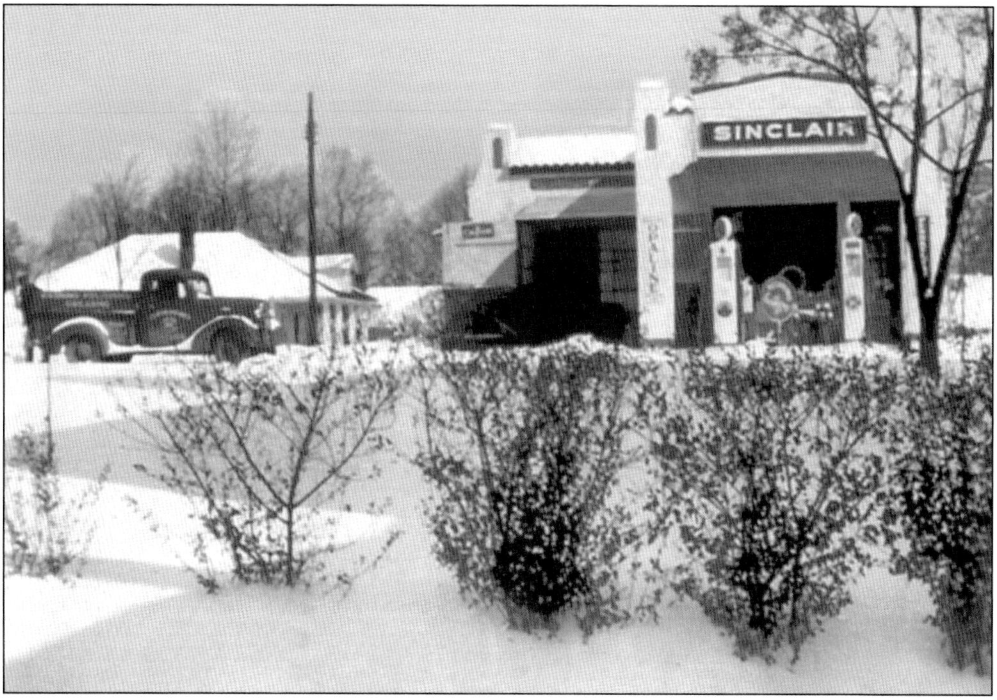

Featherstone's Service Station in East Belmont, 1946. At 122 East Catawba Street, Harry L. Featherstone and Joseph "Dutch" Featherstone worked in their service station. Besides gas, oil, free air, and minor automobile repairs, these fellows sold a broad line of fishing gear. That made Featherstone's the closest fishing equipment store to the Catawba River. There were no big-box stores in 1946. (Courtesy of Millican Pictorial History Museum.)

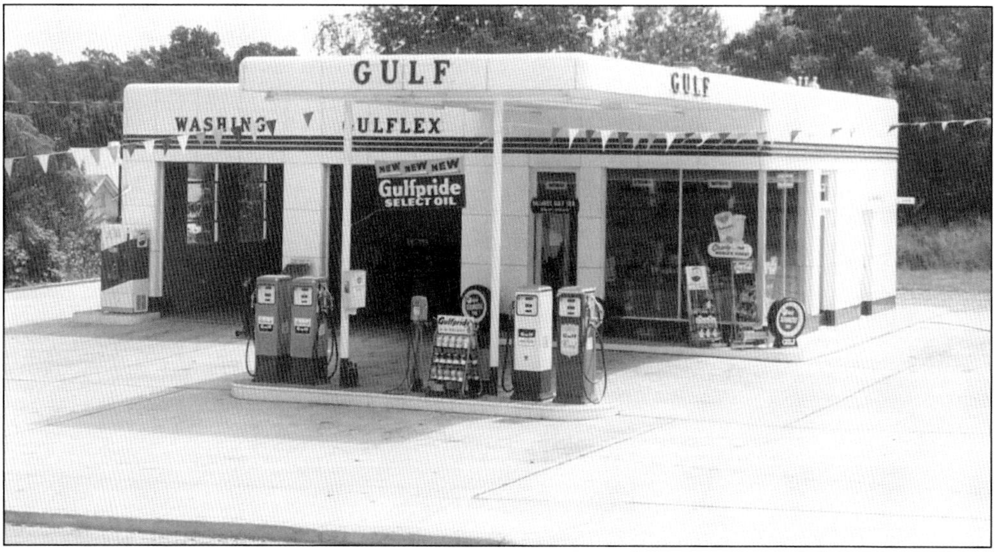

Ballard's Gulf Service Station. This brand-new station was operated by Marvin Ballard, whose brother Calvin Ballard was elected mayor of Belmont in 1969. Marvin was in great demand as a vocal soloist, particularly for weddings and funerals. In his early years at East Belmont School, when Marvin was asked by his teacher if Calvin could sing as well as he could, his answer was, "No, Calvin just 'bellers' like a bull." (Courtesy of Millican Pictorial History Museum.)

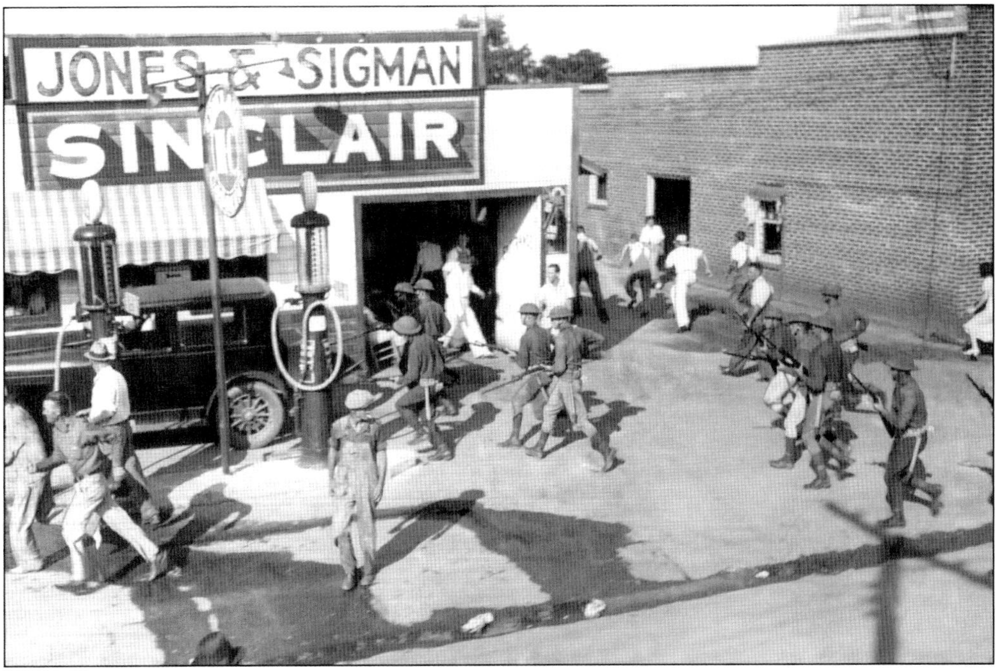

North Carolina National Guard in Action. In 1934, there were many strikes all over the nation. Sheriff Clyde Robinson of Gastonia got a call from Belmont saying that some mill workers were staging a strike and making quite a disturbance. Sheriff Robinson came to Belmont to see about it, and some of the strikers turned his car over and were ready to "beat him up," but the National Guard and police arrived just in time to keep that from happening. (Courtesy of Millican Pictorial History Museum.)

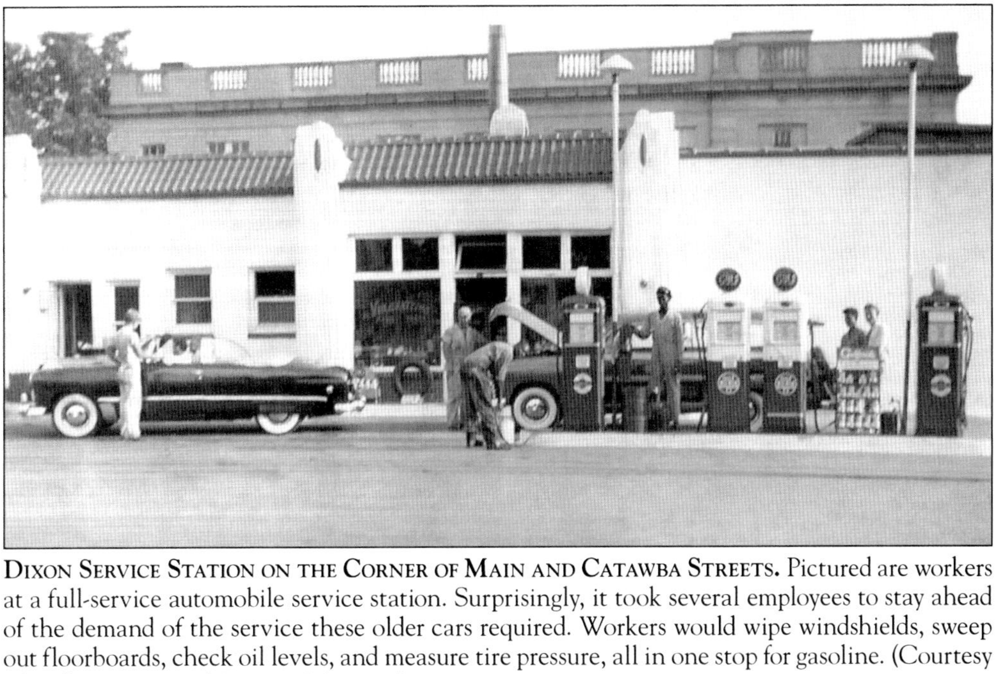

Dixon Service Station on the Corner of Main and Catawba Streets. Pictured are workers at a full-service automobile service station. Surprisingly, it took several employees to stay ahead of the demand of the service these older cars required. Workers would wipe windshields, sweep out floorboards, check oil levels, and measure tire pressure, all in one stop for gasoline. (Courtesy of Millican Pictorial History Museum.)

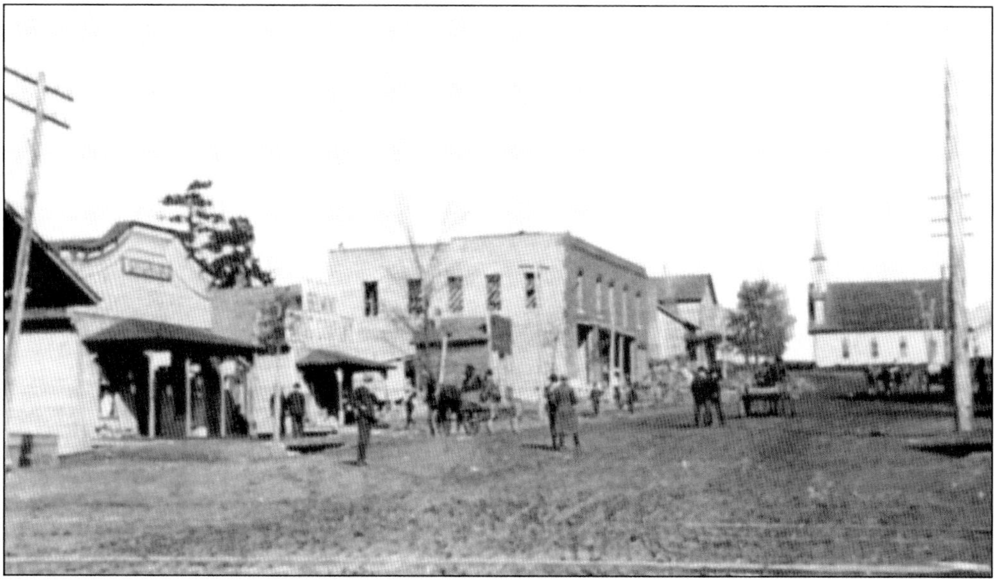

BELMONT'S MAIN STREET, 1905. In Belmont in 1905, there is no automobile to be seen. A few mules and wagons are traveling along Main Street, which, in the 1920s, became the first street to be paved. The Presbyterian church, on land donated by local physician Dr. W.W. Davis can be clearly seen. The church was later razed and rebuilt one block to the right on Catawba Street to make room for the mill office. (Courtesy of Millican Pictorial History Museum.)

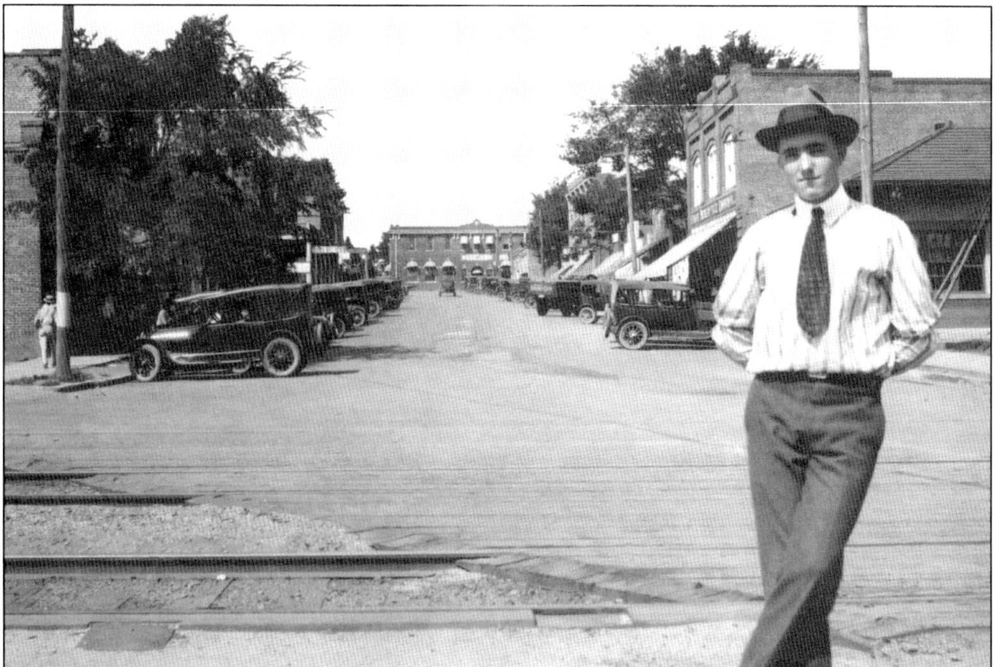

BELMONT'S MAIN STREET, 1920. Belmont's mill office building overlooks Main Street from the top of the hill. This was the only paved street in Belmont in 1920. Shortly thereafter, many streets were paved and the infrastructure, including water lines, fire hydrants, and a sewer system, was put in place. The man posing here is unidentified. (Courtesy of Millican Pictorial History Museum.)

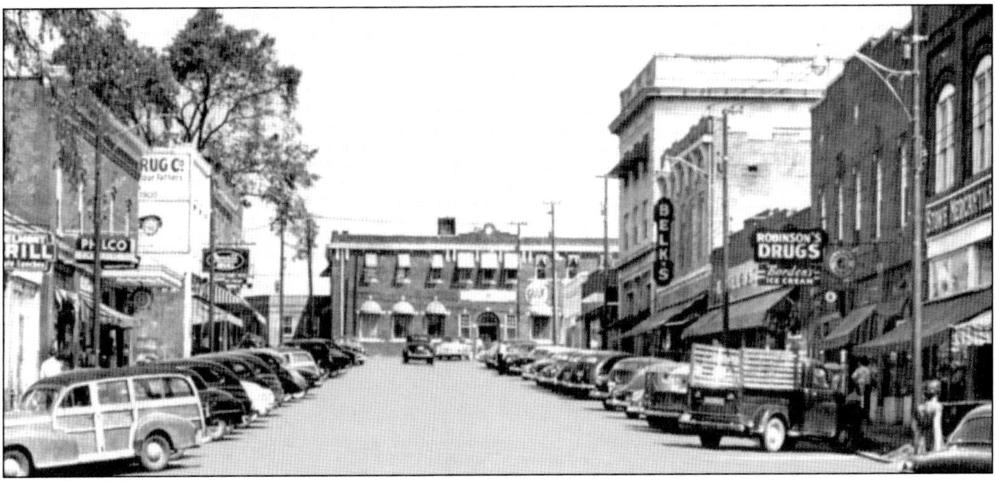

VIEW UP MAIN STREET IN BELMONT, C. 1948. Here is a view of Belmont's Main Street around 1948. The retail area on the right side of the picture features the original Stowe Mercantile, Robinson's Drug Store, the Eagle Store, Belk's department store, the Bank of Belmont, and Dixon's service station. The building seen at the top of the street is the Stowe Mill Office. On the left side of the street are the Belmont Grill, the Belmont Hotel, and the Belmont Drug Store. Other businesses are sandwiched between these prominently seen buildings. (Courtesy of Millican Pictorial History Museum.)

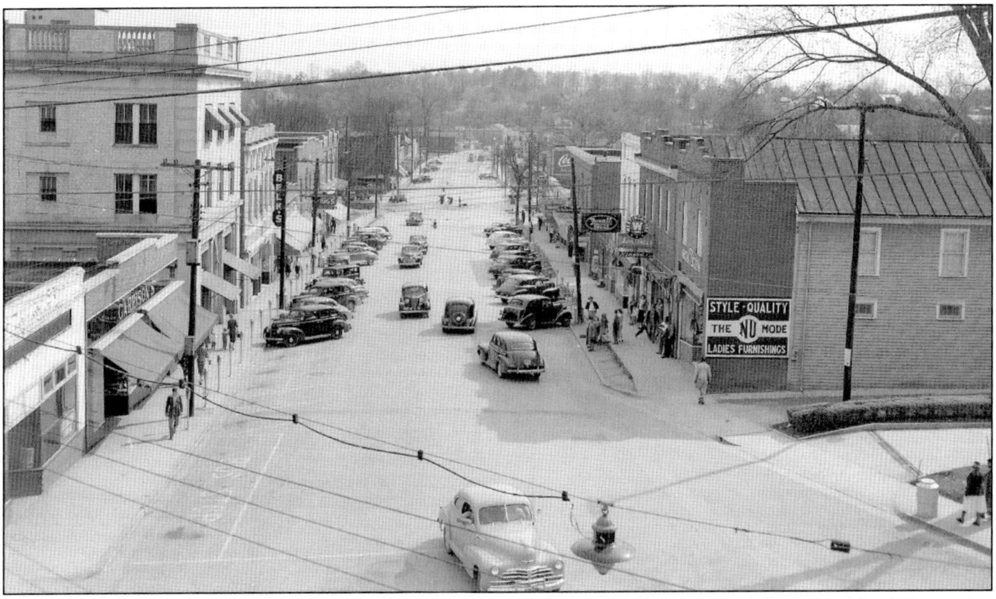

VIEW DOWN MAIN STREET IN BELMONT, C. 1948. This street scene was photographed from the Stowe Mill Office, down Main Street and toward the railroad. On the right side is the Nu Mode, which featured ladies' ready-to-wear. Farther down Main Street are W.H. and D.P. Stowe furniture store, the Belmont Drug Store, the Belmont Hotel, the Belmont Grill, the Belmont Barber Shop, Cohen's Ladies' ready-to-wear, and the G.W. Howe Company. On the left side are the corner of Dixon's Tire & Recapping, Garrison's, the Bank of Belmont, Belk's department store, the Eagle Store, Robinson's Drug Store, and Stowe Mercantile. Railroad workers are visible in the center of Main Street as they repair the tracks at the crossing. (Courtesy of Millican Pictorial History Museum.)

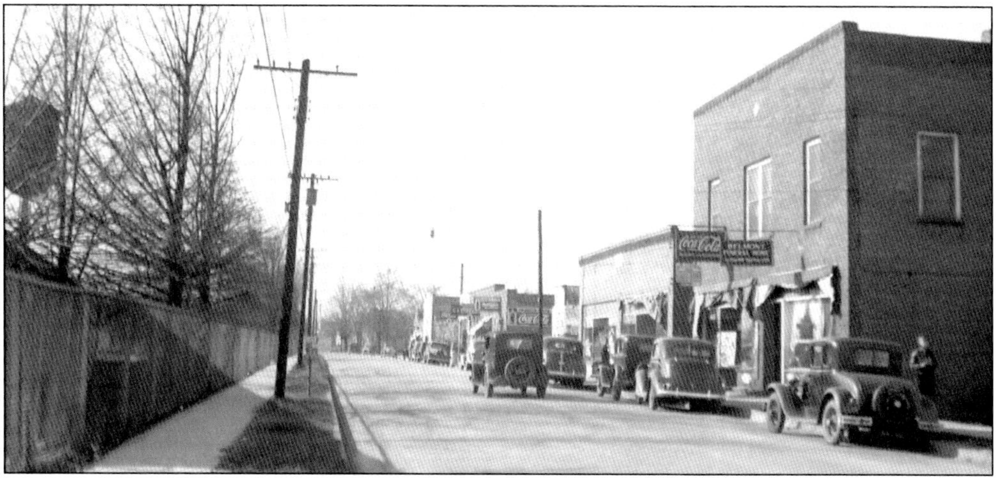

East Belmont, View Looking West, 1940s. The shopping strip pictured was the main business section of East Belmont. It contained retail stores, a beauty shop, an insurance company, a furniture store, a drugstore, and various other enterprises. Across Catawba Street stands the Majestic Mill, with its customary water tank. A chain-link fence separated the mill from public access. (Courtesy of Millican Pictorial History Museum.)

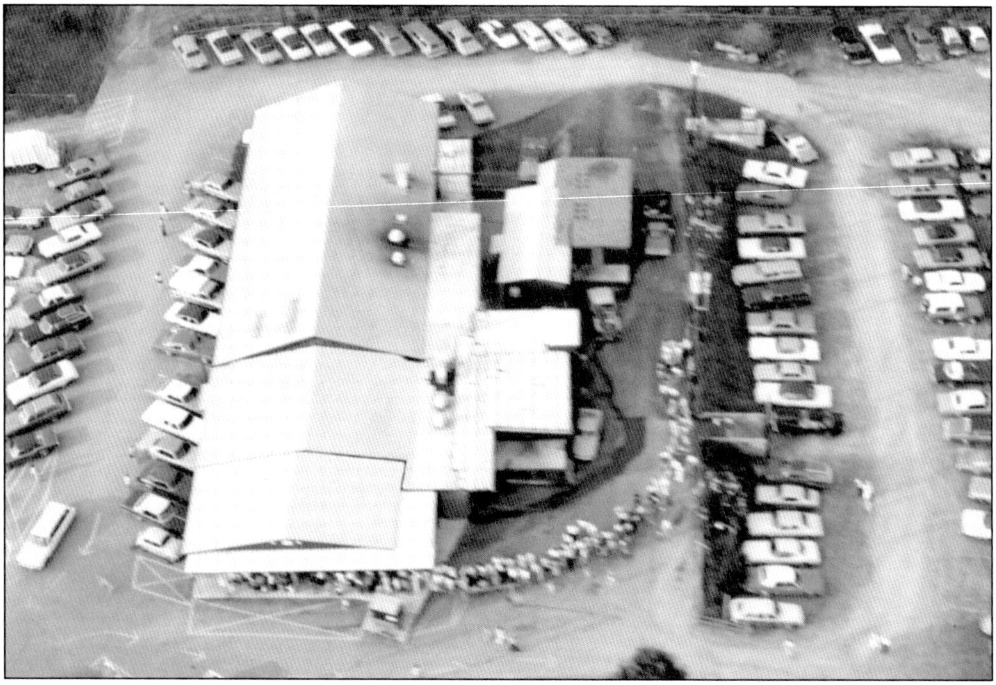

Aerial View of Lineberger's Fish Camp. Popular Lineberger's Fish Camp served customers from Gaston County, the surrounding counties, and beyond. Its popularity was so great that Gaston County police had to be posted in front of the parking lot to direct traffic on weekends. Notice the long lines of hungry people waiting patiently to be allowed to enter and be served. Parking was at a premium. This fish camp was operated by Luther Lineberger, who was one of the first men to begin frying fish in eastern Gaston County. The eating establishment gained notoriety through the news media and magazine articles and by word of mouth. (Courtesy of Millican Pictorial History Museum.)

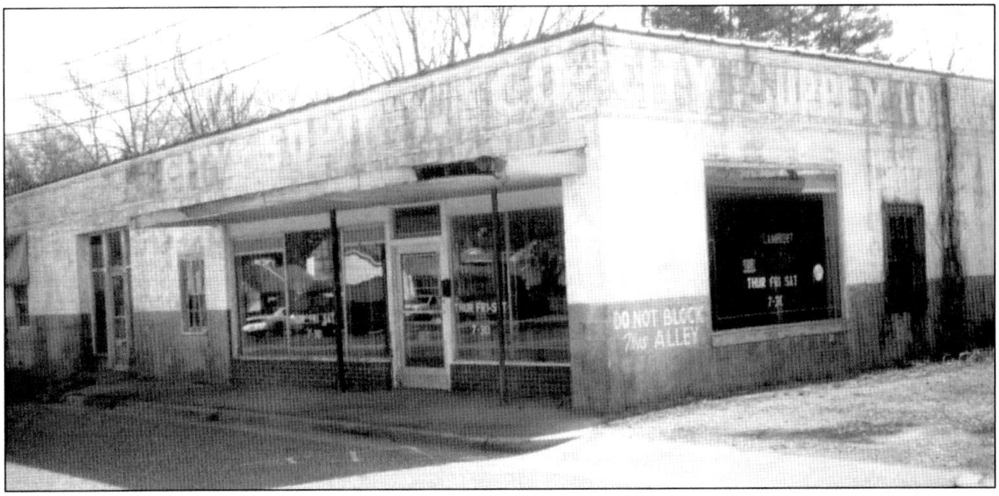

City Supply Company of Belmont. For many years, Belmont City Supply company was the main source of building materials for homes and businesses constructed following World War II. It was established by Price Hand. Several of the longtime workers were Wade Chapman, Kenneth Tate, Frank Dunn, Bill Hand, "Grover," and others. When a need for plumbing, painting, roofing, or making a sidewalk arose, one of these men could always help one know who or what was needed. This was before the days of the big-box stores like Home Depot and Lowe's. This building was converted into a restaurant called Belmont City Cafe, which was a favorite eating place for locals for several years. (Courtesy of Millican Pictorial History Museum.)

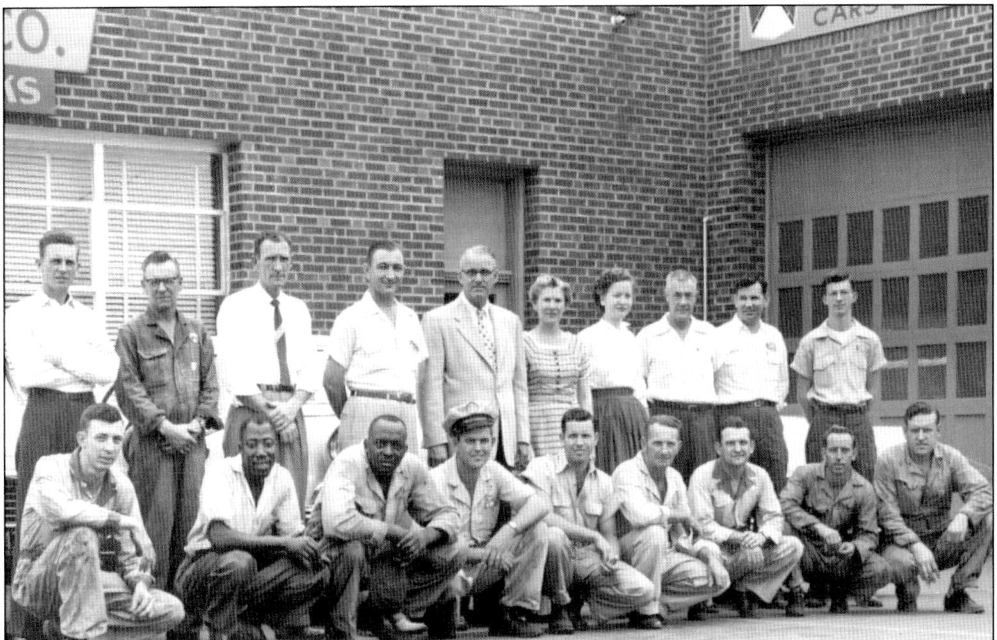

Employees at Dixon Ford Motor Company, 1955. After World War II, Dixon Motor Company thrived, as did many of the local car dealerships. It added many personnel to its workforce and opened a used-car business. It would not be long before the business outgrew this facility and moved to the corner of the Belmont/Mount Holly Road and McAdenville Road. (Courtesy of Millican Pictorial History Museum.)

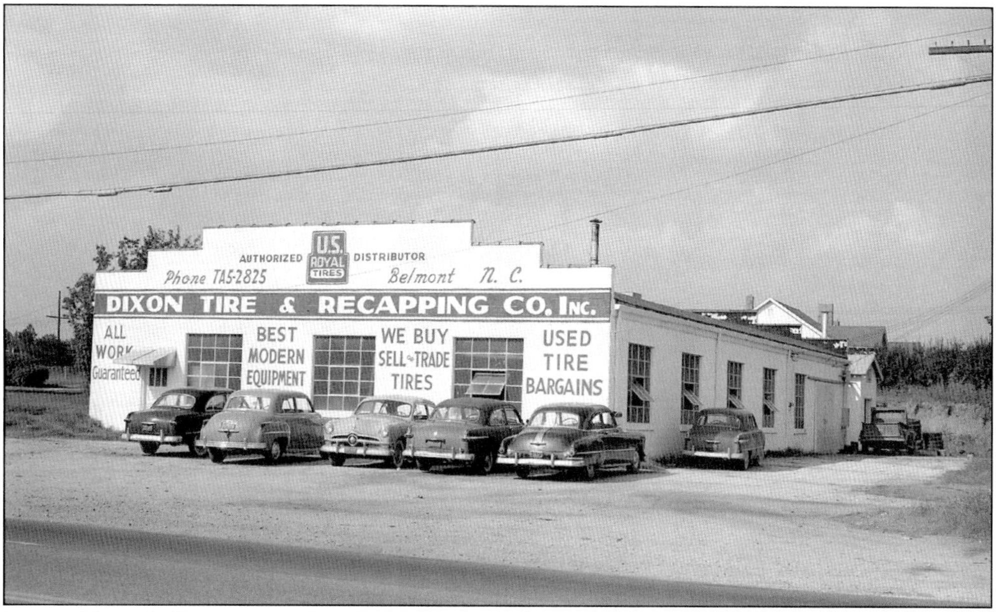

DIXON TIRE & RECAPPING CO. Dixon Tire & Recapping is pictured at its new location on Wilkinson Boulevard. For many years, this business was located at the corner of Main and Catawba Streets in downtown Belmont. During World War II, tires were scarce, so recapping old tires was a thriving enterprise. (Courtesy of Millican Pictorial History Museum.)

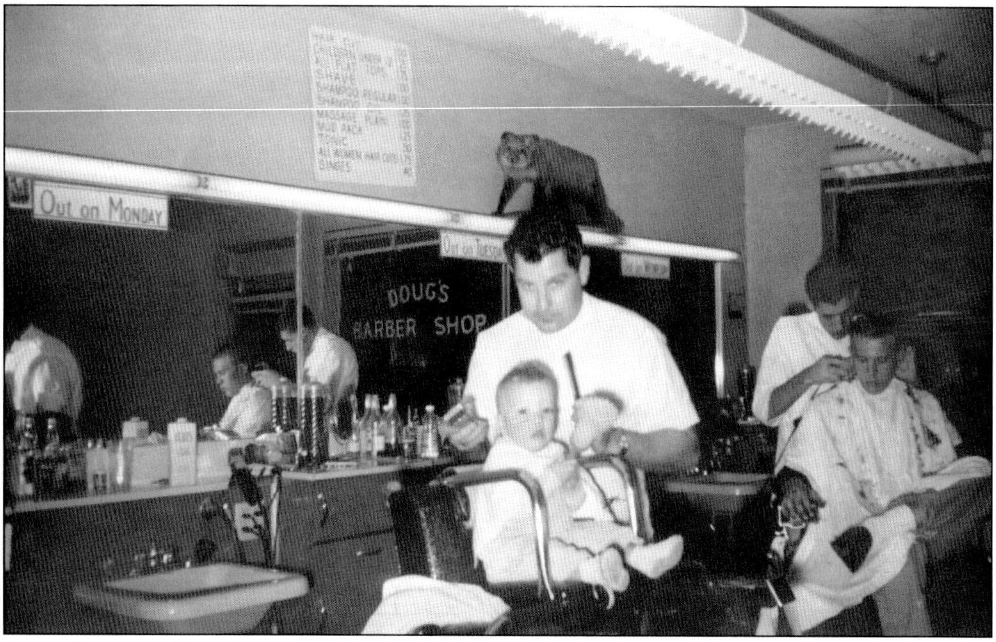

DOUG BREWER. Doug Brewer, who grew up in Belmont's East End, got his barber's license and set up shop in Belmont. His fellow barber was T.W. Ballard, pictured on the right cutting hair. The customer in Brewer's chair is Kevin Southern, who is getting his first haircut. Notice the price list on the wall behind Brewer. Now in his 80th year, Brewer is still cutting hair in his shop at the rear of the Belmont General Store, which was previously Stowe Mercantile. (Courtesy of Millican Pictorial History Museum.)

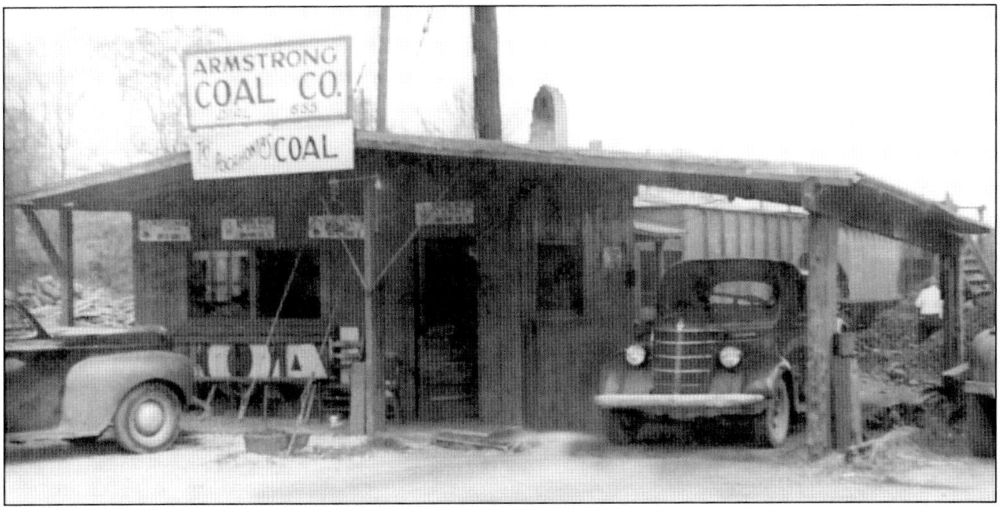

ARMSTRONG COAL COMPANY IN BELMONT. Although Jim Armstrong called his business Armstrong Coal Company, he also sold fuel oil. Coal could be delivered by the ton to the customer's home, but some people purchased coal in heavy paper craft bags that held about 50 pounds of coal. Fuel oil was generally delivered by tanker truck straight to the business or residence. Later bought and run by Clyde Clark, this business was located near the sight of the Wells Fargo drive-through bank on Glenway Avenue. (Courtesy of Millican Pictorial History Museum.)

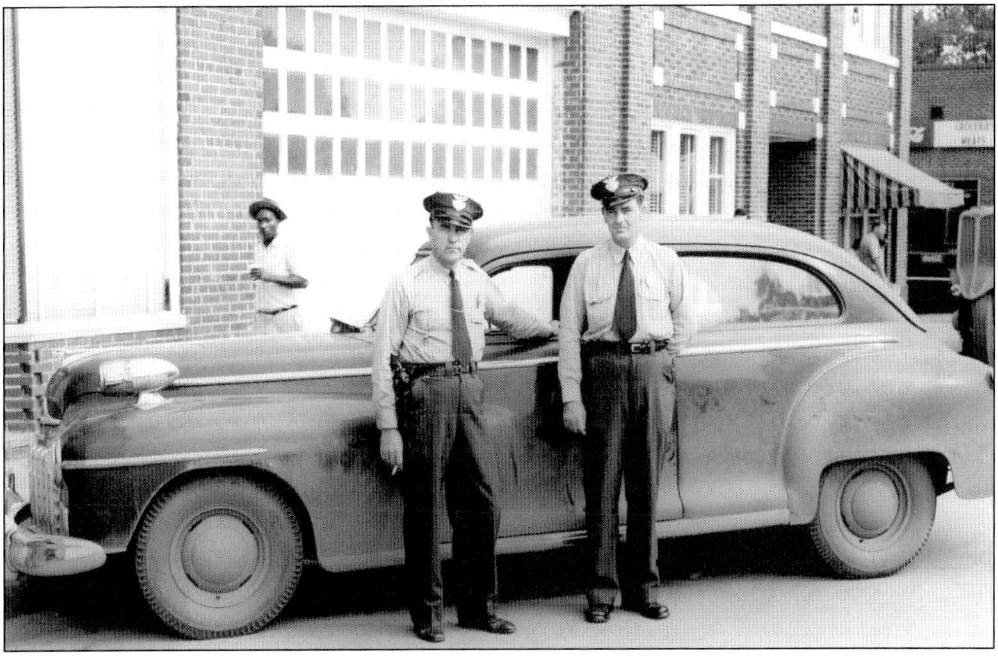

BELMONT POLICE AND FIRE DEPARTMENTS, 1940S. Civic needs got priority when vehicles became available after World War II. Here is Belmont's first postwar police car, a maroon Dodge sedan, equipped with a siren. It was heavy, slow, and probably got about 15 miles per gallon. The large door in the background belonged to the Belmont Fire Department and housed a 1920s American LaFrance fire truck. At right is Belmont City Hall, with the police station and driver's license office on the ground floor, a jail in the basement, and the recorder's court on the second floor. (Courtesy of Millican Pictorial History Museum.)

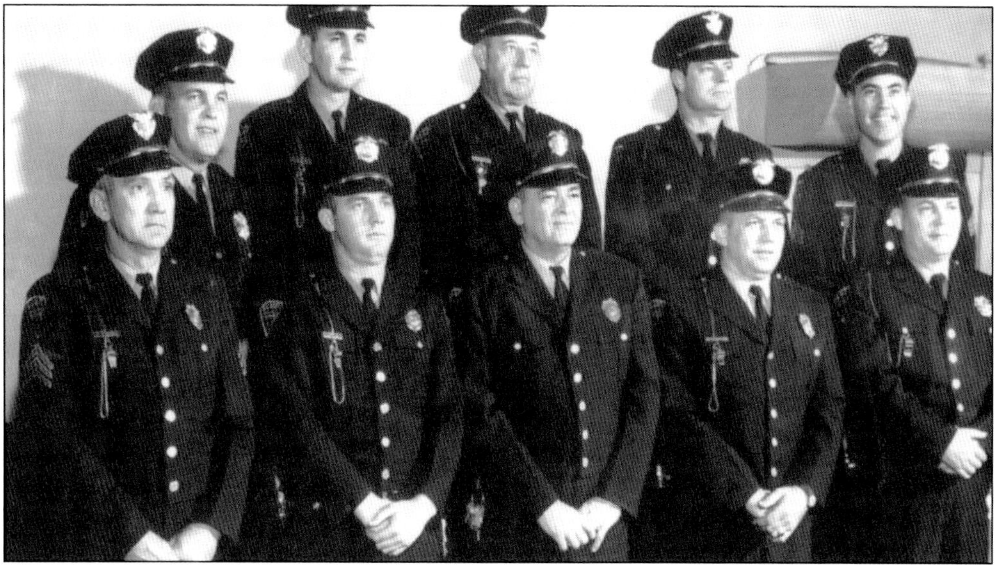

Belmont Police Department, 1963. This picture includes five future police chiefs. They are (front row) Frank Carpenter (third from left) and Tommy Hinson (fifth from left); (back row) Garrett Murphy (third from left), Bill Joye (fourth from left), and Claude Setzer (fifth from left). (Courtesy of Millican Pictorial History Museum.)

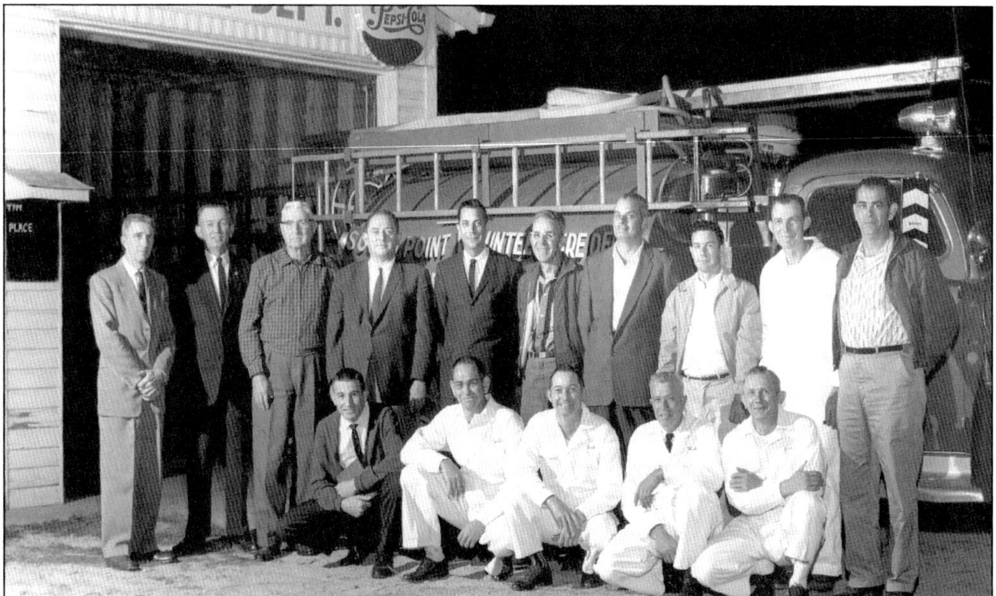

South Point Volunteer Fire Department, c. 1958. Fire protection was mandated by most people's fire insurance policies. This made it necessary for local fire departments, manned by volunteers, to be organized in areas not served by municipal fire services. The South Point Volunteer Fire Department was composed of a board of directors and firefighters who had extensive state training. Departments such as this one were supported financially by residents in the community that they served. Pictured in back of the fire department personnel is a tanker that had been placed on an Army-surplus chassis. Fortunately, most calls were to suppress grass fires. (Courtesy of Millican Pictorial History Museum.)

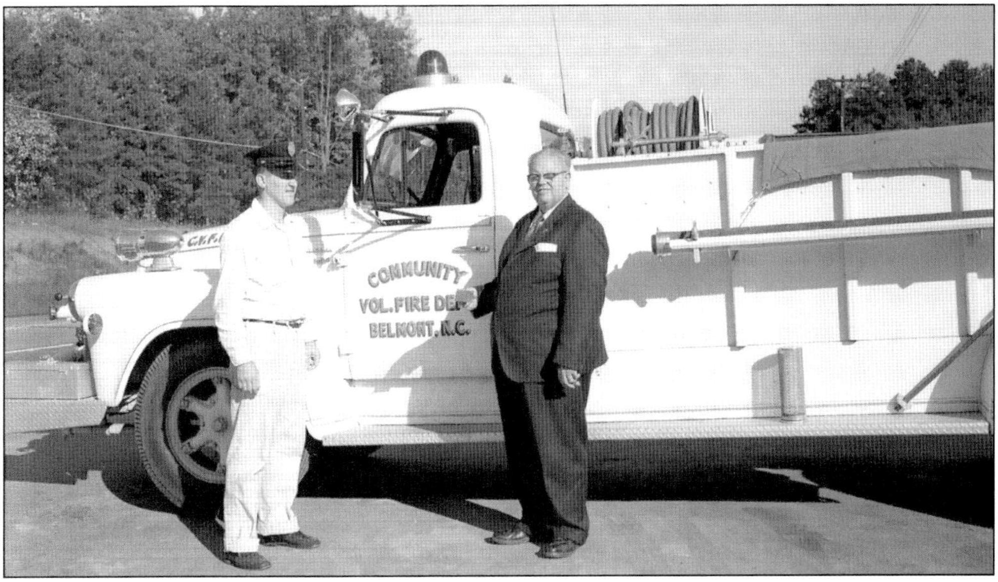

Community Volunteer Fire Department, 1950s. Before Belmont expanded its firefighting services, each of the outlying areas provided its own firefighting equipment and a department manned by trained volunteers. The departments' operation and their funding were dependent on fundraisers and volunteer firefighters. Each fire department had its own board of directors and was responsible to the Gaston County commissioners. (Courtesy of Millican Pictorial History Museum.)

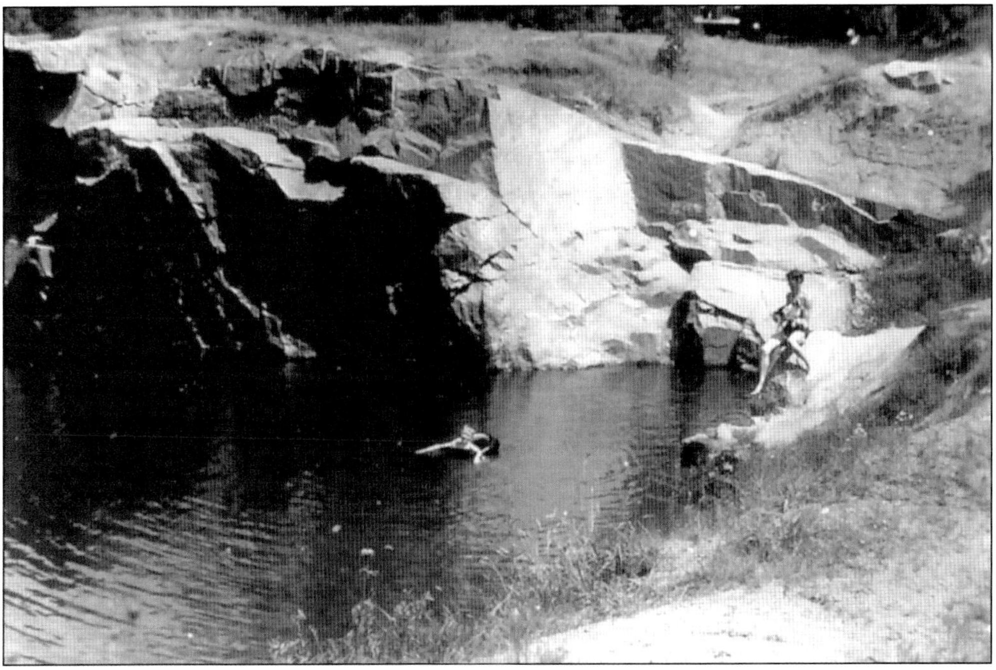

Rock Quarry off McAdenville Road. Visiting the rock quarry off McAdenville Road was strictly forbidden. However, the cold water drew some adventurous youths during hot weather. At various times, stolen vehicles ended up in the quarry's mysterious depths. (Courtesy of Millican Pictorial History Museum.)

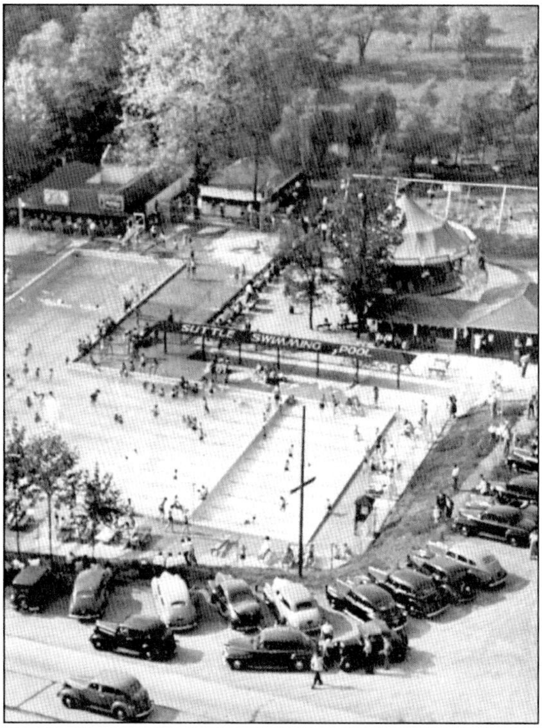

SUTTLE'S SWIMMING POOL, 1940S. Ralph Suttle provided an exceedingly popular entertainment center just across the river from Belmont in Mecklenburg County. It provided swimming, diving boards, and swimming lessons on a regular basis. There were other features on the grounds like mechanized swings, a merry-go-round, Putt-Putt golf, a grill, and arcade games. The Suttle family was very strict and allowed no smoking, drinking, profanity, or horseplay. The center's competition was across the creek: a swimming pool called Willamete. During World War II, both of these pools provided rest and recreation for soldiers stationed at Morris Field, which was just a couple of miles away. (Courtesy of Millican Pictorial History Museum.)

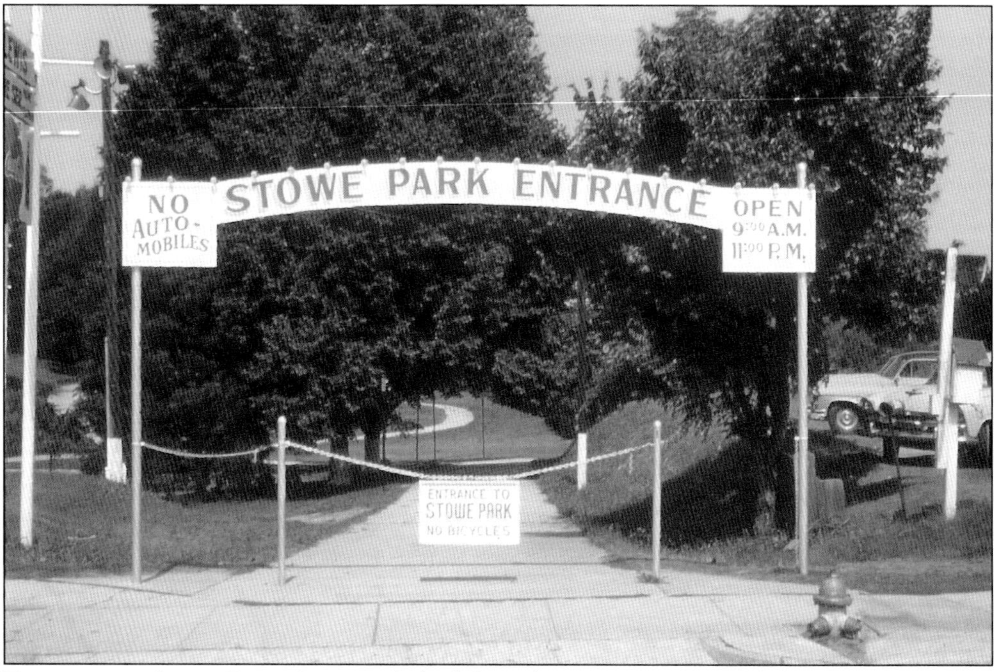

ENTRANCE TO STOWE PARK. Stowe Park, built by Robert Lee Stowe Jr., added a new dimension to recreation in the Belmont area. Not pictured is a free outdoor movie, offered once a week during the summer, weather permitting. Although the carnival pieces are gone, the park, later donated to the city, still serves Belmont as a place for a variety of events throughout the year. (Courtesy of Millican Pictorial History Museum.)

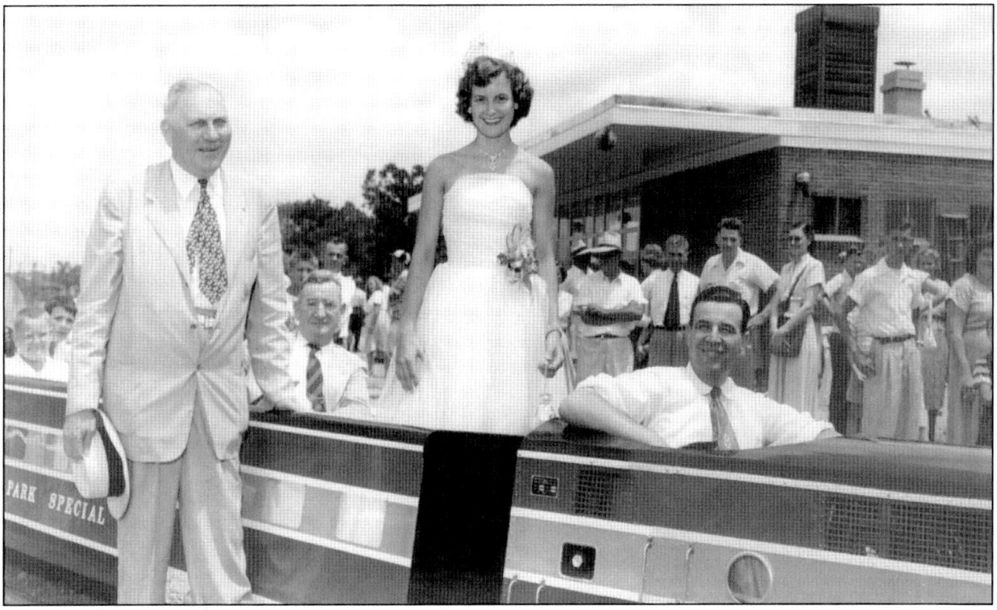

Grand Opening of Stowe Park. The grand opening of Stowe Park on July 4, 1951, was an important event in the history of Belmont. Gov. Gregg Cherry stands with his hat in his hand. City attorney Harley Gaston Sr. is seated between Miss Belmont Novella Cloninger and the governor. The engineer pictured here is textile magnate Robert Lee Stowe Jr., who conceived of the park and later donated it to the City of Belmont. Although the merry-go-round, the Ferris wheel, the train, and many other original attractions are gone, the lower portion of the park along Main Street is a vibrant area, featuring a gazebo, a fountain, swings, and other attractions. (Courtesy of Millican Pictorial History Museum.)

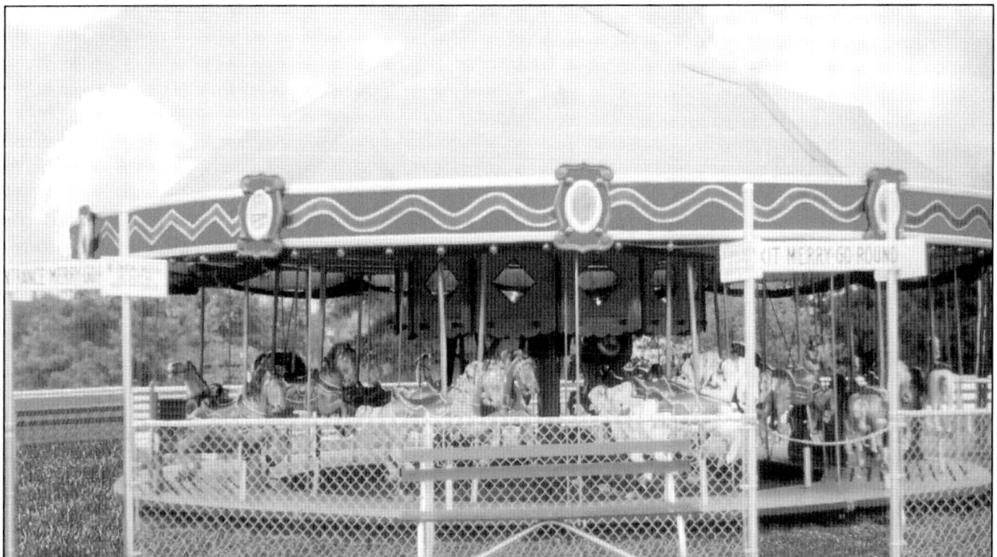

Stowe Park Carousel. Children enjoy the Stowe Park merry-go-round, which charged 10¢ per ride. This was a very popular attraction at Stowe Park, especially for the younger children. (Courtesy of Millican Pictorial History Museum.)

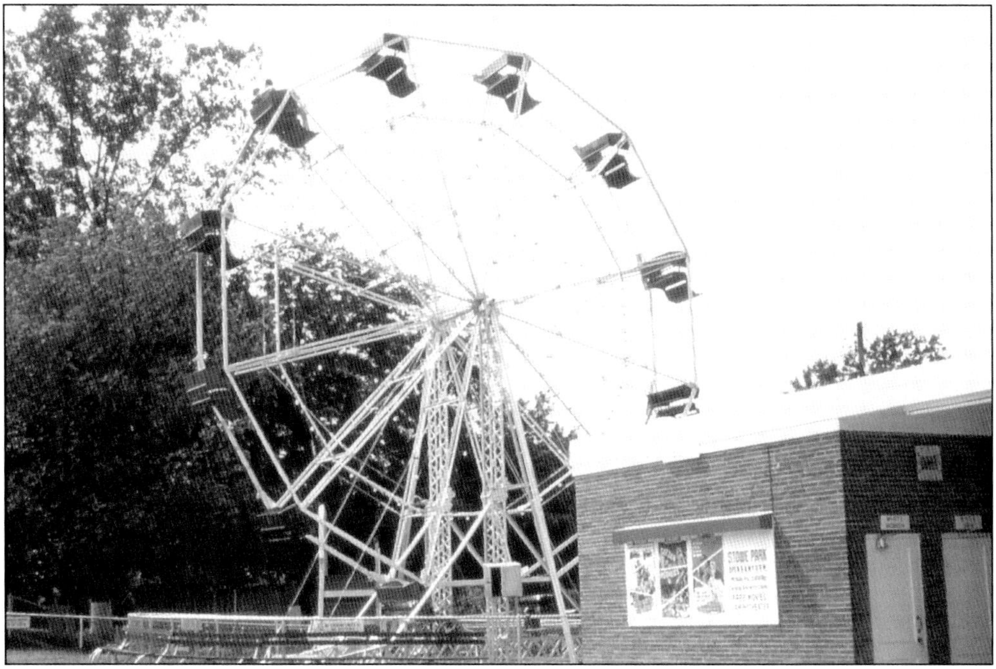

Ferris Wheel and Concession Stand at Stowe Park. From the top of the Ferris wheel, one could count around 10 water tanks. Each water tank served one mill and its village. (Courtesy of Millican Pictorial History Museum.)

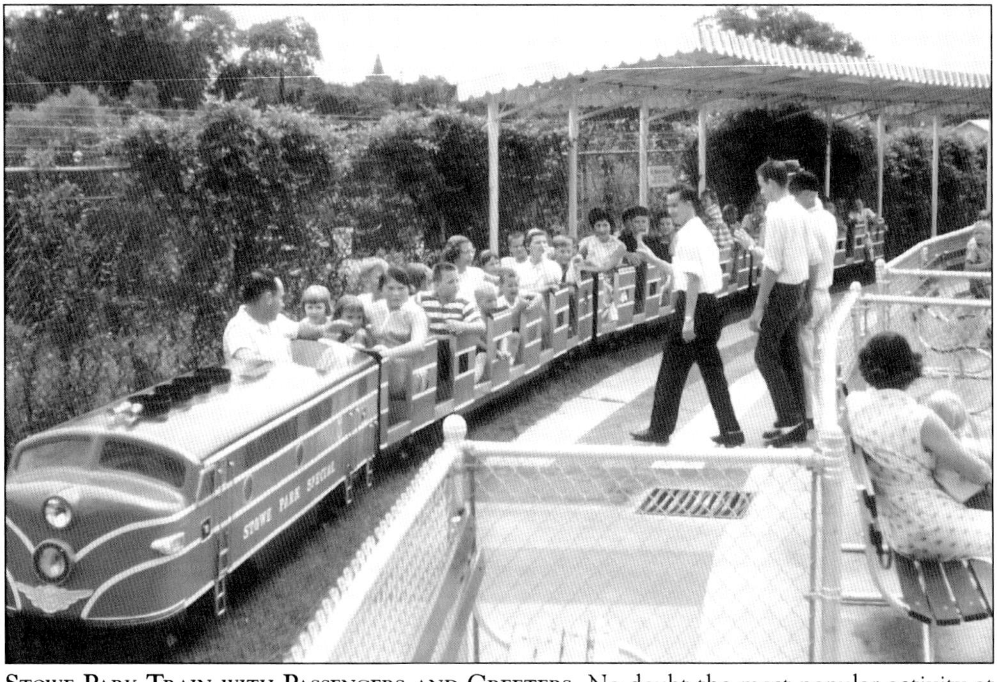

Stowe Park Train with Passengers and Greeters. No doubt the most popular activity at Stowe Park was riding the Stowe Park Special train. This was especially true for couples, as they anticipated riding through the tunnel. Children of all ages loved the train. (Courtesy of Millican Pictorial History Museum.)

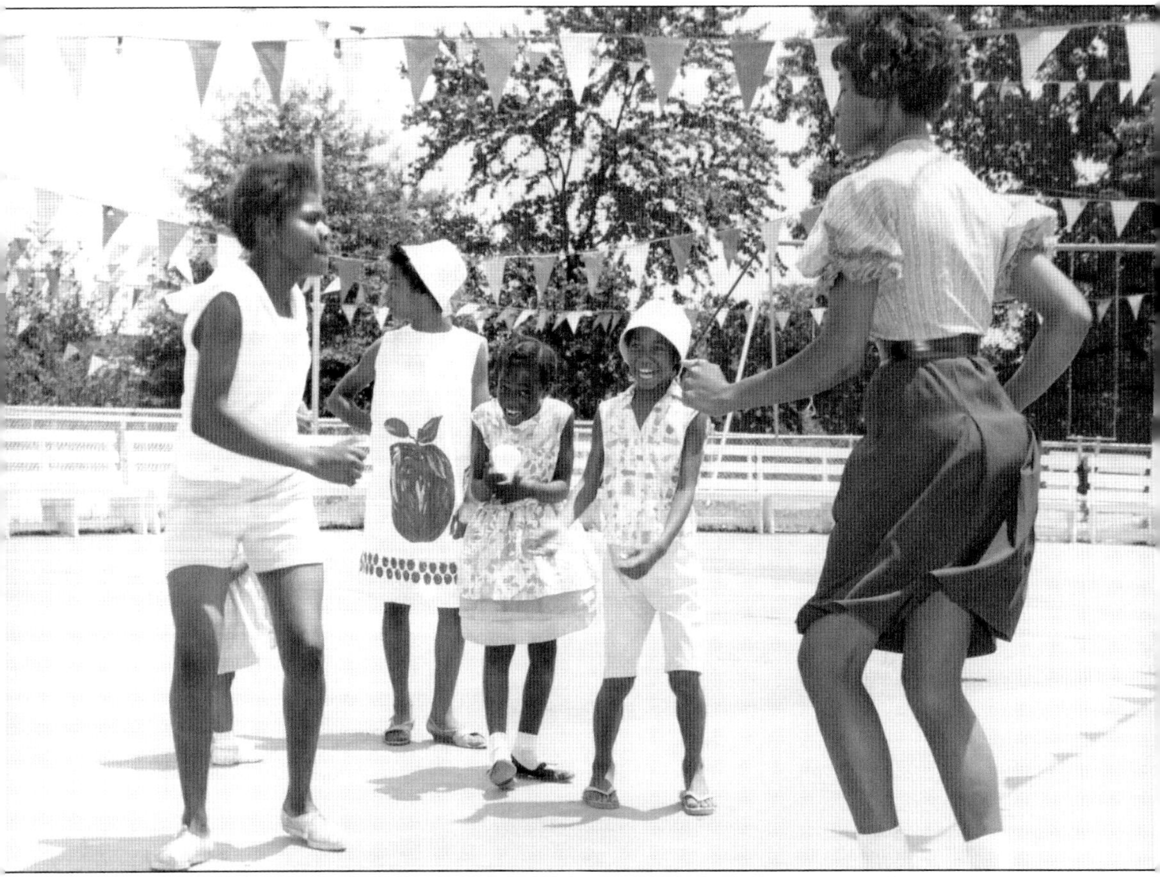

GIRLS DANCING AT STOWE PARK. Formal dancing was not in vogue in a mill town; however, the jitterbug and shag were highly popular dances—or kids would improvise their own dances. (Courtesy of Millican Pictorial History Museum.)

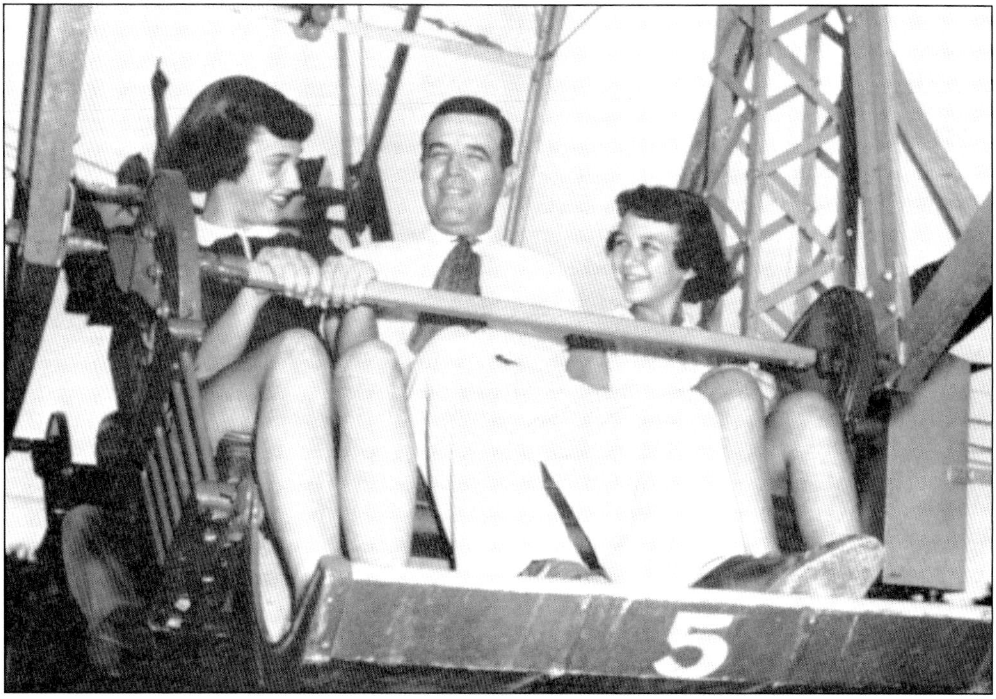

Patricia Ellington (left), Robert Stowe Jr., and Kay Nixon. A pleasant smile is on Stowe's face as he accompanies two young admirers on a trip over the Ferris wheel. His two friends' smiles reflect those of thousands of people who enjoyed Stowe Park in the 1950s and 1960s. (Courtesy of Millican Pictorial History Museum.)

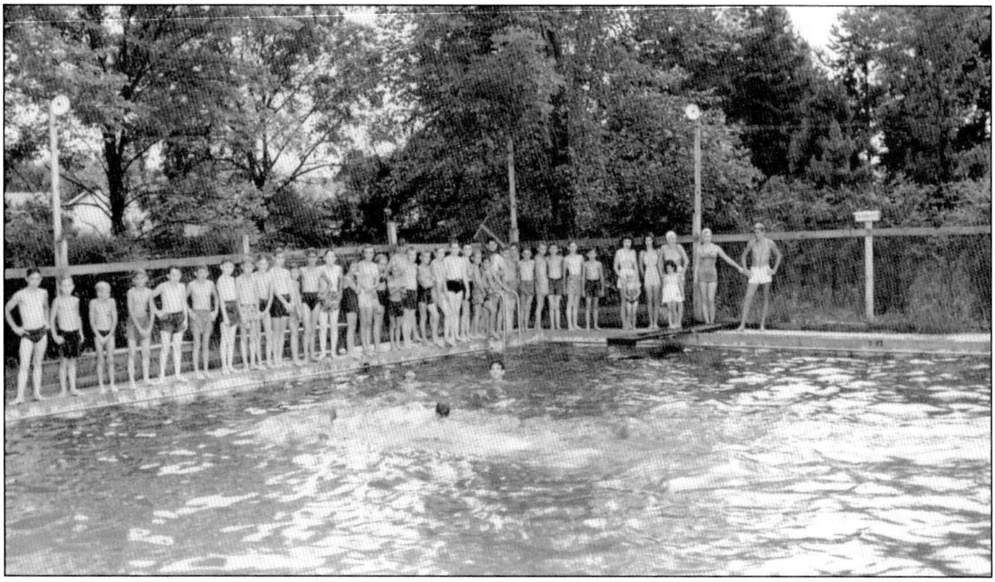

Hall's Old Swimming Pool. Recreational opportunities were limited in Belmont. Mostly, there was just tennis, softball, baseball, roller-skating, and biking until W.M. Hall built a swimming pool on the corner of Central Avenue and Todd Street. Many Belmont youngsters learned to swim or honed their skills in Hall's pool. Today, a beautiful brick ranch-style home rests on this site. (Courtesy of Millican Pictorial History Museum.)

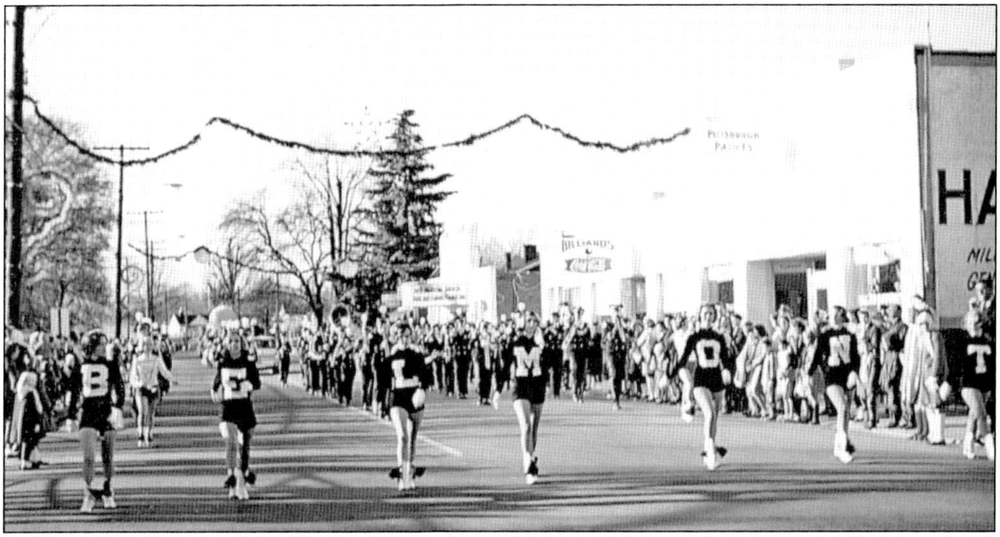

LETTER GIRLS, 1964. Pictured are the 1964 Letter Girls as they lead the Belmont High School Band in Belmont's annual Christmas parade. Along the right side of Catawba Street, one can see the Gem Theater, a billiard parlor, and Calvin Ballard's Hardware Store. Ballard served as mayor of Belmont from 1969 to 1975. (Courtesy of Millican Pictorial History Museum.)

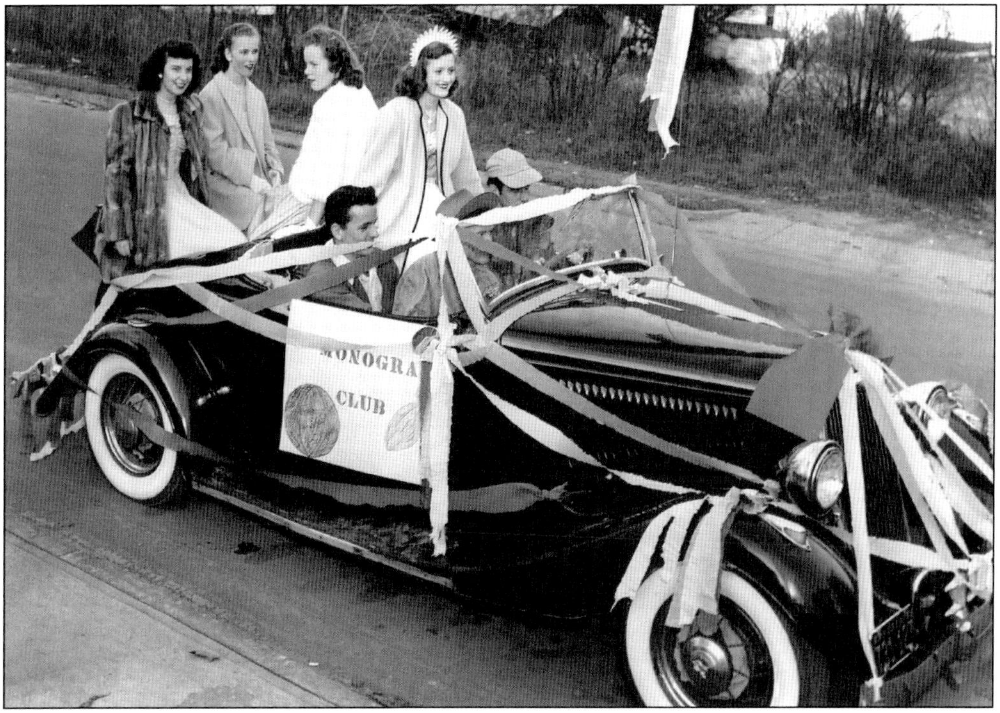

BELMONT CHRISTMAS PARADE, 1950S. Four of Belmont High School's beauties are prepared to join in Belmont's 1950 annual Christmas parade. This car was decorated and sponsored by the Belmont High School Monogram Club, which was composed of members of Belmont High School's athletic teams. The girls perched in the back are, from left to right, Carol Goodrum, Marlene Thompson, Barbara Elmore, and Bobbie Bradshaw. (Courtesy of Millican Pictorial History Museum.)

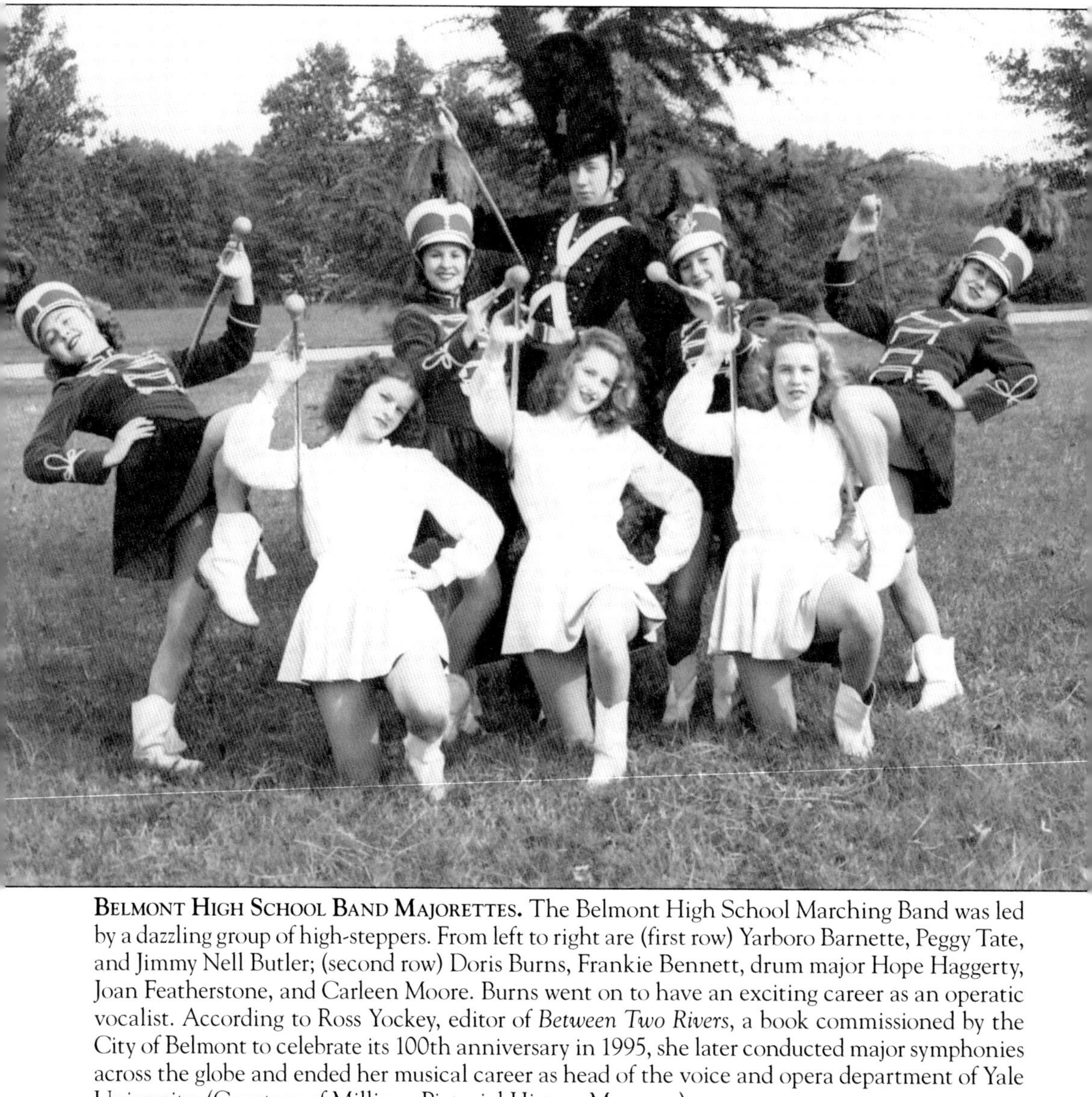

BELMONT HIGH SCHOOL BAND MAJORETTES. The Belmont High School Marching Band was led by a dazzling group of high-steppers. From left to right are (first row) Yarboro Barnette, Peggy Tate, and Jimmy Nell Butler; (second row) Doris Burns, Frankie Bennett, drum major Hope Haggerty, Joan Featherstone, and Carleen Moore. Burns went on to have an exciting career as an operatic vocalist. According to Ross Yockey, editor of *Between Two Rivers*, a book commissioned by the City of Belmont to celebrate its 100th anniversary in 1995, she later conducted major symphonies across the globe and ended her musical career as head of the voice and opera department of Yale University. (Courtesy of Millican Pictorial History Museum.)

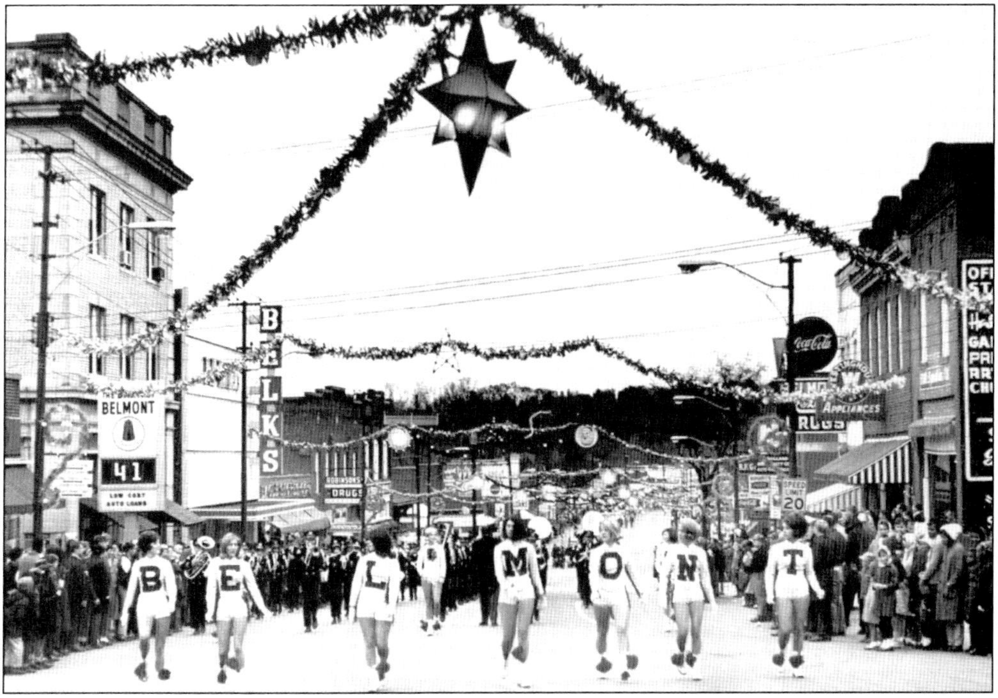

Christmas Parade, 1966. Leading the Belmont High School Band, the letter girls were the first attraction in the annual Christmas parade. This parade kicked off the official Christmas shopping season in downtown Belmont. These girls might be a little chilly in this 41-degree weather. (Courtesy of Millican Pictorial History Museum.)

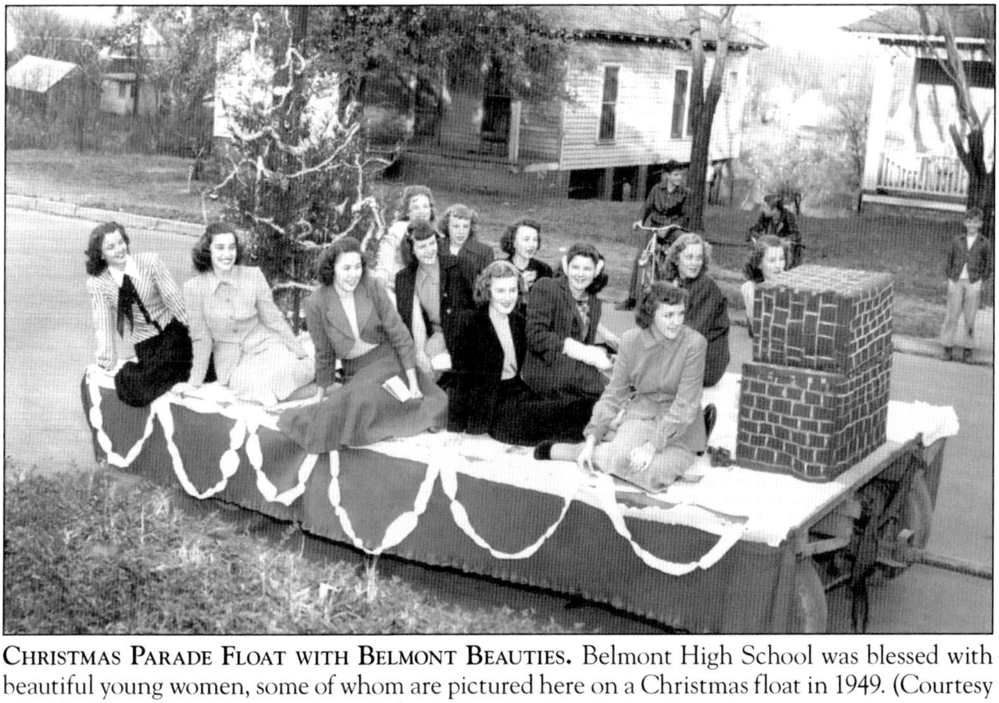

Christmas Parade Float with Belmont Beauties. Belmont High School was blessed with beautiful young women, some of whom are pictured here on a Christmas float in 1949. (Courtesy of Millican Pictorial History Museum.)

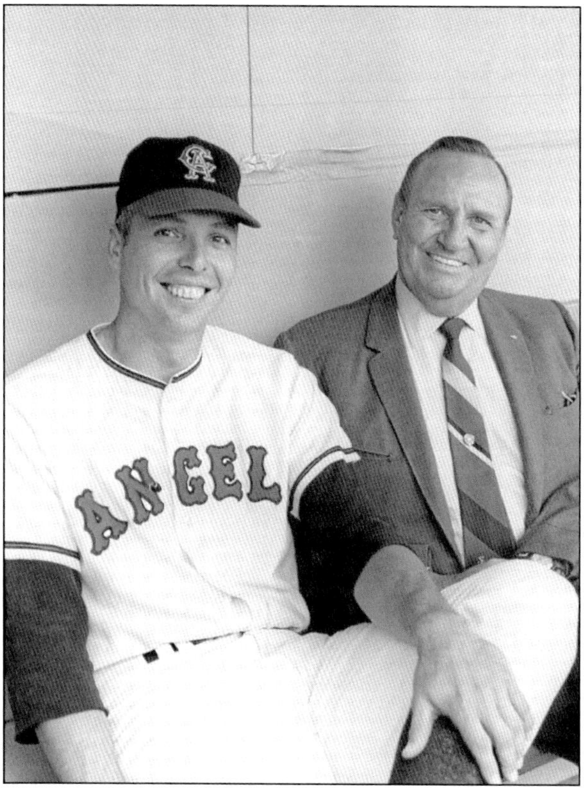

JIMMIE HALL WITH GENE AUTRY. Jimmie Hall (left) is sitting with California Angels owner Gene Autry. Hall began his baseball career at Belmont High School, and he played for the Gaston County American Legion team. He was signed in 1956 to a major-league baseball contract by the Washington Senators. He worked his way into the majors and found a home with the Minnesota Twins. There, Hall's rookie total of 33 home runs would set a career high for a first-year American League player. This record still stands. (Courtesy of Millican Pictorial History Museum.)

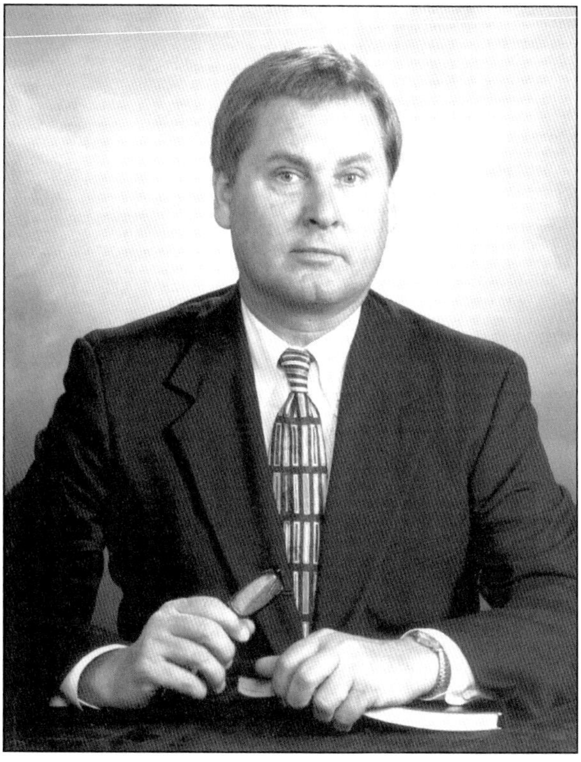

ART SHOEMAKER. Art Shoemaker, a Cramerton native, has for many years been an outstanding contributer to Cramerton, Belmont, and the surrounding areas. Art coached the Little League football team the Orangemen, who won a national championship. He also coached baseball and basketball. The Belmont Sports Hall of Fame was begun and led by Art for many years. He was also responsible for creating a small sports museum in Cramerton. The relocation of *Spirit of the Fighting Yank* was one of Art's most recent projects. (Courtesy of Millican Pictorial History Museum.)

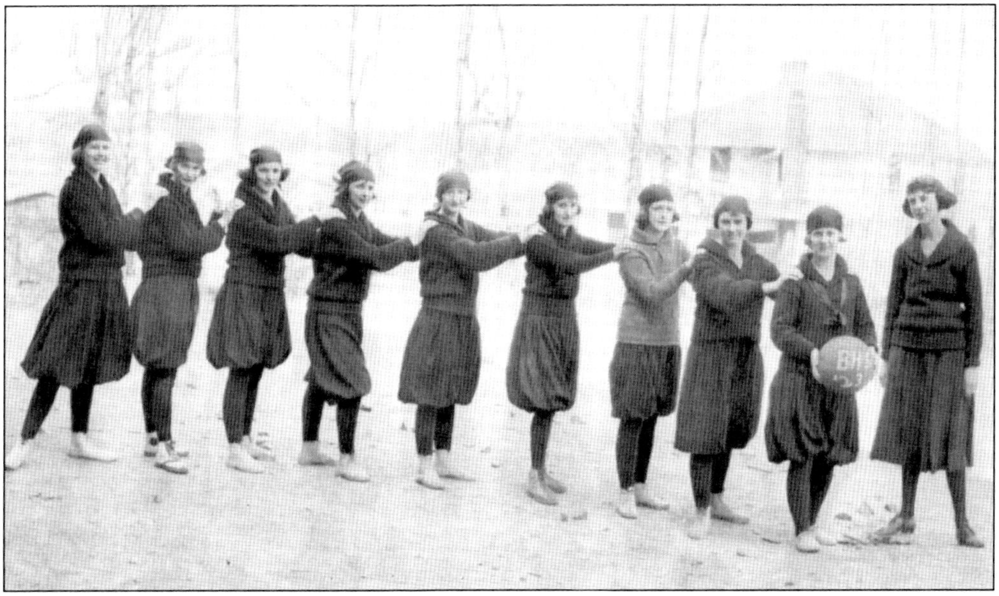

THE 1923 BELMONT HIGH SCHOOL'S GIRLS BASKETBALL TEAM. The 1923 Belmont High Girls Basketball team was required to wear modest clothing as uniforms. They played only half-court basketball. One half of the team played offense and the other half played defense. It was felt by school officials that full-court basketball was too strenuous for women. The tallest woman in the picture is the coach. (Courtesy of Millican Pictorial History Museum.)

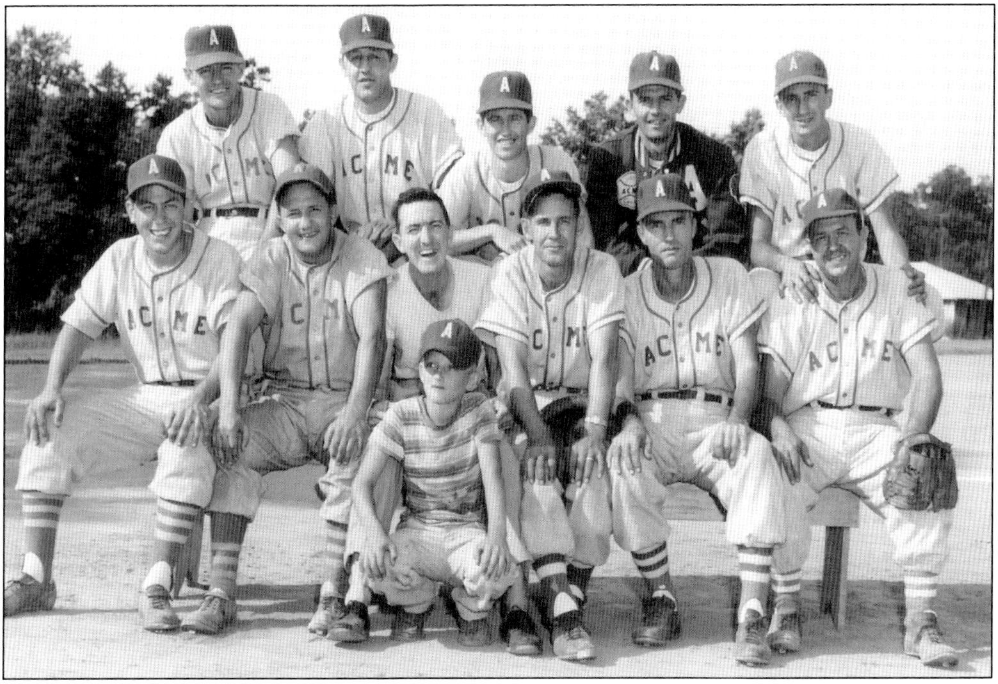

ACME BASEBALL TEAM. Many of the area mills sponsored baseball teams that competed on the diamond with other mill teams. The skill level of most players was quite high, and many engaged in minor-league or semiprofessional baseball. Stealing a prized player by offering him a job at another mill with better pay was known to happen. (Courtesy of Millican Pictorial History Museum.)

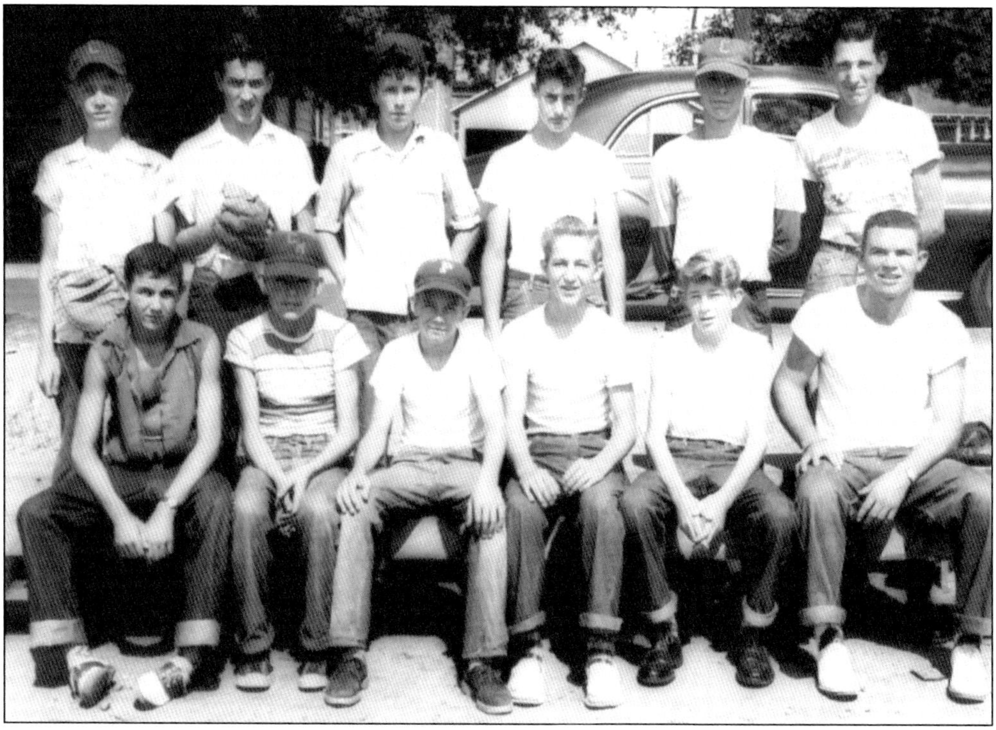

Crescent Mill Playground Baseball Team, 1950s. Baseball teams were sponsored by various textile plants. There was a lot of competition among mill hill teams. Who could predict that this team would produce major-league baseball player Jimmie Hall and North Carolina Hall of Fame football coach Jim Biggerstaff? Hall is the fifth player from the left on the back row (wearing a cap), and the player on the first row, far right is Biggerstaff. All the players contributed to the success of the team. (Courtesy of Millican Pictorial History Museum.)

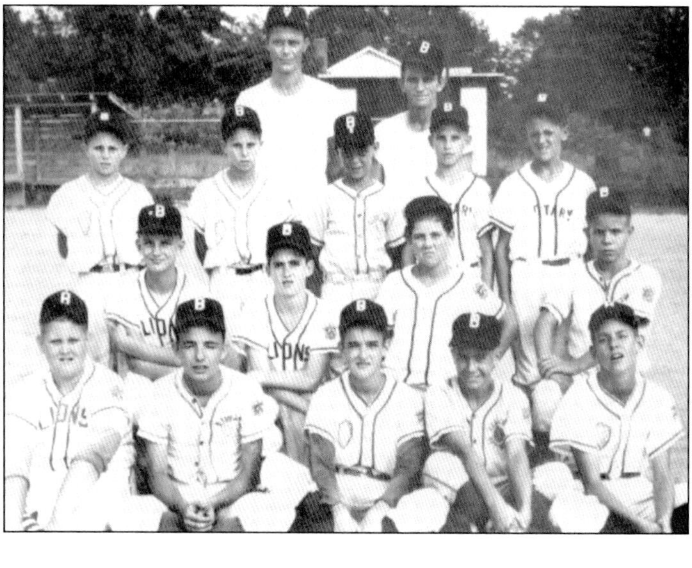

State Little League Baseball Champions, 1963. Belmont athletes won the Little League baseball state championship in 1963. Having good coaches and talented players led to this accomplishment. In years to come, these players led outstanding high school teams at South Point High School and some participated on Belmont's American Legion baseball team. (Courtesy of Millican Pictorial History Museum.)

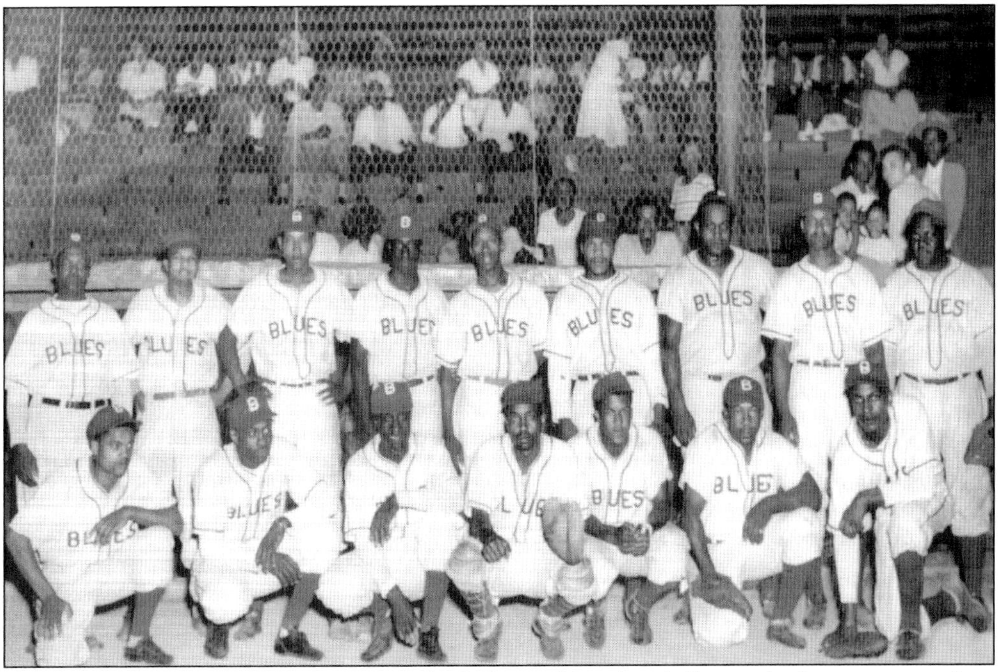

The Belmont Blues Baseball Team. The Belmont Blues baseball team had some outstanding talent and, if given a chance, some of these players may have played professionally. They played their home games at Davis Park in Belmont. Their popularity was widespread across the community, and they attracted large numbers of fans. (Courtesy of Millican Pictorial History Museum.)

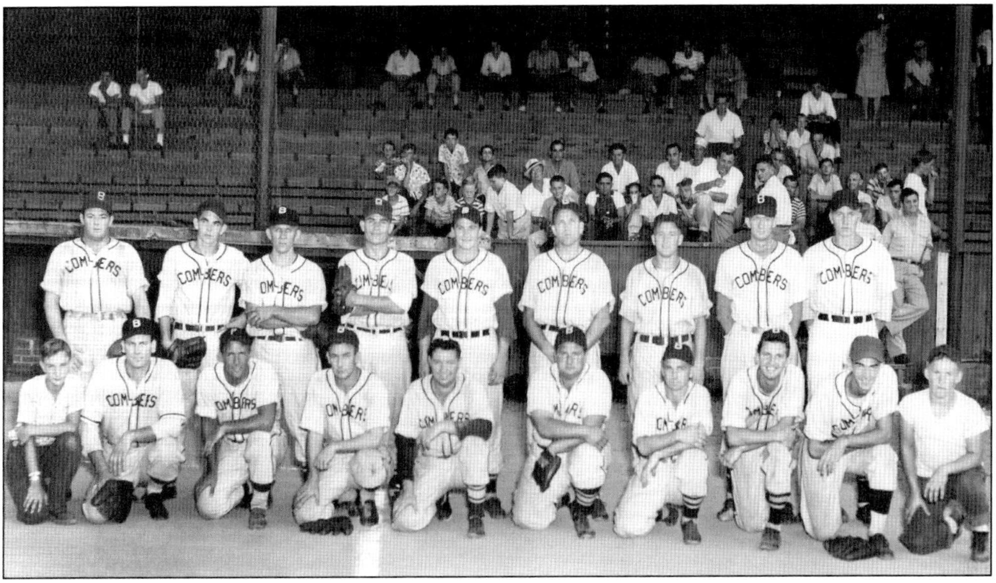

Belmont Combers, 1949. The Belmont Combers was a semiprofessional team representing Belmont in the Piedmont Textile League. Several of these players had experience in minor leagues and two or three were just out of high school. The league included Highland Park, Rex, Lance Packing Company, Cramerton, and perhaps another team or two. Playing at a time before televised baseball, this league attracted huge crowds of fans. Parking spaces around Davis Park were scarce when teams were playing. (Courtesy of Millican Pictorial History Museum.)

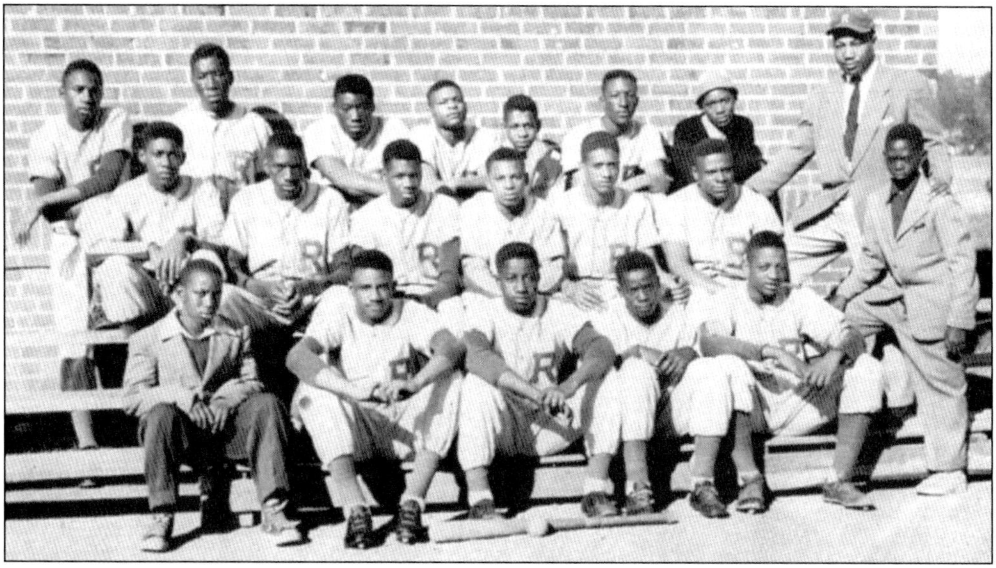

Reid High School Baseball Team, 1952. This picture shows the 1952 Belmont Reid High School baseball team. The team was blessed with talent and good coaching. From the looks on these young men's faces, they are a serious group of athletes. (Courtesy of Millican Pictorial History Museum.)

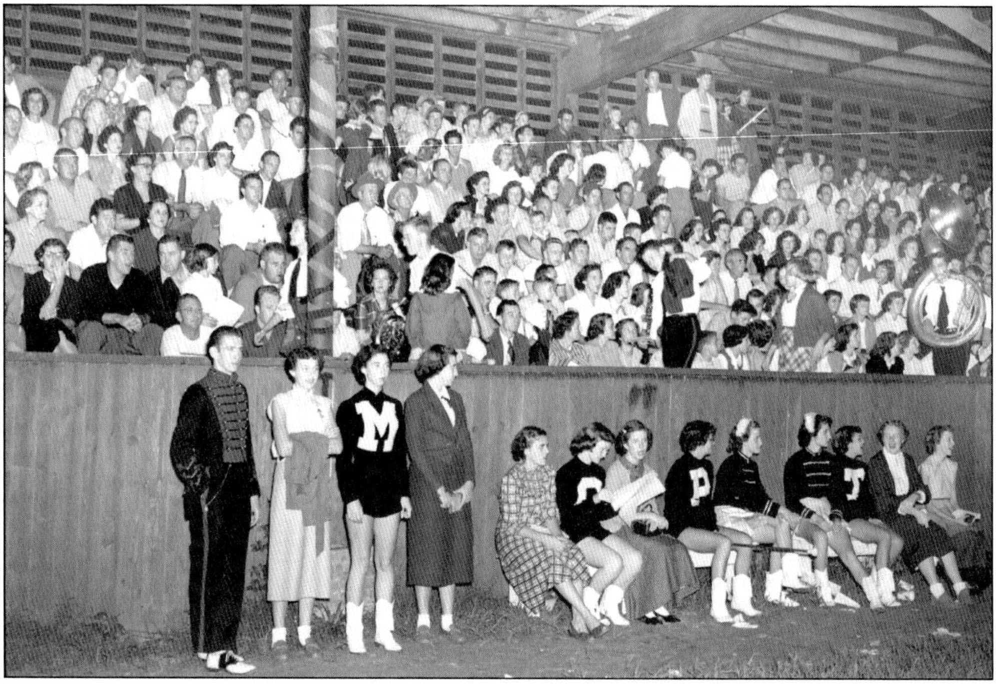

Belmont High School Football Game at Davis Park. Although the Davis Park Stadium in Belmont was destroyed by fire, many memories have been taken away by the thousands of fans who enjoyed football, baseball, and other sports here. Davis Park, built in 1939, was used for fans of Belmont High School, Belmont Abbey College, Reid High School, and Belmont Combers, Belmont's semiprofessional baseball team, which was a member of the Piedmont Textile League. (Courtesy of Millican Pictorial History Museum.)

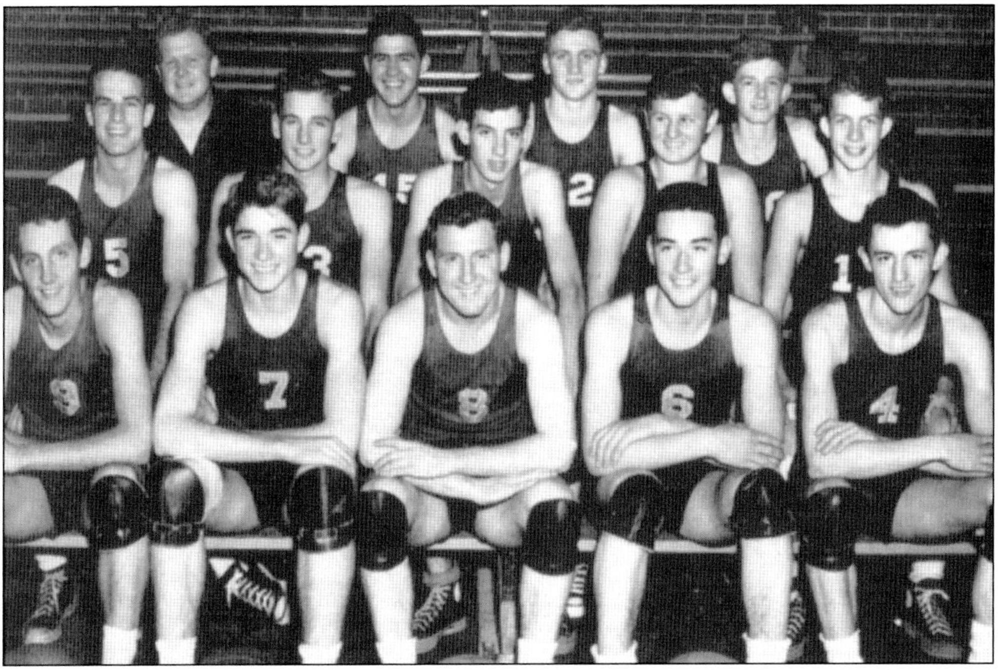

Belmont High School Basketball Team, 1950. Under the leadership of Wrather Johnson and Gerald Cortner, this group of young men, which includes a number of former football players, had an outstanding basketball season in 1950. These men were highly successful in life as well as in sports. Two of them became medical doctors, one became a Hall of Fame softball player, another was a successful banker, and yet another, an outstanding high school coach. One of these men became a public school educator for whom a school in Georgia was named. In addition, three of the players became valuable employees of Duke Power Company. (Courtesy of Millican Pictorial History Museum.)

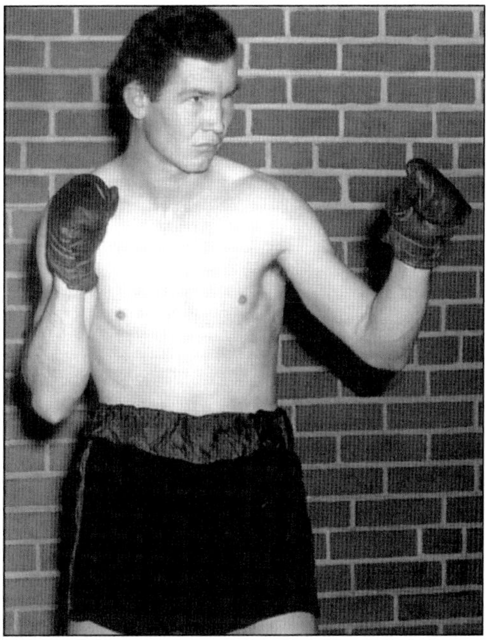

Boxer Guy Brown, 1940. East Belmont's Guy Brown strikes a pose before working out in the boxing ring. He fought all comers, and it has been reported that he once had two fights on the same night. The acme of his boxing career was attaining the Southern Middleweight Championship title. (Courtesy of Millican Pictorial History Museum.)

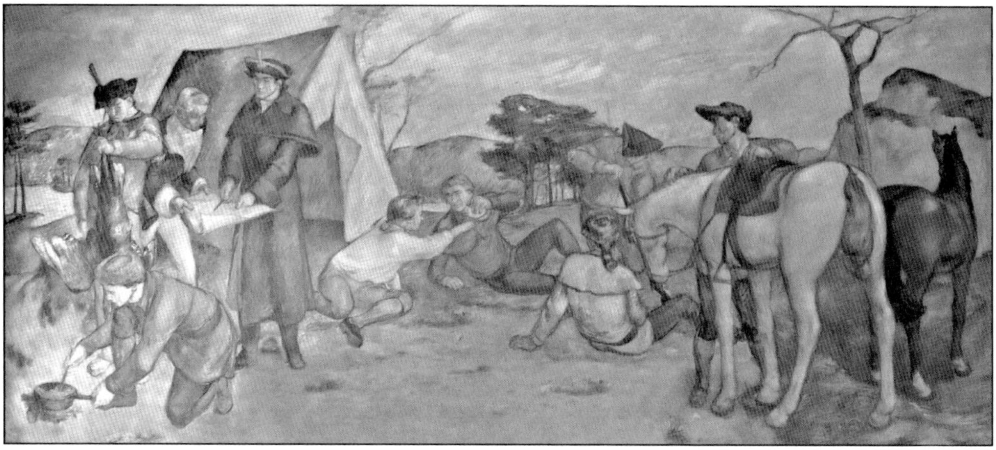

Maj. William Chronicle Mural. This mural on the wall of Belmont City Hall, formerly the Belmont Post Office, was commissioned by the Works Progress Administration (WPA) in an effort to employ artists as a part of Pres. Franklin D. Roosevelt's Back to Work Plan to lift the American economy out of the Depression. The artist was Peter DeAnna, who was urged to depict the local history of the South Point area. This scene depicts Maj. William Chronicle preparing the South Fork Boys to engage the Tories in the Battle of Kings Mountain. (Courtesy of Millican Pictorial History Museum.)

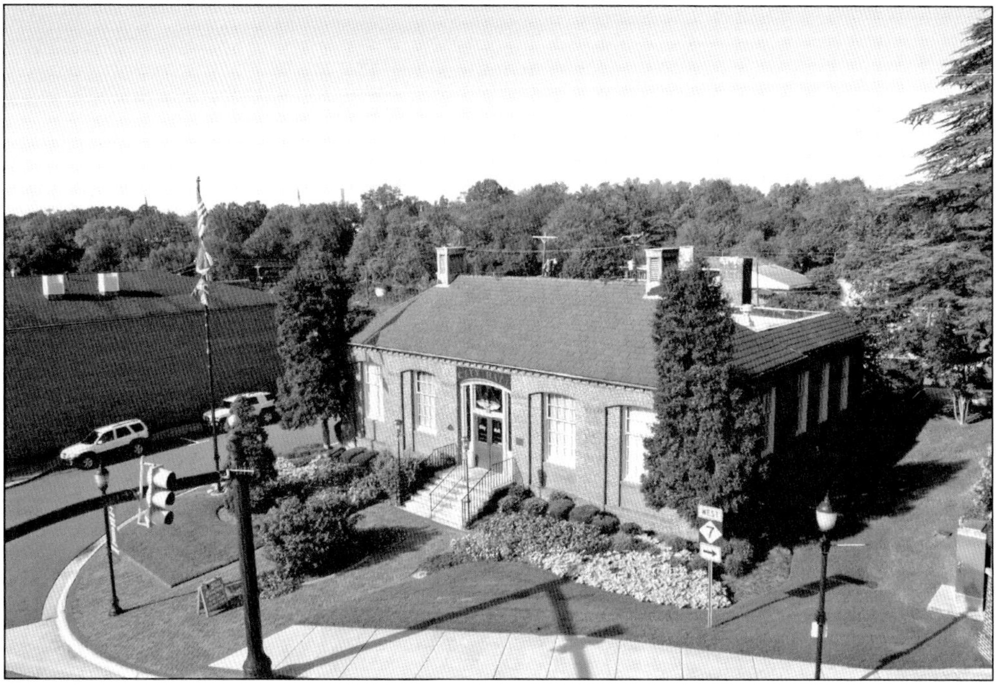

Aerial View of City Hall. The site of Belmont City Hall was once the location of the James P. Stowe House on Main Street. The house was moved backwards to make room for a new Belmont Post Office in 1939. In 1970, another new post office was built and the city moved into the vacated building, now city hall, in 1973. (Courtesy of Millican Pictorial History Museum.)

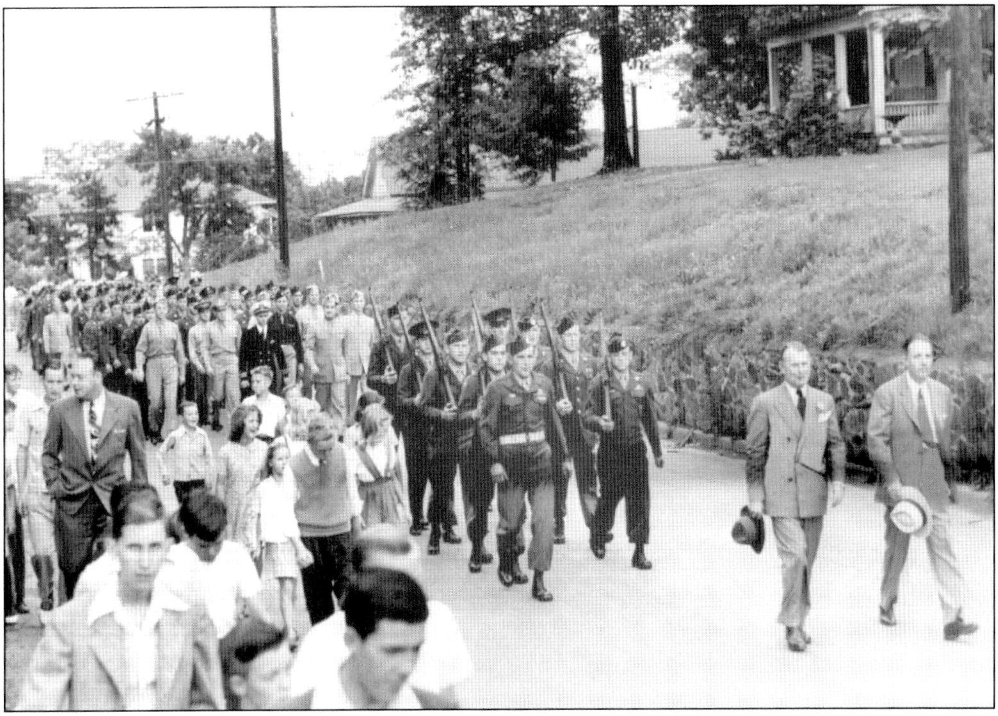

Veterans Day Parade. This 1946 parade, led by Bill Pharr and Walter Warren, has just crossed the Central Avenue and Main Street intersection and is proceeding to Greenwood Cemetery, where a memorial service will be conducted. Veterans from all military branches are represented and in uniform. The property behind the stone wall belongs to the First Presbyterian Church and will soon be graded to street level and become the site of the present church. (Courtesy of Millican Pictorial History Museum.)

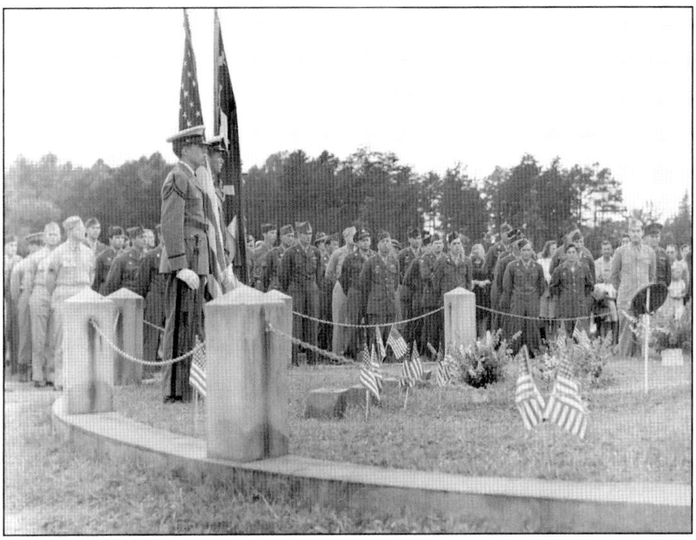

World War II Veterans at Greenwood Cemetery. The veterans at Greenwood Cemetery are standing at parade rest. They are giving their full attention to the memorial services. (Courtesy of Millican Pictorial History Museum.)

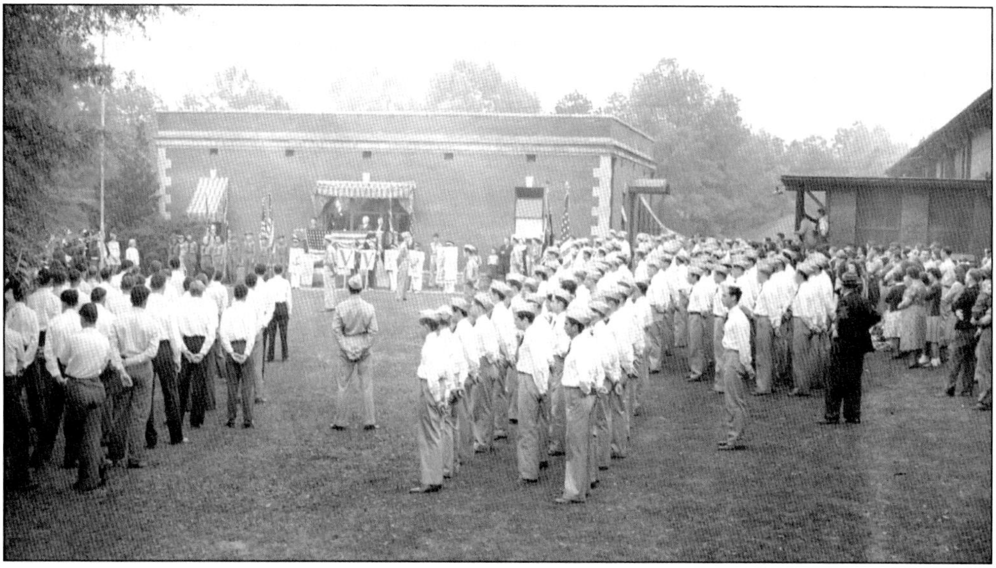

Aberfoyle Mill Bond Drive. A bond drive parade featured the Belmont High School Band, cadets from St. Leo's School for Boys, Boy Scouts, the Civil Air Patrol (CAP), and other organizations. Band members from the elementary school, who were too young to participate in the music, carried signs promoting the sale of bonds. Some of the cadets from St. Leo's, while wearing wool uniforms, fainted because of the heat and fell backwards from the bleachers on which they stood. Events like this parade generated enthusiasm for purchasing war bonds. (Courtesy of Millican Pictorial History Museum.)

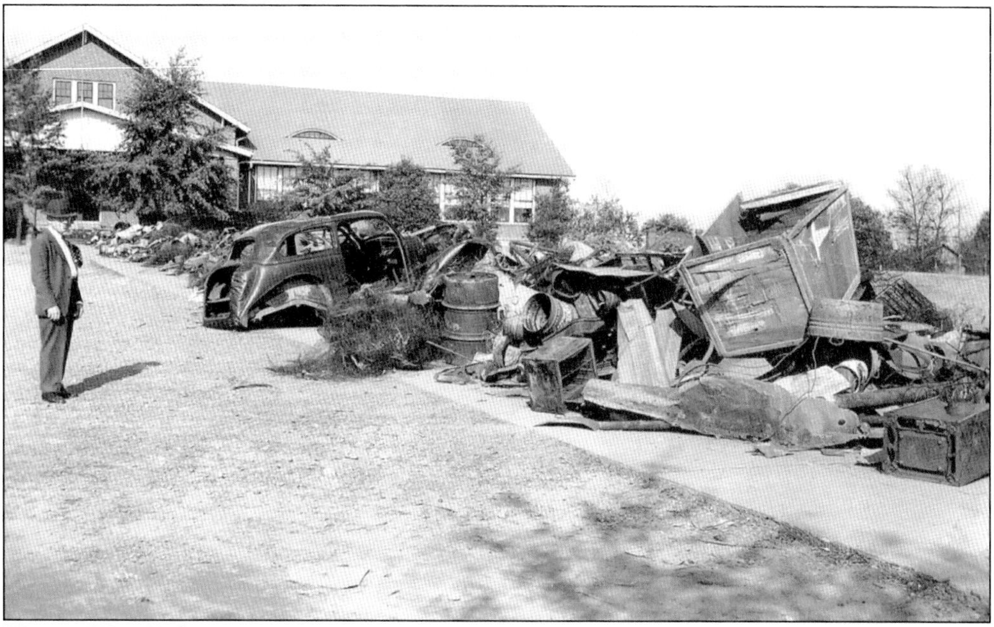

World War II Scrap Metal Drive. A scrap metal drive in 1943 sponsored by the Belmont Jaycees was enthusiastically promoted by all Belmont elementary schools. Armbands and sweatshirts were awarded to students indicating the student's rank based on the weight of the metal turned in. Here, principal J.B. Page inspects the East Belmont School's students' contribution to the World War II scrap metal drive. (Courtesy of Millican Pictorial History Museum.)

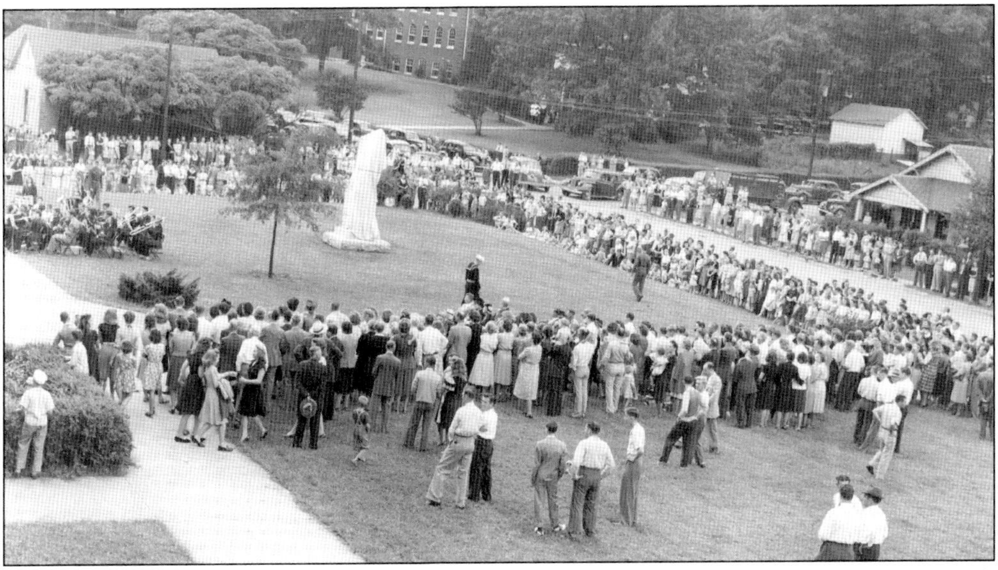

DEDICATION OF THE WORLD WAR II *FIGHTING YANK*. The *Fighting Yank* was unveiled on the grounds of Belmont High School in 1946. The high school band played patriotic songs as preparations were made to unveil the statue. The *Fighting Yank* was moved in 2014 to a site in Stowe Park. Former North Carolina governor Gregg Cherry gave a stirring and complimentary speech. The new statue site has been enhanced with plantings, benches, and a sidewalk surrounding the area; and the statue is prominently displayed facing Main Street. (Courtesy of Millican Pictorial History Museum.)

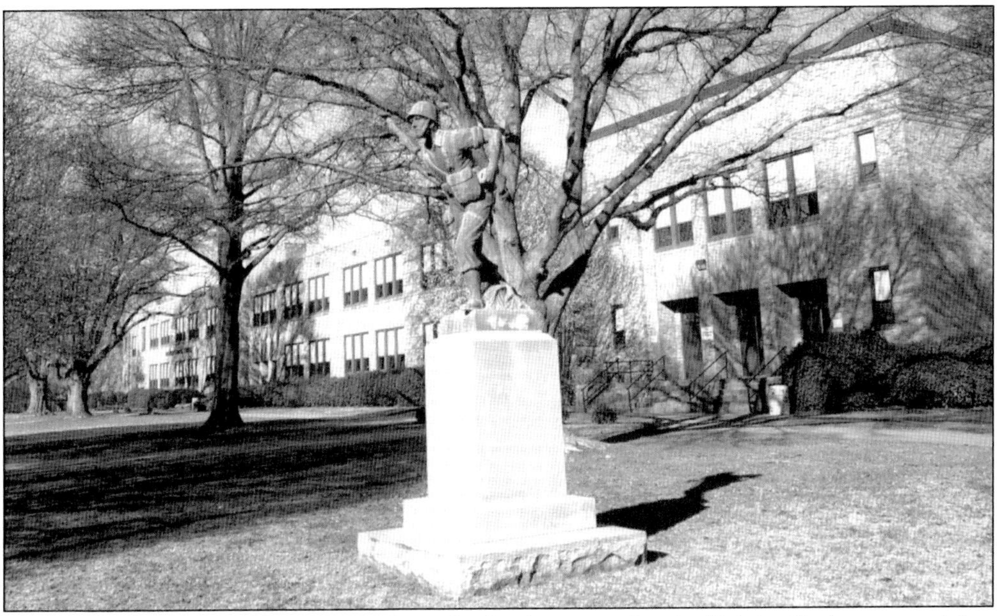

BELMONT HIGH SCHOOL'S *FIGHTING YANK*. In the foreground is the *Fighting Yank*, a memorial to the servicemen from this area who lost their lives in World War II. The statue was erected in 1946 on the grounds of Belmont High School. In the background, the 1939 Belmont High School is pictured. The statue was moved to Stowe Park, facing Main Street, in 2014 and now commemorates all branches of the armed services. (Courtesy of Millican Pictorial History Museum.)

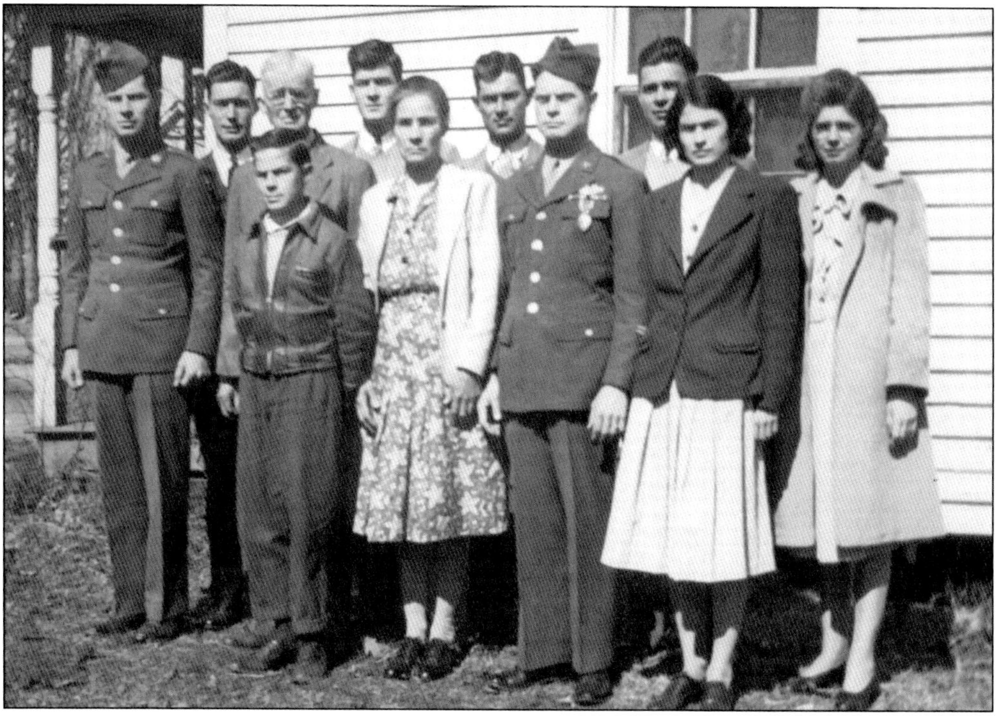

THE JOYE FAMILY AT THEIR MAJESTIC MILL VILLAGE HOME, 1945. Here are nine children of the Joye family who occupied a mill home on the Majestic Mill Village. Two of the young men are dressed in their military uniforms, having just been discharged from the Army. (Courtesy of Millican Pictorial History Museum.)

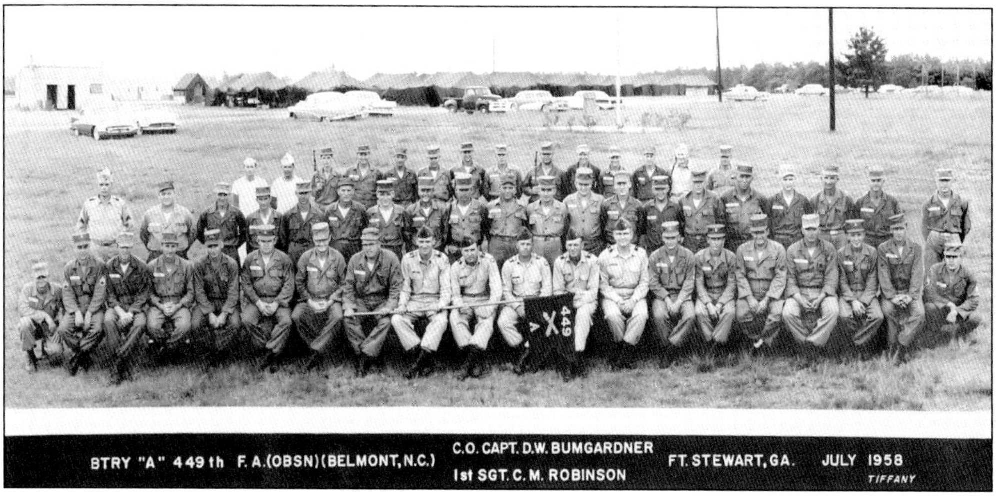

BELMONT NATIONAL GUARD, 1958. Belmont's National Guard is pictured while on maneuvers at Fort Stewart, Georgia. The annual maneuver was a required activity along with weekly local meetings at the Belmont Armory. Before being added to the roster, each man was required to have eight weeks of basic training at Fort Jackson, South Carolina. Many of the Guardsmen had prior military experience. Guardsmen had a six-year military obligation. (Courtesy of Millican Pictorial History Museum.)

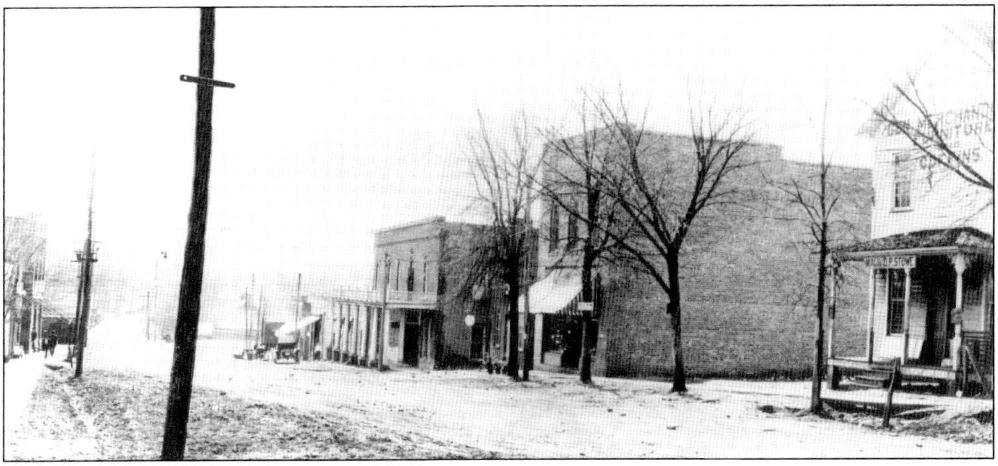

BELMONT'S UNPAVED MAIN STREET, C. 1909. In the building at far right, W.H. and D.P. Stowe operated a general merchandise and furniture store that also sold coffins. The next building to the left has served as a drugstore as well as many other uses. The building with the colonnade is the hotel building, erected by George M. Gullick at the request of the textile mill owners of Belmont. On the other side of the street, the tallest building is Stowe Mercantile General Store. Belmont's first paved road was Highway 7, which turned down Catawba Street, just above the part of Main Street shown here, and led across the Catawba River and into Mecklenburg County. Main Street remained unpaved for several more years. (Courtesy of Millican Pictorial History Museum.)

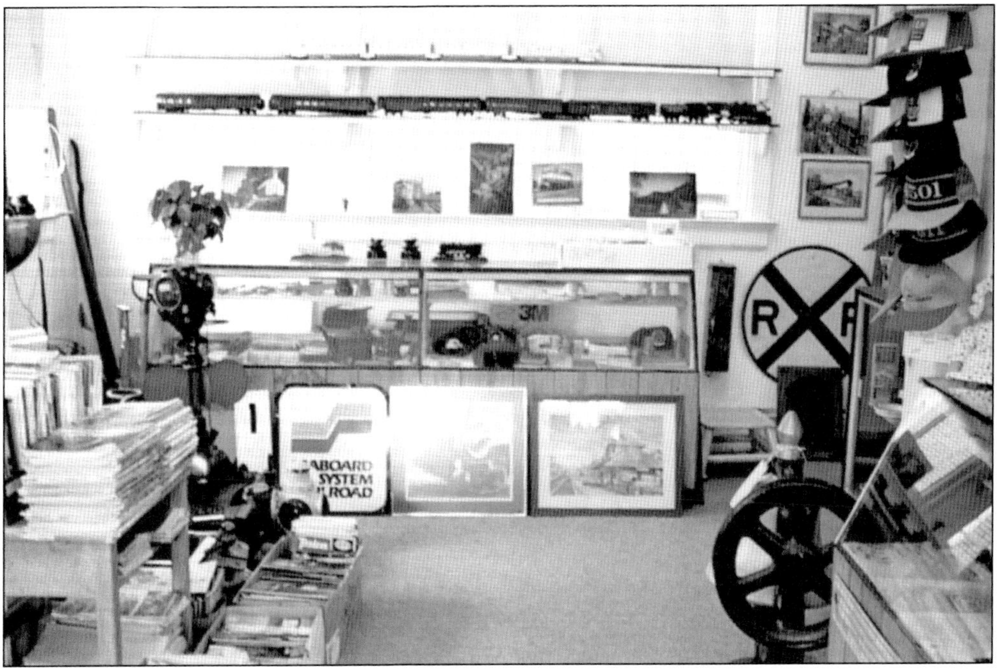

PIEDMONT CAROLINA TRAIN MUSEUM, BELMONT. The former Piedmont and Northern depot and the Western Union offices were housed in this building. After standing empty for several years, the building housed a dress shop. When the dress shop closed, the property was leased to train enthusiasts and was used as the Piedmont Carolina Train Museum. It attracted many visitors from throughout Piedmont North Carolina, who found much interest in the train memorabilia. The structure presently houses a bicycle shop. (Courtesy of Millican Pictorial History Museum.)

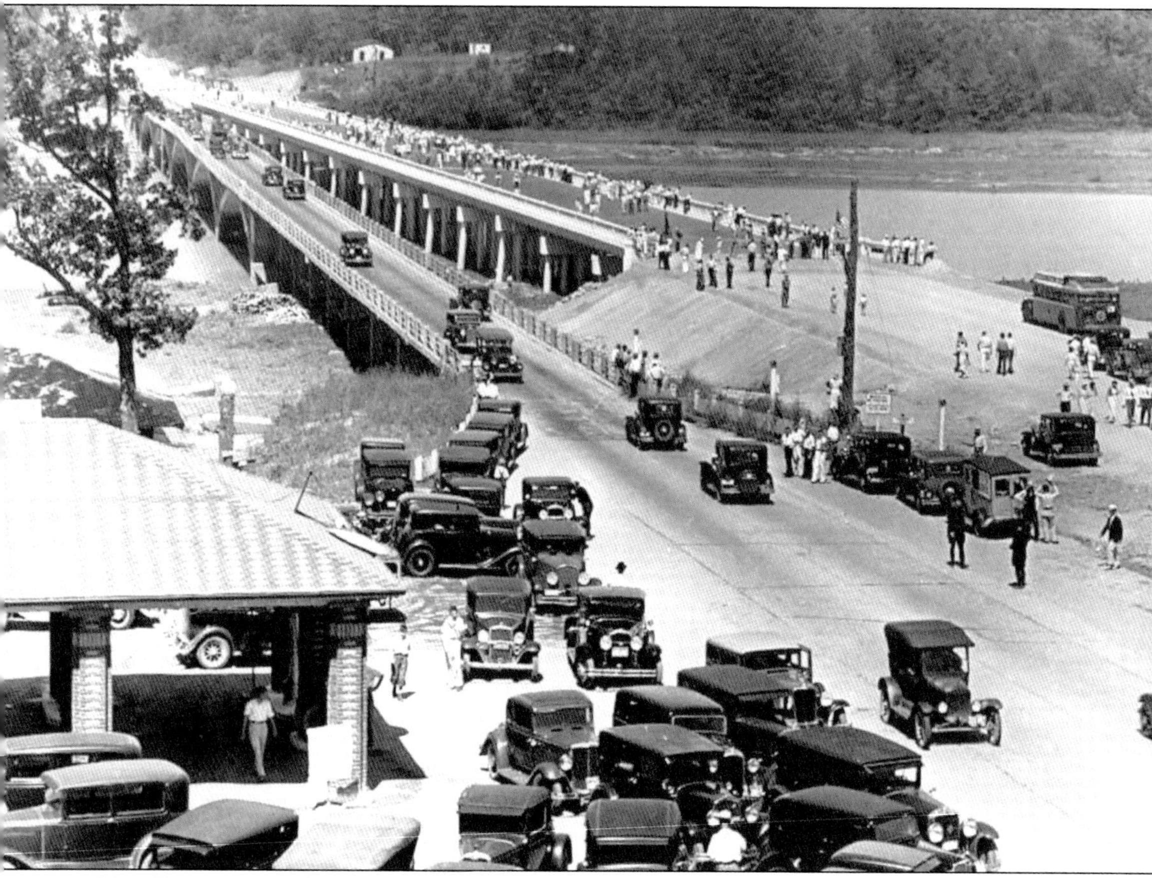

New Bridge over Catawba River. When Wilkinson Boulevard was constructed in 1926, this handsome bridge spanned the Catawba River. This was probably the third bridge at this location. Prior to the construction of these bridges, this was the site of Sloan's Ferry, which served as transportation across the river for many years. (Courtesy of Millican Pictorial History Museum.)

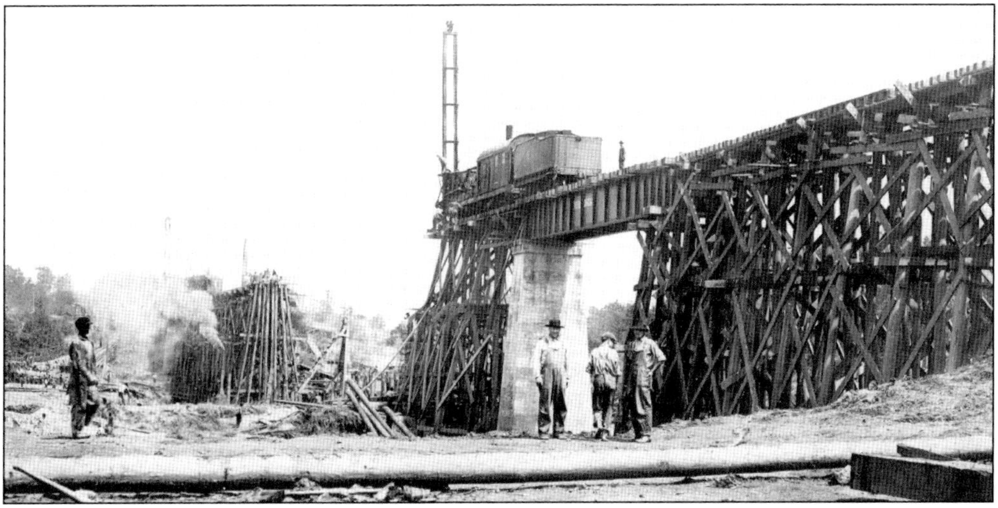

Crew Working on Railroad Trestle, 1916. A pile driver sits atop a railroad car as workers reinforce the foundation for the Catawba River trestle. The 1916 flood had destroyed the previous bridge. Debris from mills and barns upstream piled against the Southern Railway trestle, causing great weight to come to bear on the bridge. There had been an attempt to reinforce it by rolling boxcars loaded with cotton onto the span. This effort failed, and the bridge went down, along with the railroad cars and the workers that were trapped there. (Courtesy of Millican Pictorial History Museum.)

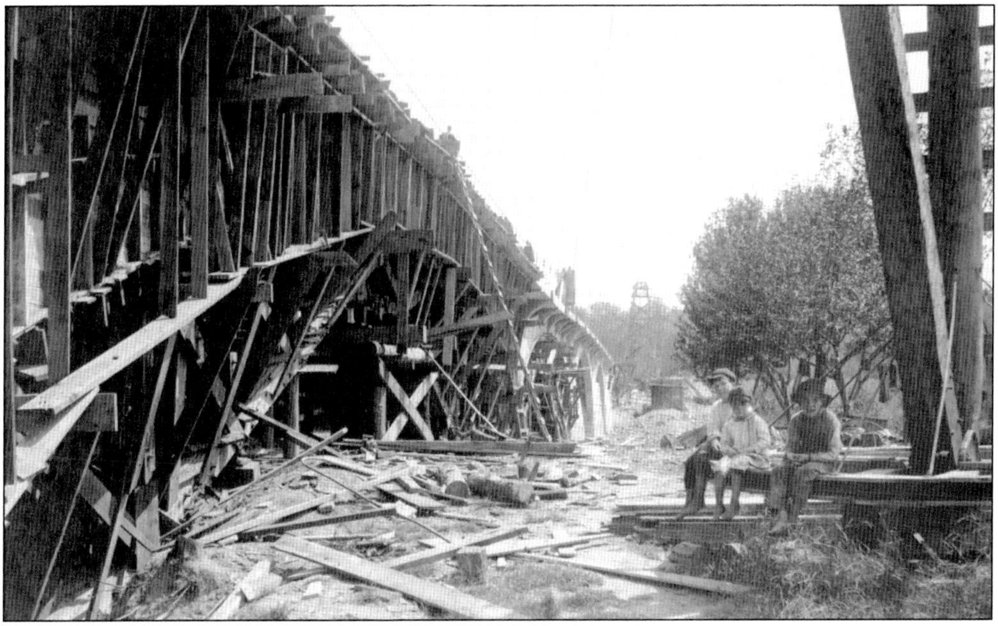

Rebuilding the Bridge over the Catawba, 1917. A disastrous flood of the Catawba and South Fork Rivers in July 1916 destroyed mills, bridges, and all of the agricultural bottomland in their paths. An unknown number of train workers were washed down the river, some to their deaths. Some were rescued as they clung to tree branches along the riverbanks. Six men were rescued by Peter Stowe and Fons Ross, two African American men who had helped construct a hastily built boat. For their bravery, these men were the recipients of a collection sponsored by the *Charlotte Observer.* (Courtesy of Millican Pictorial History Museum.)

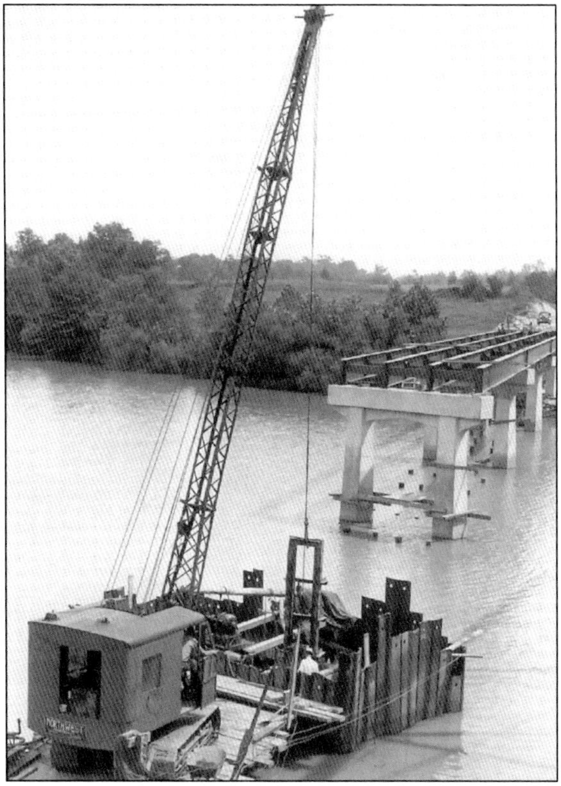

Building Catawba River Bridge. A construction crew is using a pile driver to lay the foundation for a new bridge for Highway 29/74 across the Catawba River. The new bridge seen here under construction replaces the bridge that washed away in the flood of 1916. (Courtesy of Millican Pictorial History Museum.)

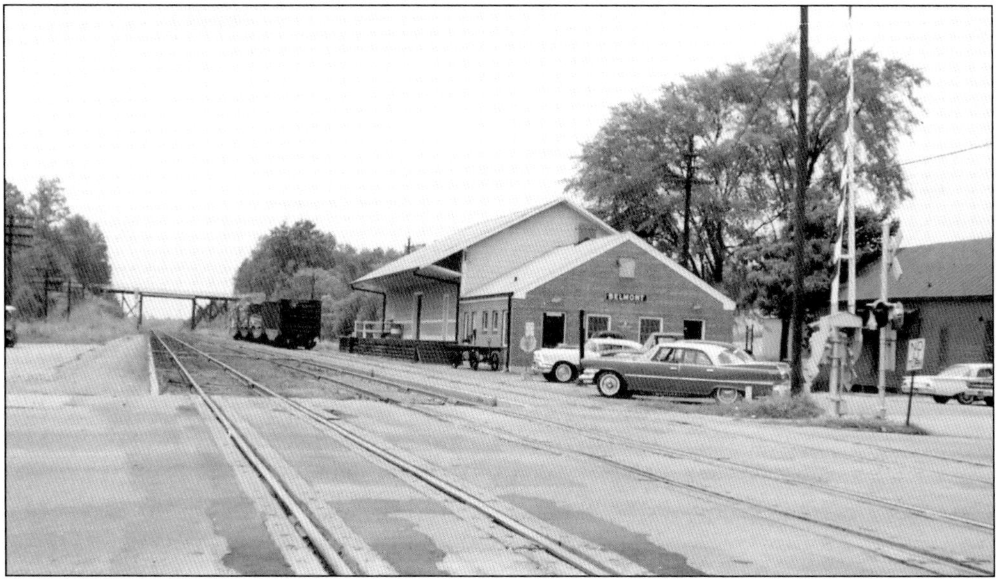

Southern Railway Depot and Freight Warehouse. The Southern Railway's passenger and freight depot was razed and a new one built across the tracks as a freight warehouse only. All manner of heavy goods were unloaded or shipped out from this warehouse. The stationmaster was Claude Albright. Far down the tracks is the overhead bridge that spans a cut through the hillside. A new bridge replaced the old bridge and was named in honor of Clyde Deitz. (Courtesy of Millican Pictorial History Museum.)

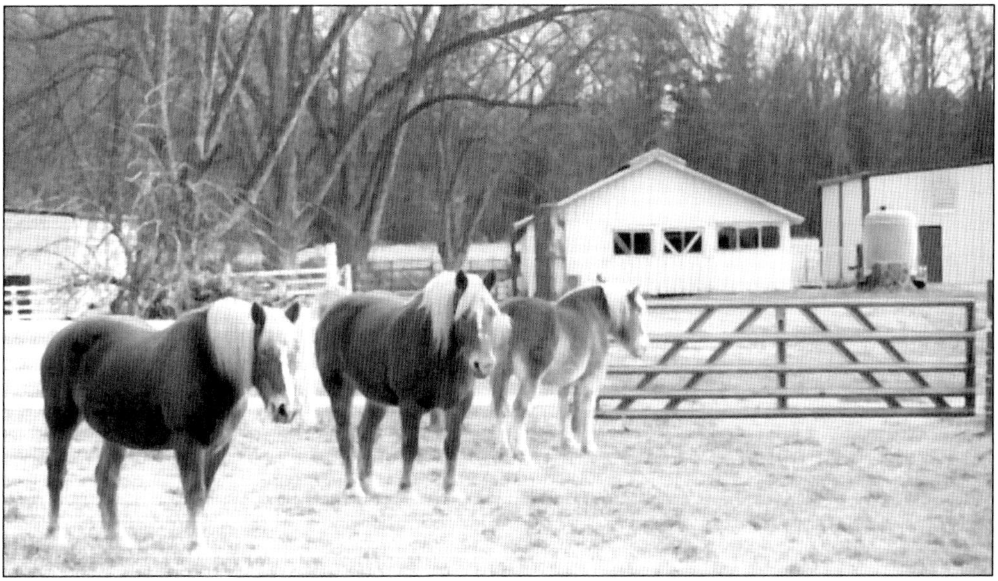

Seven Oaks Farm. Seven Oaks Farm was one of Dan Stowe's pet projects. The farm had a variety of livestock, including the horses pictured here. The property has now been parceled between Stowe Botanical Gardens, which is home to a world-class orchid conservatory; many other unique garden features; and an upscale housing development. (Courtesy of Millican Pictorial History Museum.)

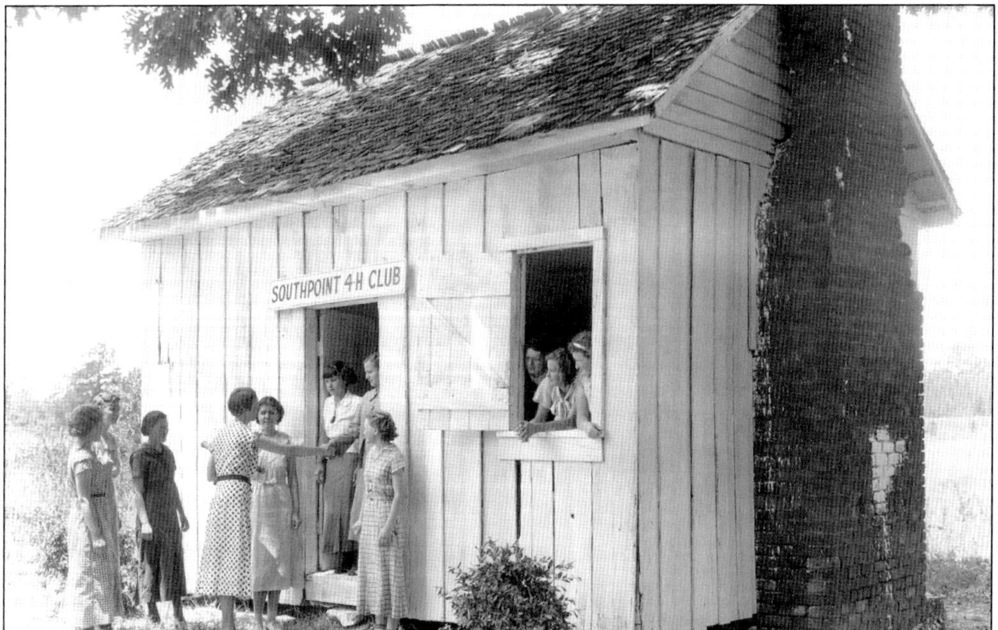

South Point 4-H Clubhouse, 1928. This image of the South Point 4-H clubhouse depicts young ladies who support the 4-H ideals of Head, Heart, Hands, and Health. The South Point 4-H club is thought to be one of the earliest clubs organized in this part of North Carolina. The clubs operate under the umbrella of the North Carolina Agricultural Extension Department. (Courtesy of Millican Pictorial History Museum.)

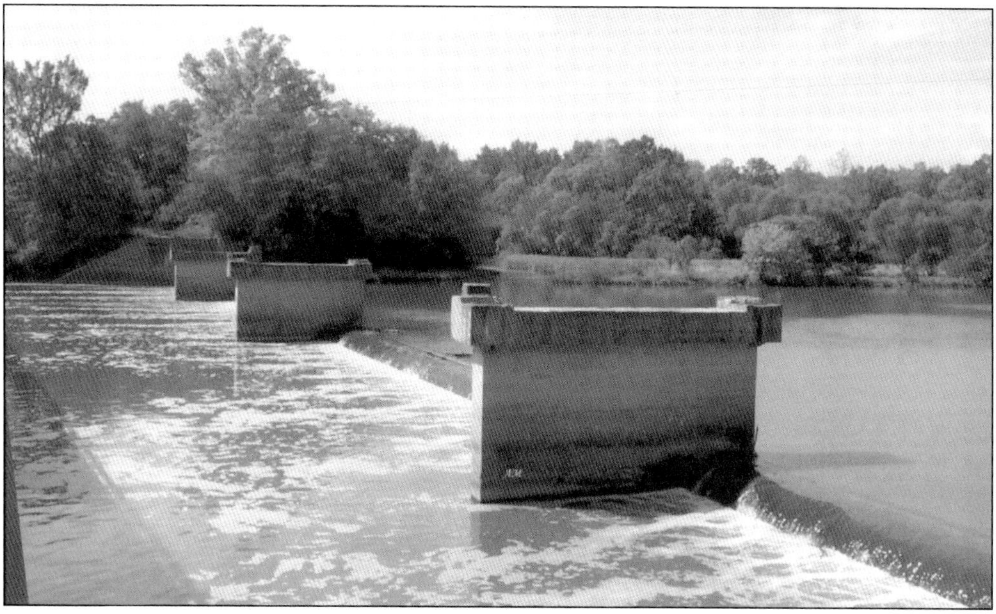

Foundation of Upper Armstrong Bridge. This is a picture of the foundation and supports of the previous Upper Armstrong Bridge, which was replaced in the 1960s. Textile pioneer Stuart Cramer prevailed on the state to include a dam under the bridge that backed up the South Fork River, creating a broad lake that could be used for recreational purposes. In recent years, the lake has narrowed as silt from upstream has settled along the riverbank. (Photograph by Jack Page.)

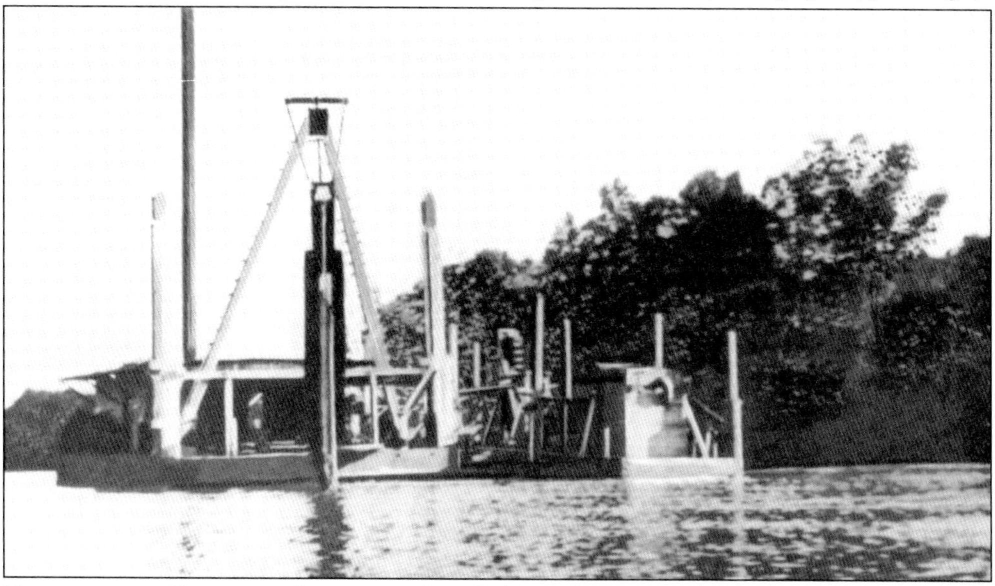

Dredging for Gold near Belmont, 1910. Belmont lies in North Carolina's Piedmont Gold Belt. For the most part, gold is found in noncommercial amounts in Belmont's streams and rivers. Pictured is a gold dredge, whose owner is attempting to obtain gold by pumping sand and mud from the bottom of the Catawba River. The dredge probably cost more to construct than any gold obtained. There were several gold mines in the vicinity of Belmont, including the Stowe-Leeper mine on the Point and the mine on Fite's Creek in Catawba Heights. (Courtesy of Millican Pictorial History Museum.)

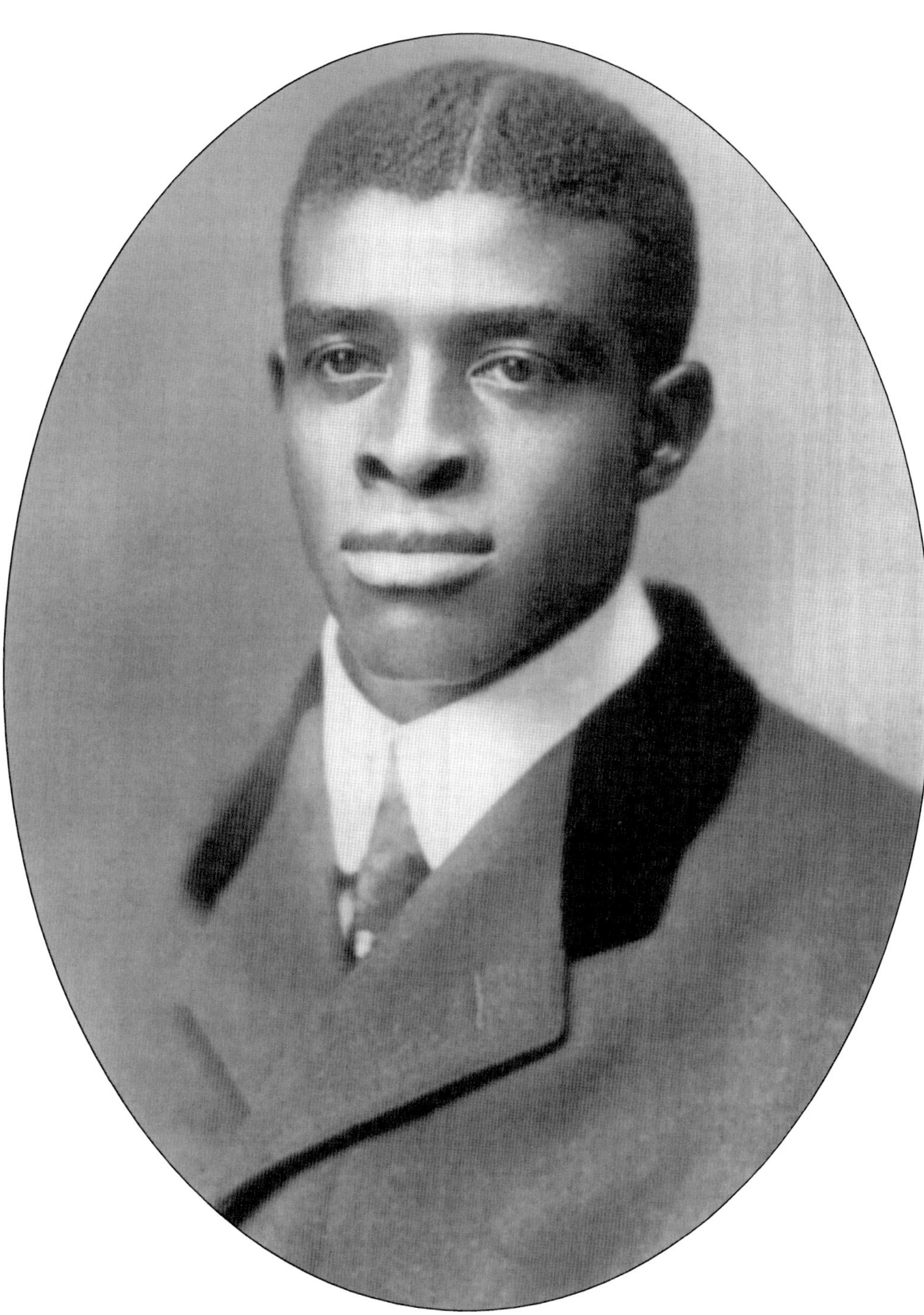

Prof. C.J.B. Reid. Charles Jesse Bynum Reid was the principal of the Reid School in the black community that was later named for him. He was educated at Knox College in Tennessee. In his early years as a Belmont educator, Professor Reid lived in Lowell and rode a bicycle to Belmont each day to the school that also eventually bore his name. (Courtesy of Millican Pictorial History Museum.)

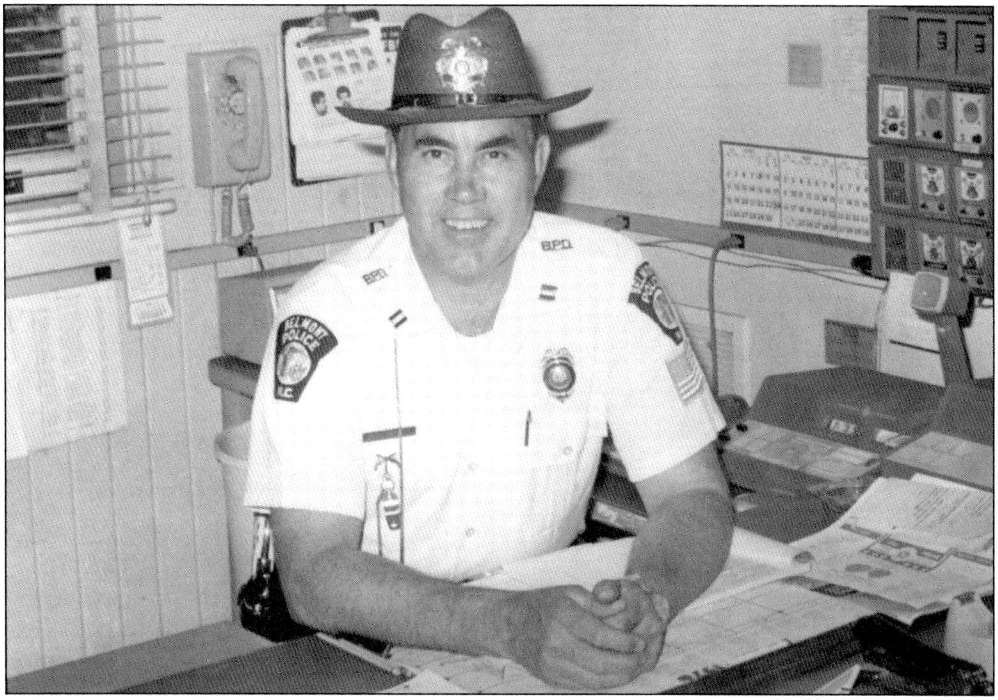

CAPT. CLAUDE SETZER. At a time when Belmont was growing rapidly, Capt. Claude Setzer was an effective chief of police. Under his direction, Belmont added personnel, more advanced training, and more up-to-date equipment for the police department. (Courtesy of Millican Pictorial History Museum.)

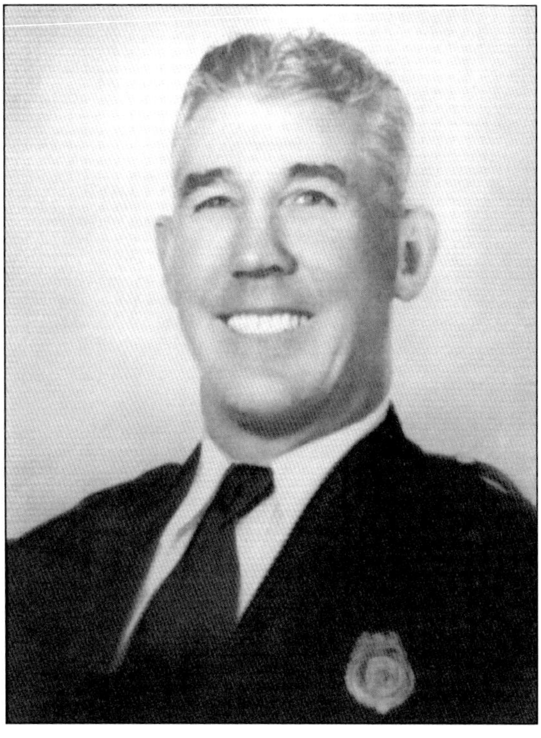

ROY COSTNER, CONSTABLE. Constable Roy Costner served as the local law enforcer in North Belmont. He was a very popular and highly respected individual. He also was a part-time instructor at Belmont Abbey College, where he supervised the rifle range and instructed students in marksmanship and firearms safety. It has been said that no one could outrun Costner on foot, so few tried. (Courtesy of Millican Pictorial History Museum.)

CHIEF OF POLICE GILES HOOVER. Chief Giles Hoover was a practical man and a strong police chief in Belmont for 30 years, having been responsible for helping, along with the National Guard, to maintain peace during the textile strike in 1934. It was reported in the *Belmont Banner* that "if any community in the state has a better police and safety record than Belmont we would like to hear about it!" His home on Central Avenue was removed and was replaced by Belmont High School in 1939. (Courtesy of Millican Pictorial History Museum.)

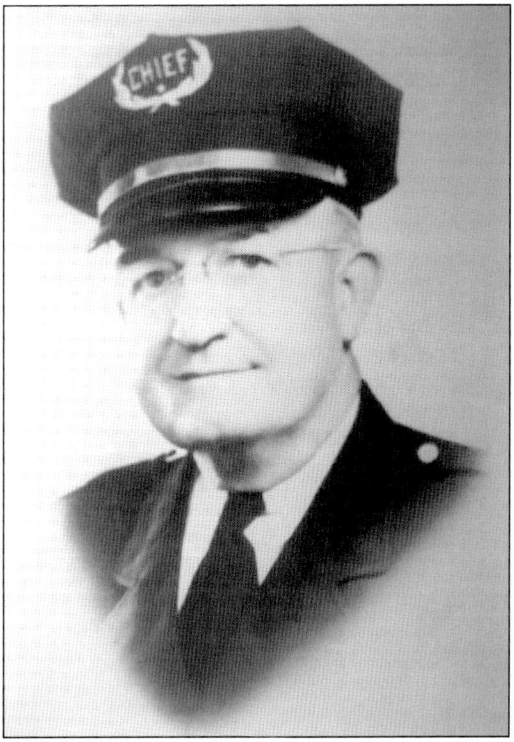

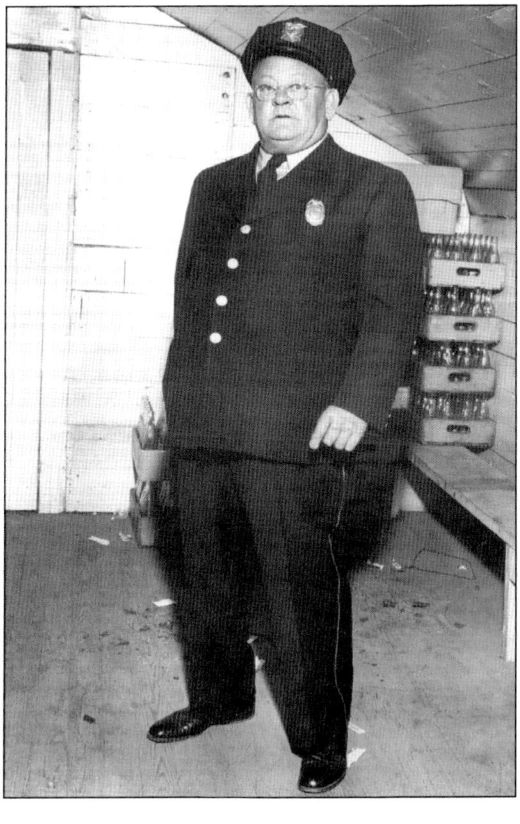

JULIUS JENKINS, CARETAKER OF DAVIS PARK. Julius Jenkins was the official caretaker of Davis Park in 1954. His duties included taking care of the infield, preventing damage to the stadium, and preventing any "hippies" from camping out under the shelter provided by the stands. He took his Davis Park duties and his duties as a school crossing guard seriously. (Courtesy of Millican Pictorial History Museum.)

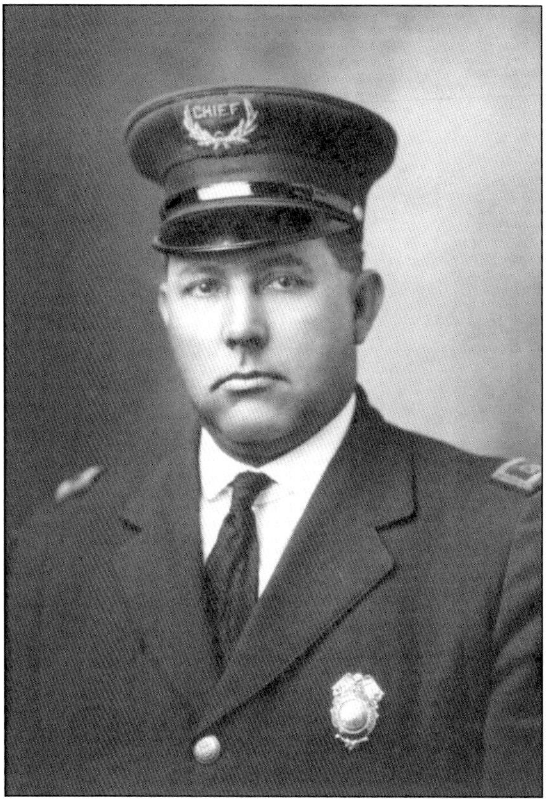

Robert Hall Mingus, Chief of Police, 1915–1927. It is told that after many complaints about a woman preaching on Main Street, Chief Mingus told her to stop her street preaching. However, he died the next day. His successor, Giles Hoover, informed the police officers of Belmont that she could preach anytime or anyplace she wanted to. Mingus had served Belmont for 12 years. (Courtesy of Millican Pictorial History Museum.)

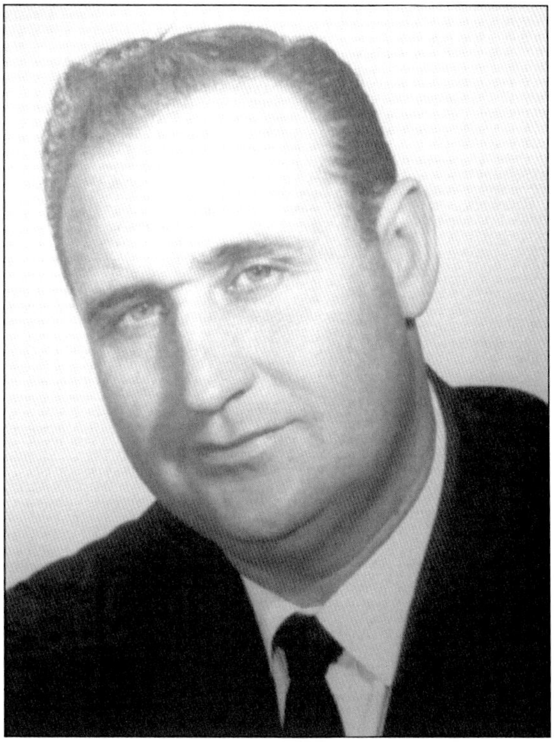

Everette Gantt, Boxing Coach, Early 1950s. Everette "Ebb" Gantt played football for the Belmont High School Cardinals and Belmont Abbey College. While in military service, he discovered boxing. After being released from the military, he organized a boxing team in Belmont that worked out under the Belmont City Hall and in a section of Davis Park. Known as a "friend of the boy," he coached the Belmont Peewees in football. Ebb was the sports announcer for WCGC in Belmont. He was elected to the Belmont Sports Hall of Fame in 1989, and was recognized for his work as an announcer by being awarded the J. Robert Marlowe Merit Award. (Courtesy of Millican Pictorial History Museum.)

DWIGHT FRADY, SPORTSWRITER. Encouraged by his English teacher Paul Neal, Dwight Frady became a professional sportswriter. He became sports editor of the *Gastonia Gazette* and later editor of the *Belmont Banner.* Among his many awards are his induction into three Halls of Fame: first, in 1990, the Belmont Sports Hall of Fame; in 1993, the American Legion Baseball Hall of Fame; and in 2006, the Gaston County Sports Hall of Fame. Frady enjoyed coaching Little League baseball. Upon Frady's retirement after 53 years in the newspaper industry, a Belmont street and an athletic park were named for him. He was one of the most well-known and beloved citizens of Belmont. (Courtesy of Millican Pictorial History Museum.)

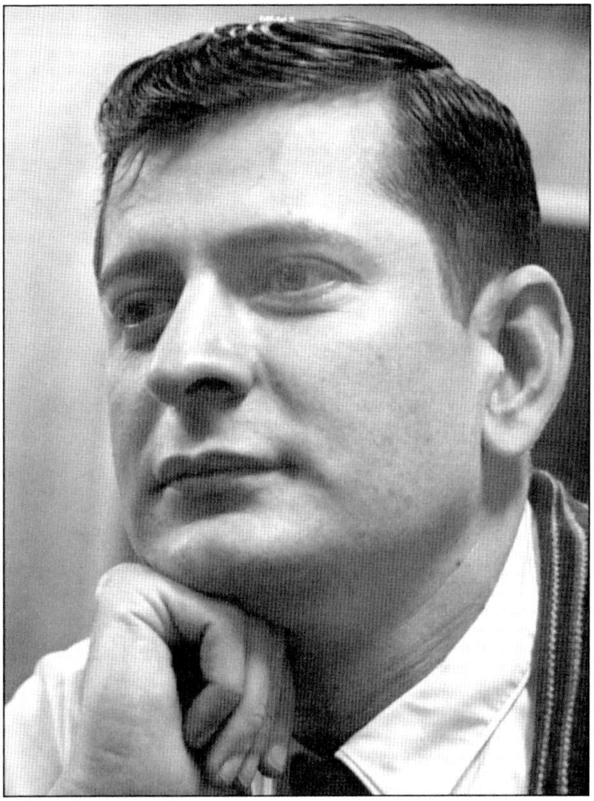

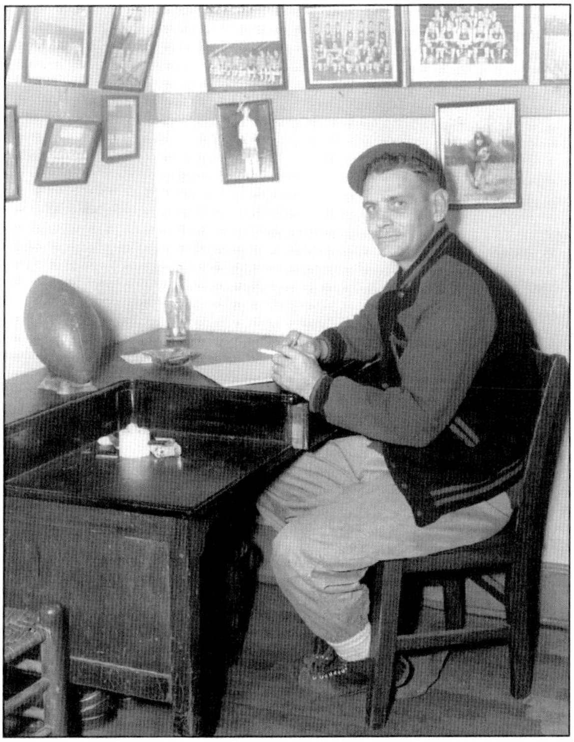

GERALD CORTNER. Gerald Cortner came to Belmont High School as a biology teacher, athletic director, and head football coach in the fall of 1946. He immediately established a winning athletic program that, over the years, attracted hundreds of boys and girls. Students were able to participate on outstanding football, baseball, and men's and women's basketball teams. After having graduated from Tennessee Technological University, Cortner served as a Coast Guard commander. He became the Belmont High School principal in the fall of 1953. The auditorium of South Point High School is named in his honor. (Courtesy of Millican Pictorial History Museum.)

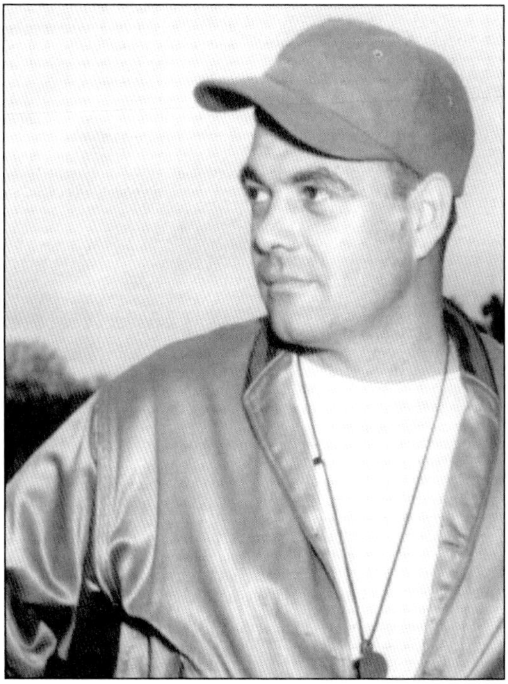

Wrather Johnson, Belmont Coach, 1946–1950s. Wrather Johnson, a graduate of Tennessee Technological University, came to Belmont in 1946 as a physical education teacher, the head coach of girls' basketball, and assistant football coach. Later, he became head football coach. His outgoing personality endeared him to the school's staff as well as the student body. Johnson was a successful coach before going into administration as principal of the newly opened New Hope Elementary School. (Courtesy of Millican Pictorial History Museum.)

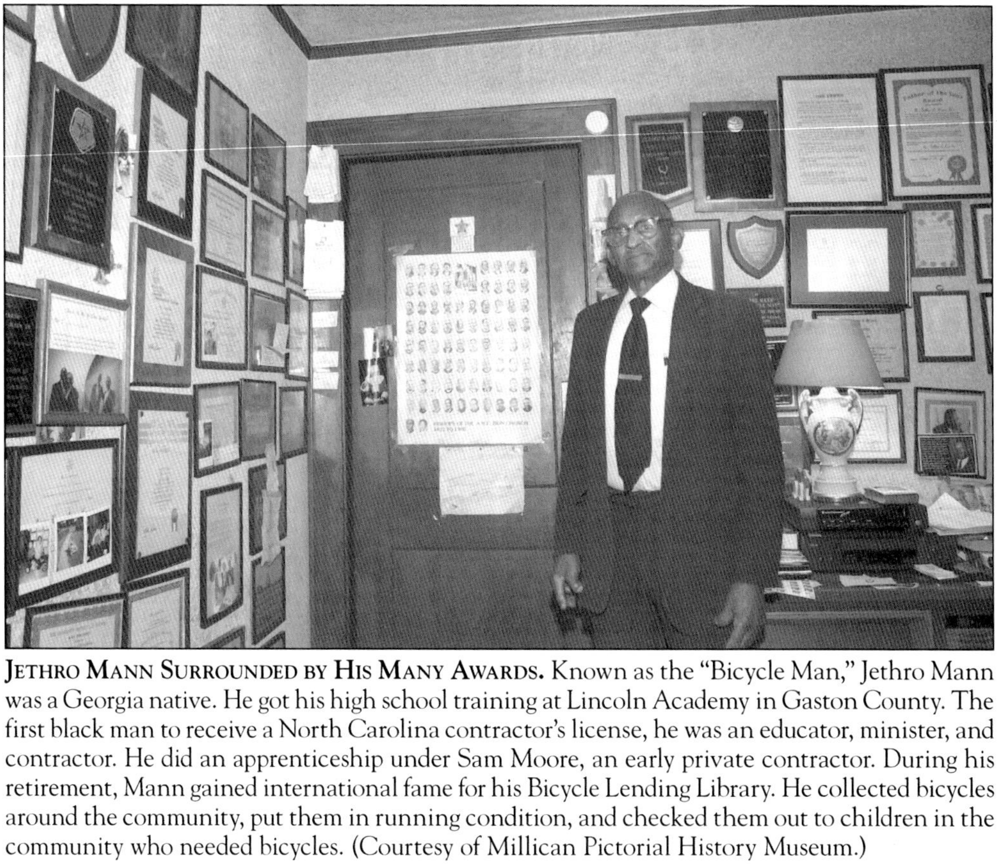

Jethro Mann Surrounded by His Many Awards. Known as the "Bicycle Man," Jethro Mann was a Georgia native. He got his high school training at Lincoln Academy in Gaston County. The first black man to receive a North Carolina contractor's license, he was an educator, minister, and contractor. He did an apprenticeship under Sam Moore, an early private contractor. During his retirement, Mann gained international fame for his Bicycle Lending Library. He collected bicycles around the community, put them in running condition, and checked them out to children in the community who needed bicycles. (Courtesy of Millican Pictorial History Museum.)

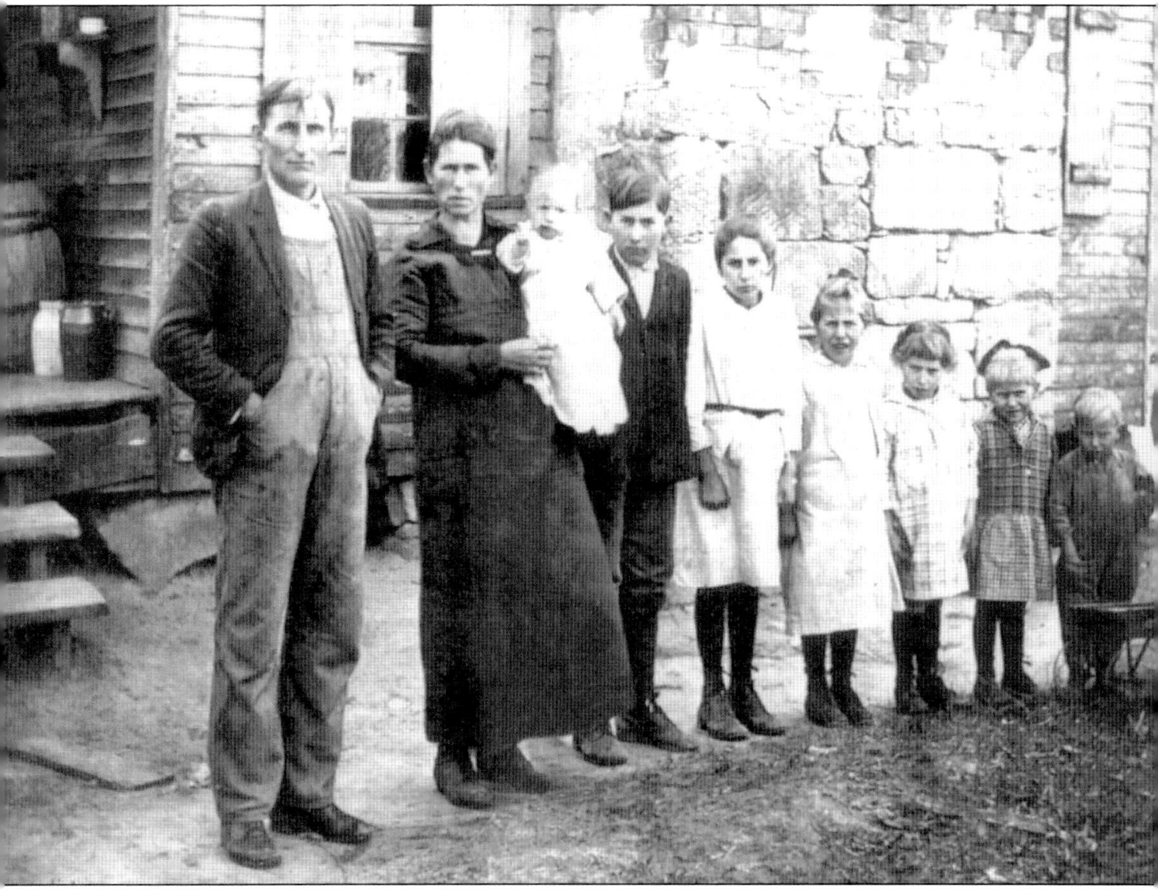

THE WILLIAM EMMETT WENTZ FAMILY, 1923. The Wentz family tradition holds that this family rented property from the Hall family off South Point Road. This picture was made in 1923 before the home was flooded when the Catawba River was dammed up below Fort Mill. This destroyed their home and flooded their farmland. From left to right are William Emmett Wentz and his wife, Lucy Jane Brimer—both allegedly part Cherokee—and their children. There were ten children; three are not pictured. (Courtesy of Millican Pictorial History Museum.)

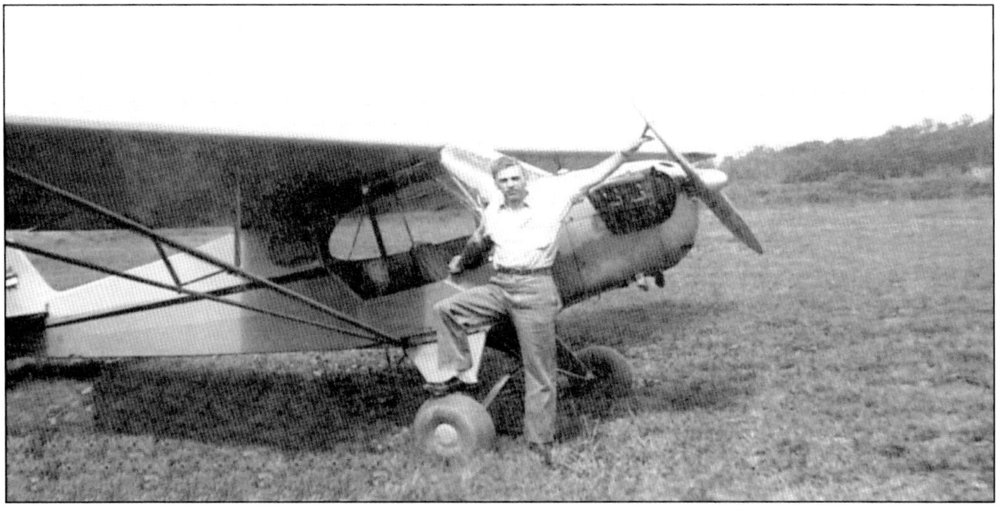

Brown Town Airstrip. The airstrip located in the Brown Town area of Belmont was popularly called "Manson Arrowood Airport." The runway was located on Belmont Abbey property through which Interstate 85 now passes. Arthur Hawkins is pictured with a "tail dragger." The airstrip was grassed and slanted eastward toward the Catawba River. (Courtesy of Millican Pictorial History Museum.)

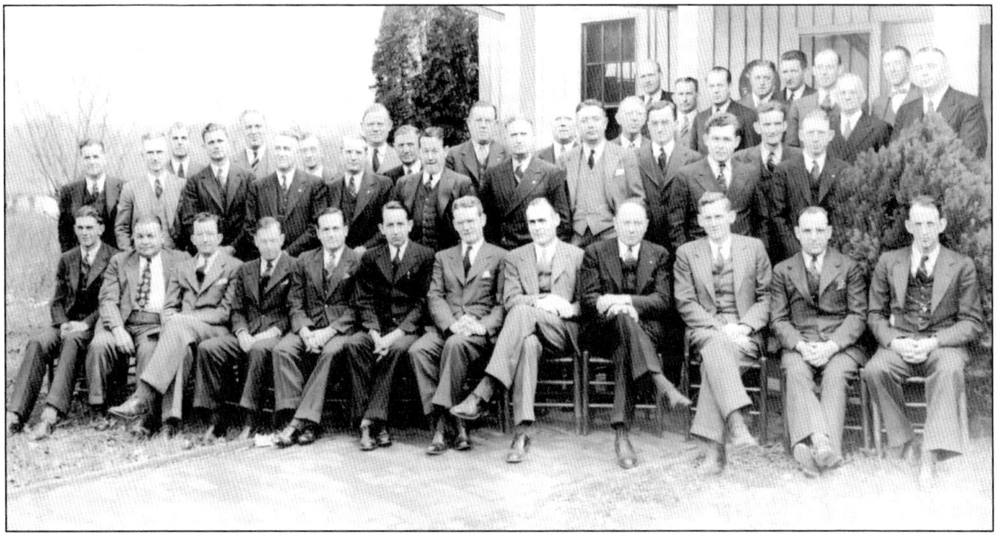

Belmont Business Men's Portrait at the Library, 1930s. Among this array of movers and shakers of Belmont in the 1930s are Roy Moore, Dr. Wade Breeland, Ike Howe, Prep Hall, Raymond Garrison, Eli Cohen, Paul Neal, Johnny Johnson, "Doc" Robinson, David Bumgardner Sr., Ray Buckner, Leonard Laye, Dr. Preston Taylor, Harvey Elmore, and Rev. Richard Kelly. The building in the background is Belmont's first public library, built by Minnie Stowe Puett. It presently houses Oak Ridge Dental Arts, Inc. (Courtesy of Millican Pictorial History Museum.)

Three

Evolution of Belmont
1970s–Present

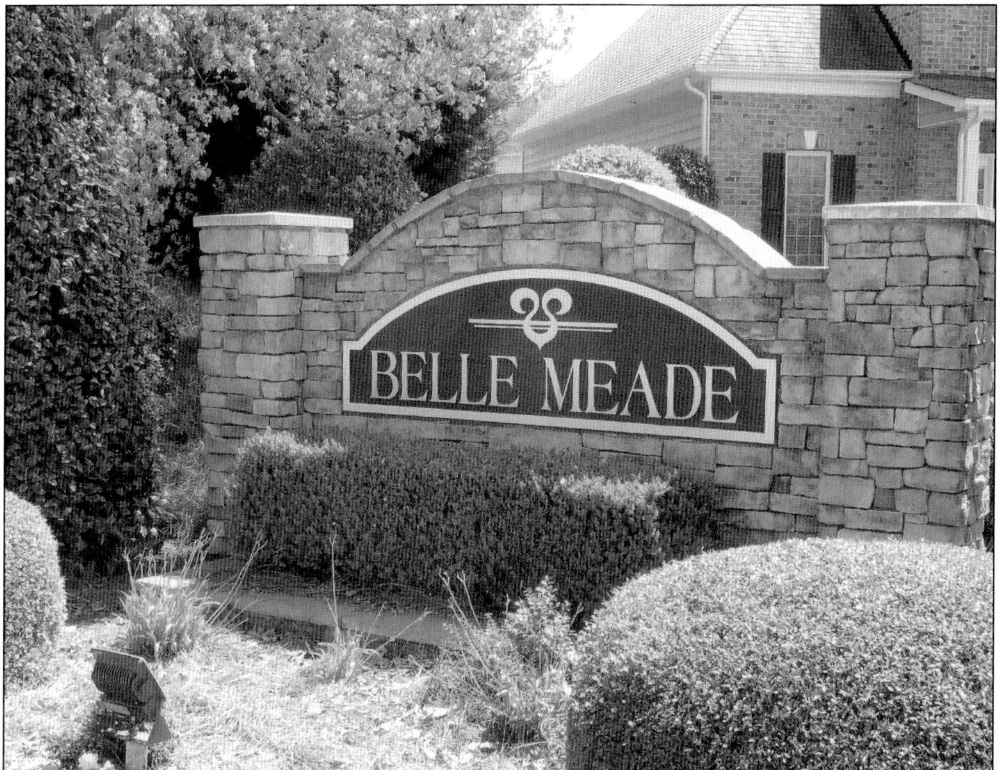

Belle Meade. This attractive entrance marker is one of some 20 that lead into developments that have replaced farmland on the South Point peninsula and the south New Hope Road. Most of these developments have homes that are unique. People come to this area from Mecklenburg County, out-of-state environs, and uptown Belmont, seeking more space in which to live and raise their families. (Photograph by Jack Page.)

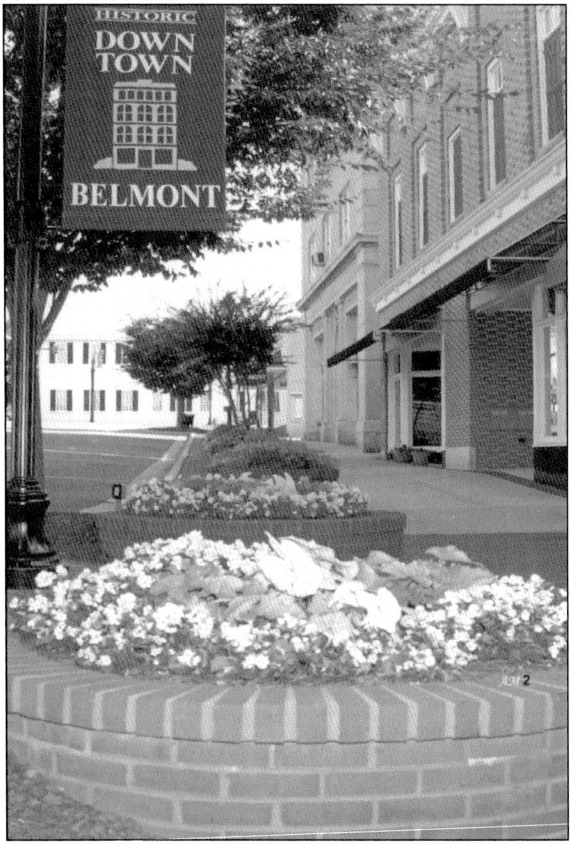

Downtown Belmont, 2003. After considerable prodding of the city council by Mayor Kevin Loftin, the council approved a plan to enhance the appearance and the utility of downtown Belmont. This included upgrading the water system, burying all telephone and electric lines, repaving sidewalks, and the building of planters for flowers. The project drew a great deal of attention and was largely responsible for attracting new citizens and businesses to the community. Note that in the top left corner, there is a banner proclaiming downtown Belmont as a historic city. Also enhanced is the Stowe Mill Office at the top of the Main Street. (Courtesy of Millican Pictorial History Museum.)

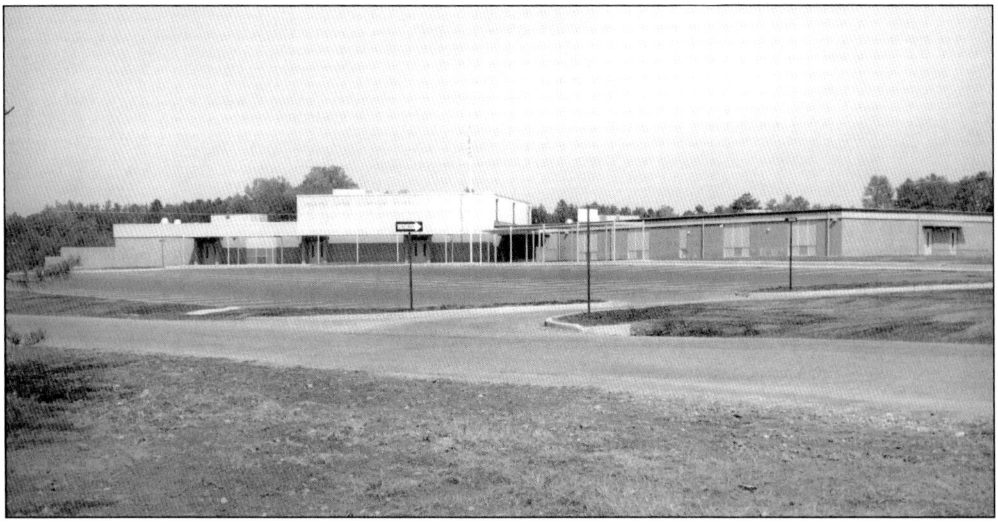

Belmont Central Elementary School. Built in 1969 on the Eagle Mill's baseball field, this modern structure is quite an update over the previous worn-out facility. The former elementary school/high school had served Belmont students since well before World War I. Very soon, the grounds were enhanced with plantings of shrubs and flower beds. Longtime principal Paul Houser continued as principal of the new school until he retired. (Courtesy of Millican Pictorial History Museum.)

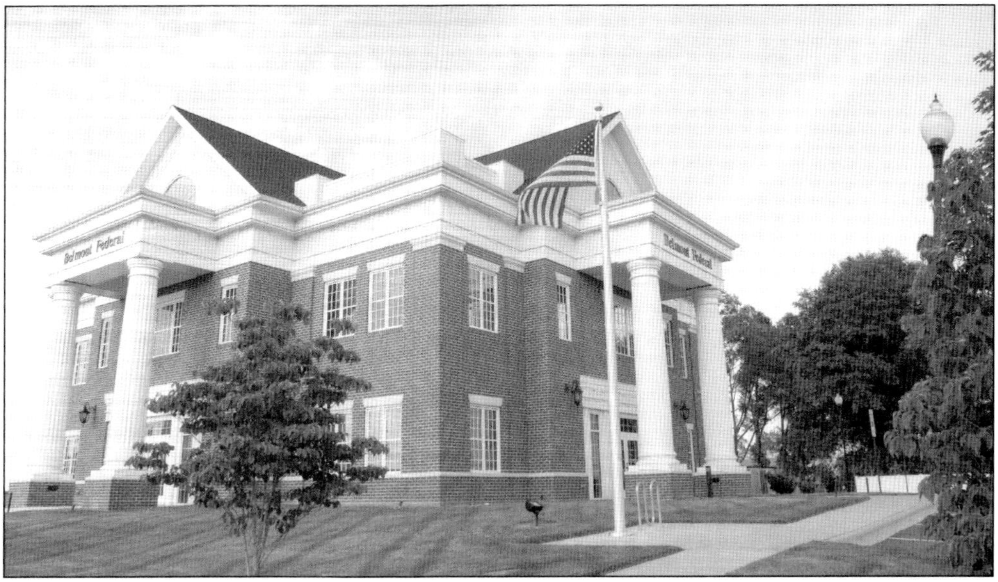

Belmont Federal Savings and Loan. The new Belmont Federal Savings and Loan is an imposing building at the top of the hill overlooking the intersection of Park Street and Wilkinson Boulevard. Longtime president Bart Hall was succeeded by Betty Lewis and subsequently by Michael Anthony. The services of Belmont Federal Savings and Loan have enabled many families to become proud homeowners. (Courtesy of Millican Pictorial History Museum.)

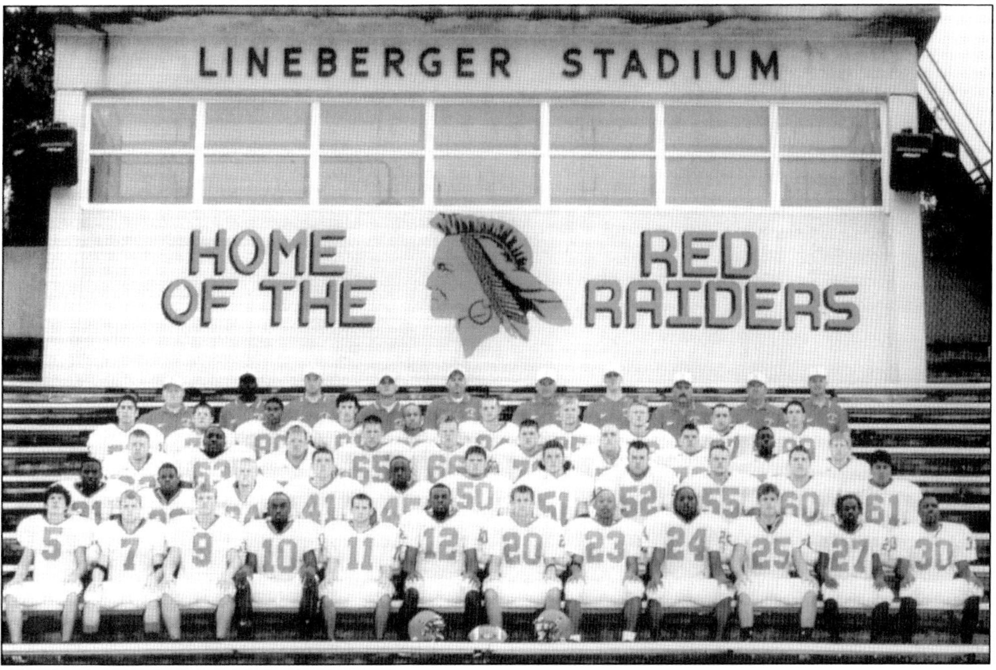

South Point Red Raiders, 2003. Without a superstar on the team, these players pulled together to such a degree that they were successful in winning the North Carolina State 3A championship. They were fortunate to have a full staff of professional coaches in addition to a large number of volunteer coaches, most of whom were former South Point Red Raiders. (Courtesy of Millican Pictorial History Museum.)

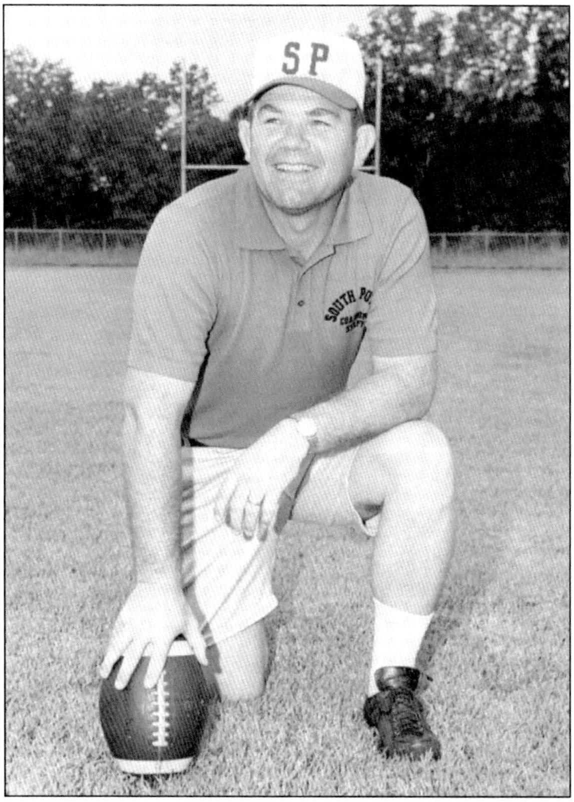

Coach Jim Biggerstaff, South Point High School. Jim Biggerstaff, also known as "Coach Big," invigorated the Red Raiders after several years of lackluster play. Coach Biggerstaff had played for the Raiders under coaches Gerald Cortner and Wrather Johnson, and in his senior year, the team was undefeated, with a 10-0 record. Also during his senior year, he was voted Most Valuable Player and received the Dr. Wade Breeland Award. After graduating from Western Carolina University, Biggerstaff coached and taught in Rockingham, North Carolina, for 10 years. In 1969, he became head football coach, athletic director, and biology teacher at South Point High School. Over his career, he had many outstanding teams and coached the North Carolina Shrine Bowl team as well as the West team in the North Carolina East-West All-Star game. (Courtesy of Millican Pictorial History Museum.)

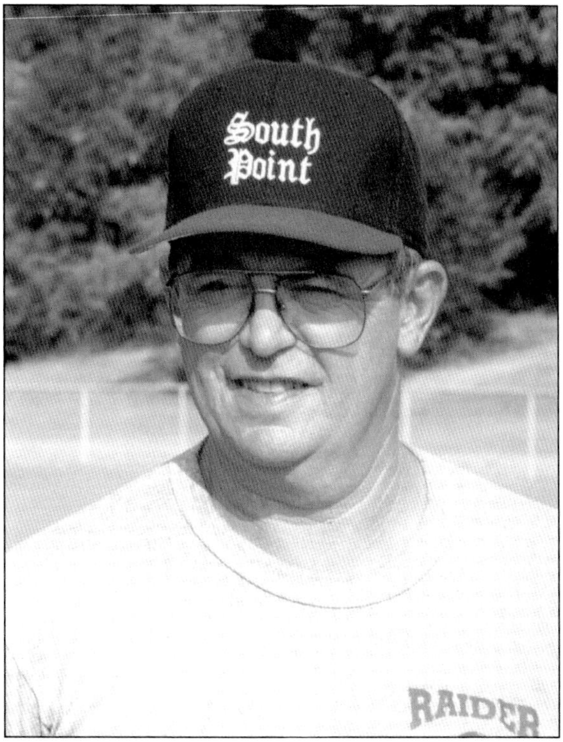

Coach Phil Tate, South Point High School. Phillip A. "Phil" Tate came to Belmont when he was 12 years old. His family moved to the Duke Power Village off South Point Road. He excelled in football and baseball. After graduating from Western Carolina University, Tate secured employment at Hunter Huss High School. Shortly thereafter, he moved to South Point High School, where he was highly successful as a baseball coach, with a record of 219 wins and 81 losses. Tate has been inducted into the Belmont Sports Hall of Fame and the Gaston County Sports Hall of Fame. He continues as a volunteer football coach at South Point High School. He is not only respected but also loved by "his boys." (Courtesy of Millican Pictorial History Museum.)

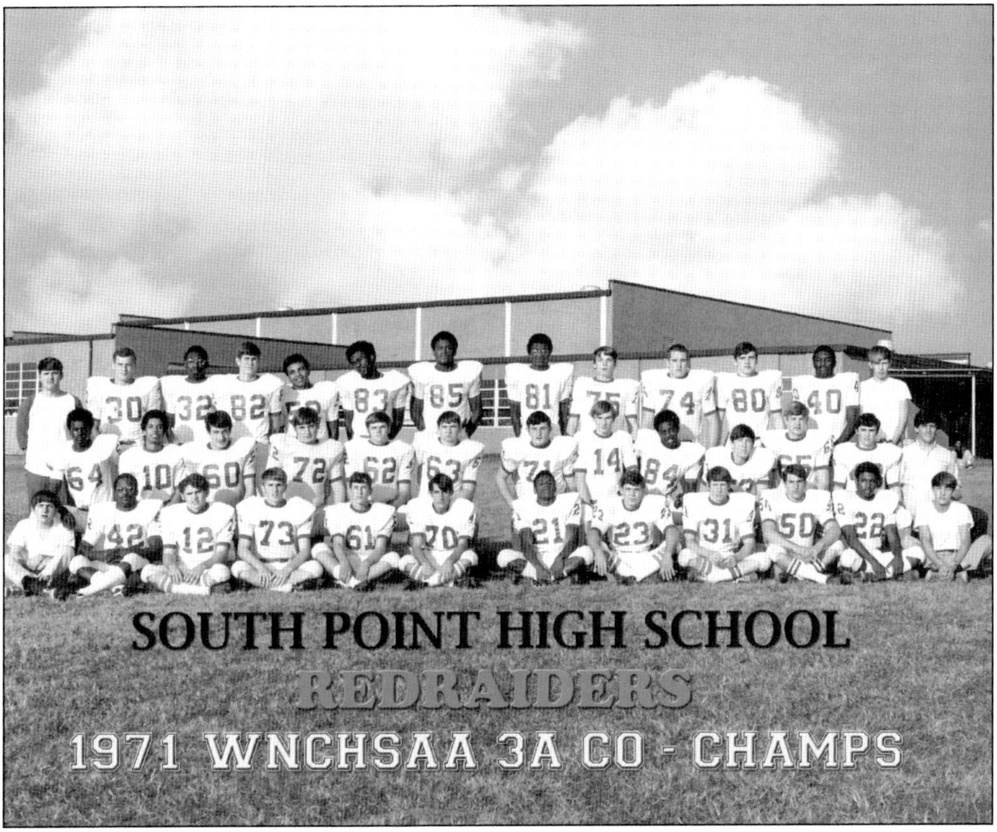

RED RAIDERS FOOTBALL TEAM. The South Point High School Red Raiders football team of 1971 was undefeated in conference play. Led by Scott Crawford, the team rose through the play-offs to meet Salisbury High School for the WNCHSAA (Western North Carolina High School Activities Association) 3A championship. This game ended in a tie. The players on this team set a winning standard for teams to come, culminating in 1979 with the Red Raiders winning the state championship. (Courtesy of Millican Pictorial History Museum.)

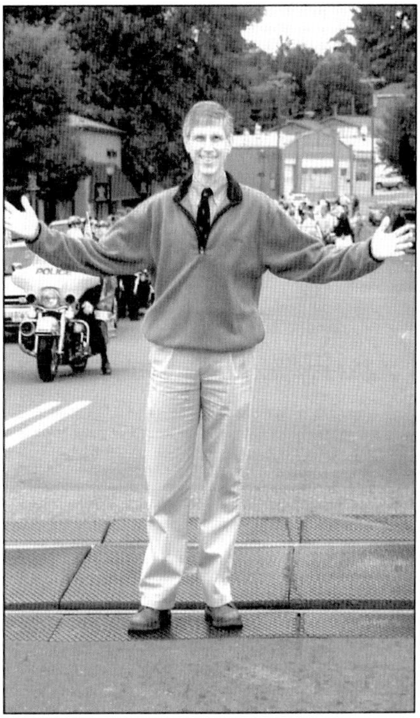

MAYOR RICHARD BOYCE. Rev. Richard Boyce, pastor of Belmont's First Presbyterian Church from 1993 to 2003, served Belmont as mayor from 2005 to 2013. Currently, he is the dean of Union Presbyterian Seminary in Charlotte. Boyce was a Charlotte native and a third-generation pastor. He grew up in Virginia and is a graduate of Davidson College. His wit and humor endear him to the public and cause him to be asked to be a speaker and a moderator for various functions in the Belmont area. (Courtesy of Millican Pictorial History Museum.)

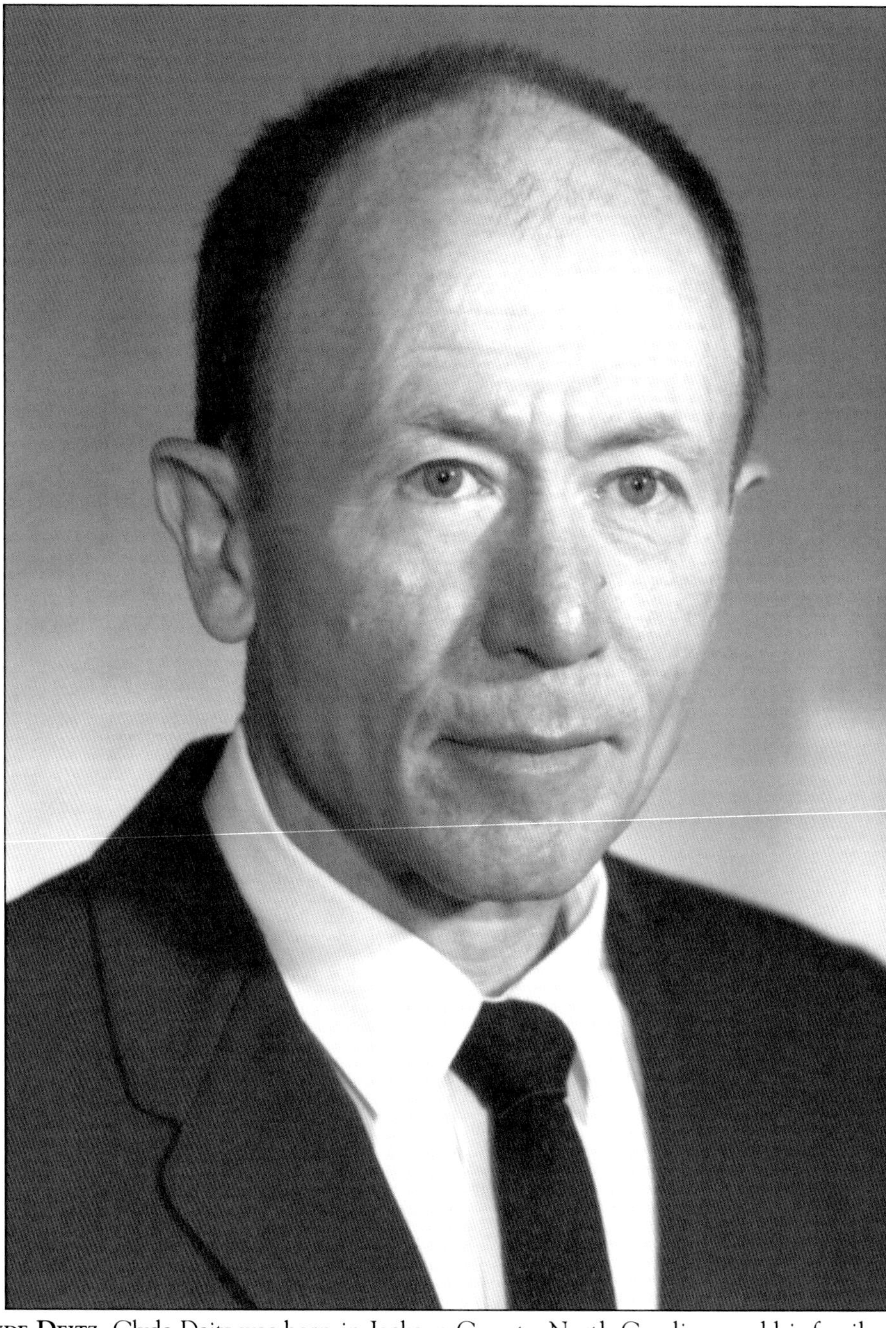

Clyde Deitz. Clyde Deitz was born in Jackson County, North Carolina, and his family moved to Belmont's Majestic Mill Village when he was a small boy. Deitz served in the US Coast Guard during World War II. Upon returning to Belmont, he became heavily involved in the Belmont Hosiery Company, where he spent the rest of his career. Deitz was elected to the Belmont City Council, where he served for 22 years. He was greatly responsible for the smooth desegregation of the Belmont schools. He was named as Belmont's Citizen of the Year in acknowledgment for his service to Belmont. The overhead bridge adjacent to the Belmont Library was named in his honor. (Courtesy of Millican Pictorial History Museum.)

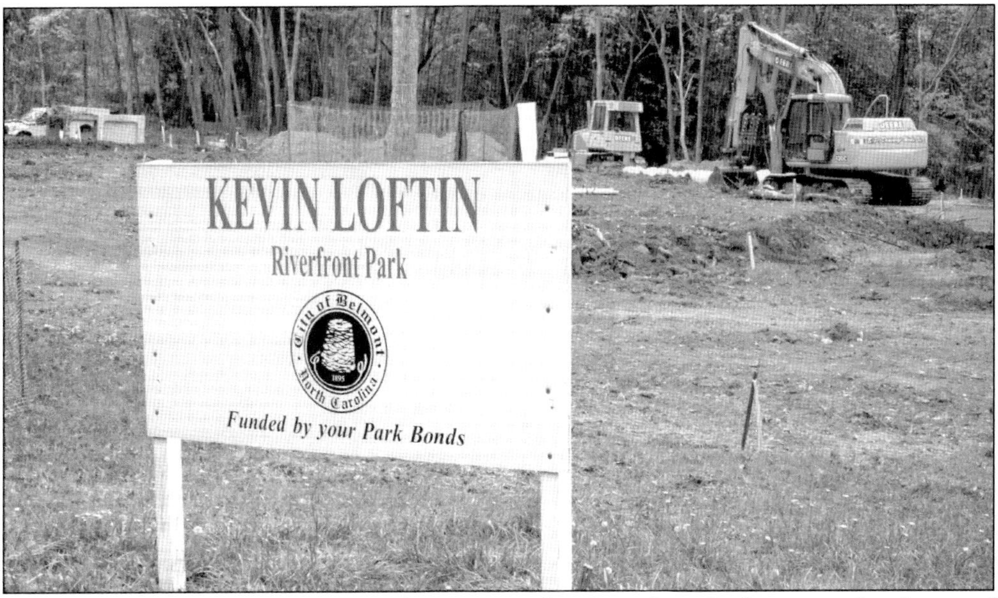

KEVIN LOFTIN RIVERFRONT PARK. The Kevin Loftin Riverfront Park is named in honor of Mayor Kevin Loftin, who was one of the most forward-thinking of Belmont's political leaders. His foresight led to the construction of Belmont's modernized downtown infrastructure. Flower boxes were constructed on the widened sidewalk, all utility lines have been buried, and the 1920s-era water and sewer lines have been replaced. This revitalization of downtown's Main Street led to what has become a mix of vibrant, expanding, and competitive local retail shops, eating establishments, antique stores, jewelry stores, and more. Furthermore, the beauty of the town and a strong Montcross Chamber of Commerce have brought about many new housing developments along the South Point Peninsula and New Hope Road. (Photograph by Jack Page.)

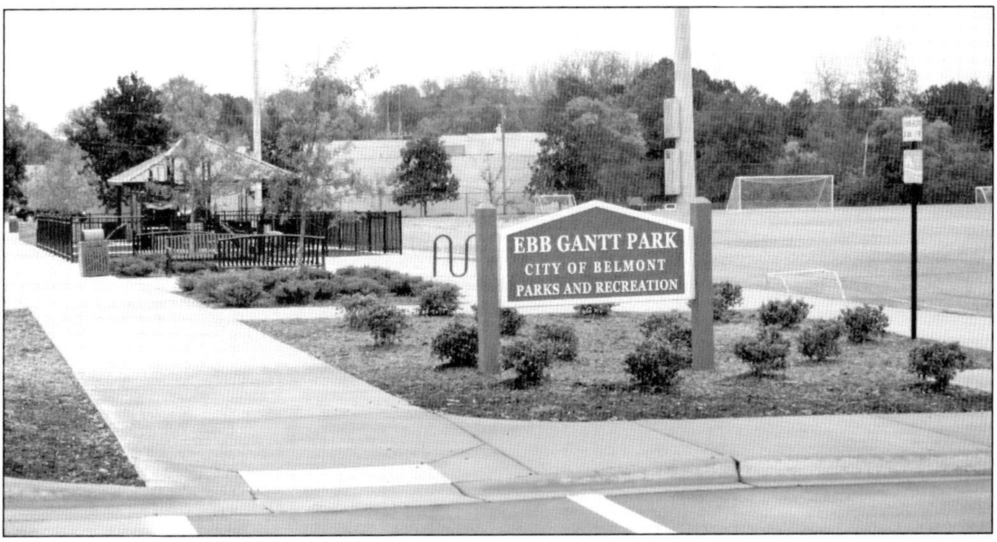

EBB GANTT PARK. Ebb Gantt, a Belmont native, served in the military, where he learned to box. As a civilian, he was a US mail carrier, a boxing coach, Little League football coach, public address sports announcer, and was a broadcaster for WCGC radio in Belmont. The soccer complex pictured here consists of three full-sized soccer fields and is named in honor of Gantt in gratitude for his contribution to the sports community of Belmont. (Photograph by Jack Page.)

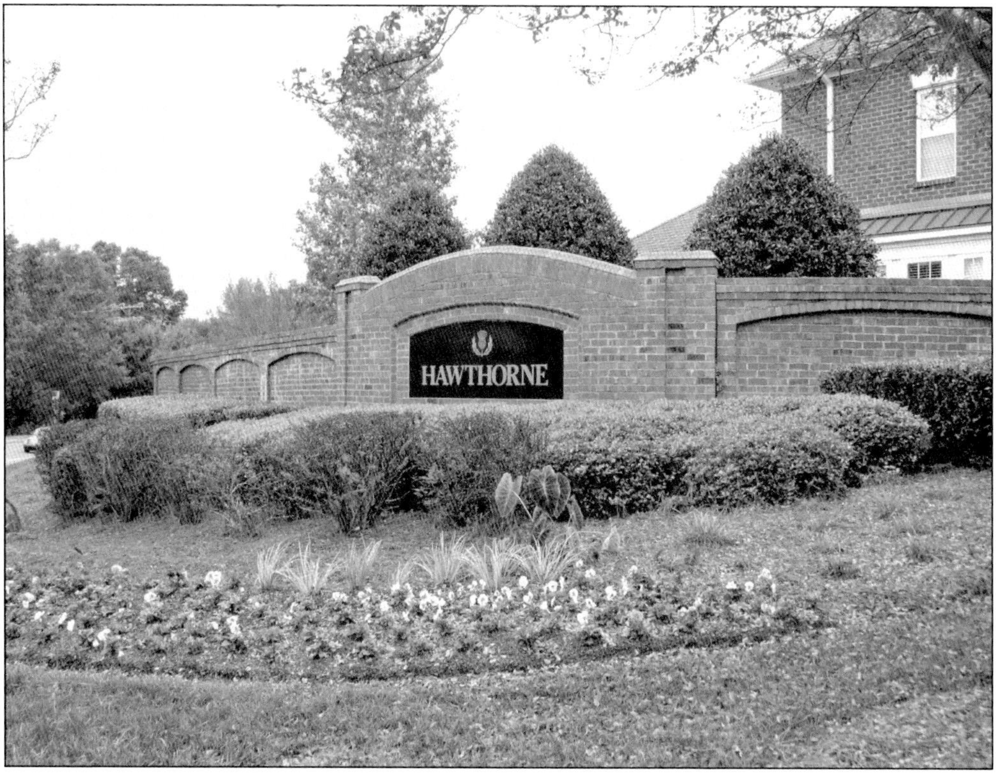

Hawthorne Housing Development. The upscale homes in Hawthorne sit on property that once housed the Imperial Mill Village, which was commonly known as the Imperial Mill Hill. The homes for the mill workers sat amidst some very old majestic trees. To make a transition to this present housing development, the mill houses were burned by local fire departments as training exercises and the trees and land were completely recontoured to suit the needs of those who designed and built Hawthorne. In earlier days, this property contained the sites of Stockade Hill, a primitive schoolhouse that Robert Lee Stowe Sr. attended as a boy, and a brush arbor that was the genesis of what has become Belmont's First Baptist Church. (Photograph by Jack Page.)

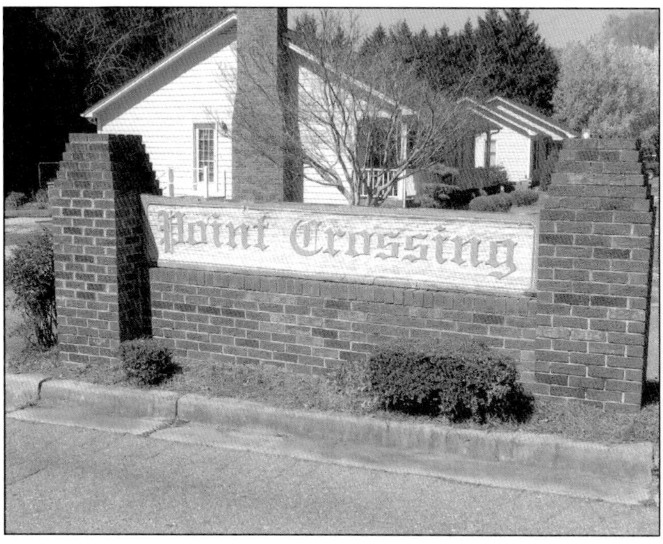

Point Crossing. This entrance marks the development of homes on property that was once the farmland of the Neil Mellon family. This acreage has been divided many times over the years. (Photograph by Jack Page.)

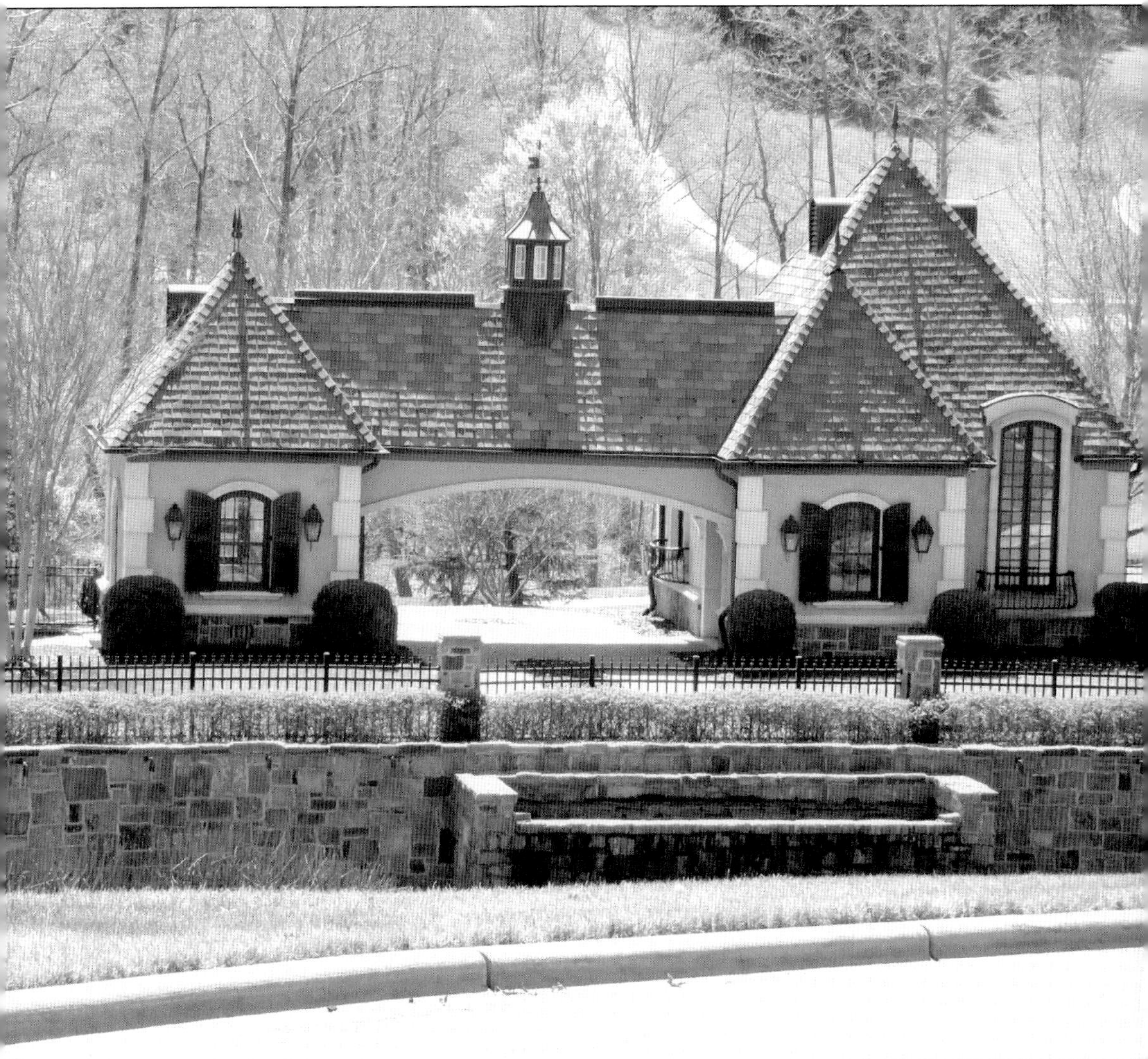

ENTRANCE TO REFLECTION POINTE. Reflection Pointe, a gated residential community, sits astride the confluence of the South Fork and Catawba Rivers. It was in this area that Robert Leeper and James Kuykendall, with the help of neighbors, erected a log fort around 1750. This property for many years was known by the local inhabitants as "Hurricane Hill." All of the 350 homesites have houses that are individually customized. In addition, there are many added amenities including sidewalks, a swimming pool, and other recreational areas. (Photograph by Jack Page.)

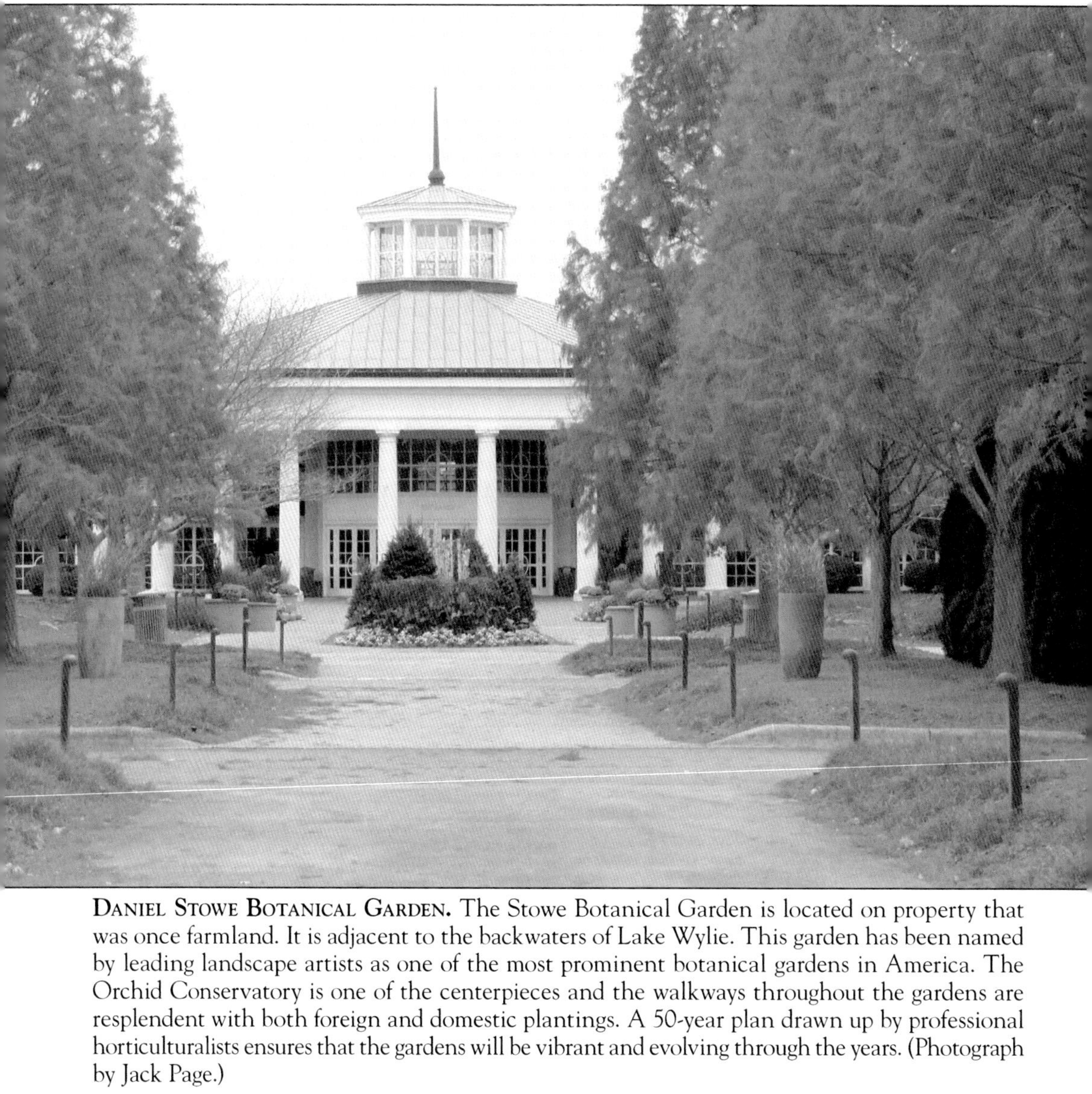

DANIEL STOWE BOTANICAL GARDEN. The Stowe Botanical Garden is located on property that was once farmland. It is adjacent to the backwaters of Lake Wylie. This garden has been named by leading landscape artists as one of the most prominent botanical gardens in America. The Orchid Conservatory is one of the centerpieces and the walkways throughout the gardens are resplendent with both foreign and domestic plantings. A 50-year plan drawn up by professional horticulturalists ensures that the gardens will be vibrant and evolving through the years. (Photograph by Jack Page.)

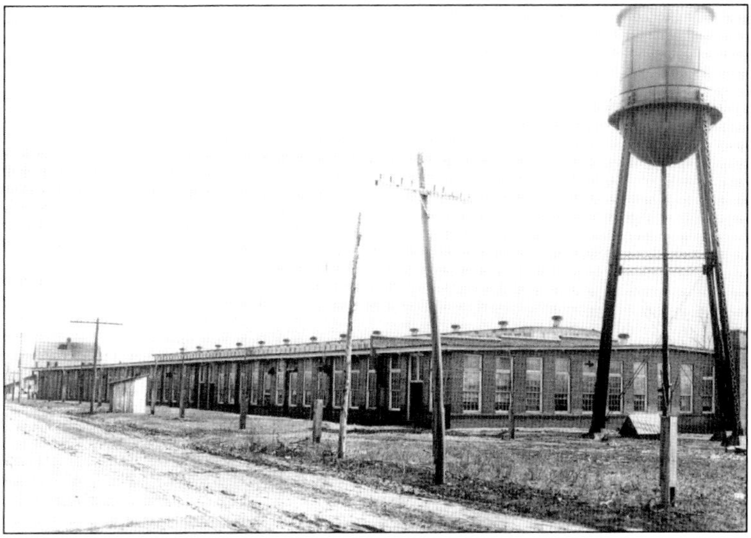

The Majestic Mill, 1914. Situated along the muddy Catawba Street, the Majestic Mill provided employment for dozens of workers. The water tank provided water for the mill and its surrounding village. Today, the mill has been converted into the Catawba River Antique Mall, which attracts shoppers and lookers from miles around.

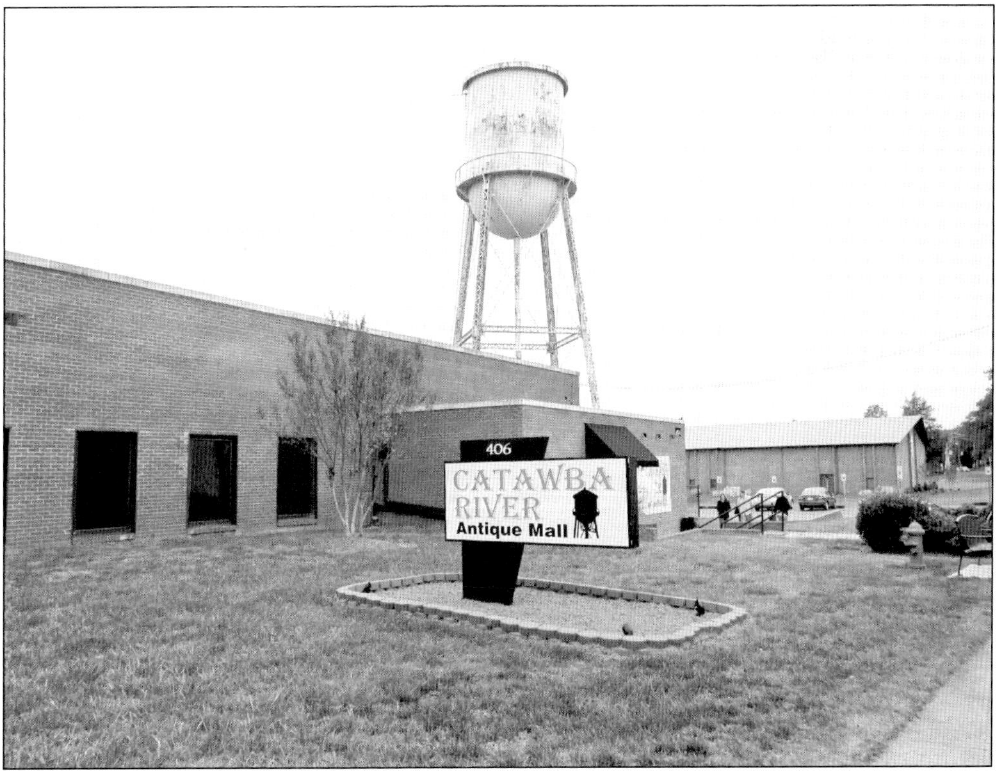

Catawba River Antique Mall. The Catawba River Antique Mall is housed in what was originally the Majestic Manufacturing Plant, the third-oldest cotton mill in Belmont. The mill processed cotton that came in one door as a bale and went out another door as spools of cotton yarn. Today, this is one of the largest antique malls in this portion of North Carolina. Areas can be leased for vendors to display their collections that are for sale. People come from all over Piedmont North Carolina and other states to discover their personal treasures. (Photograph by Jack Page.)

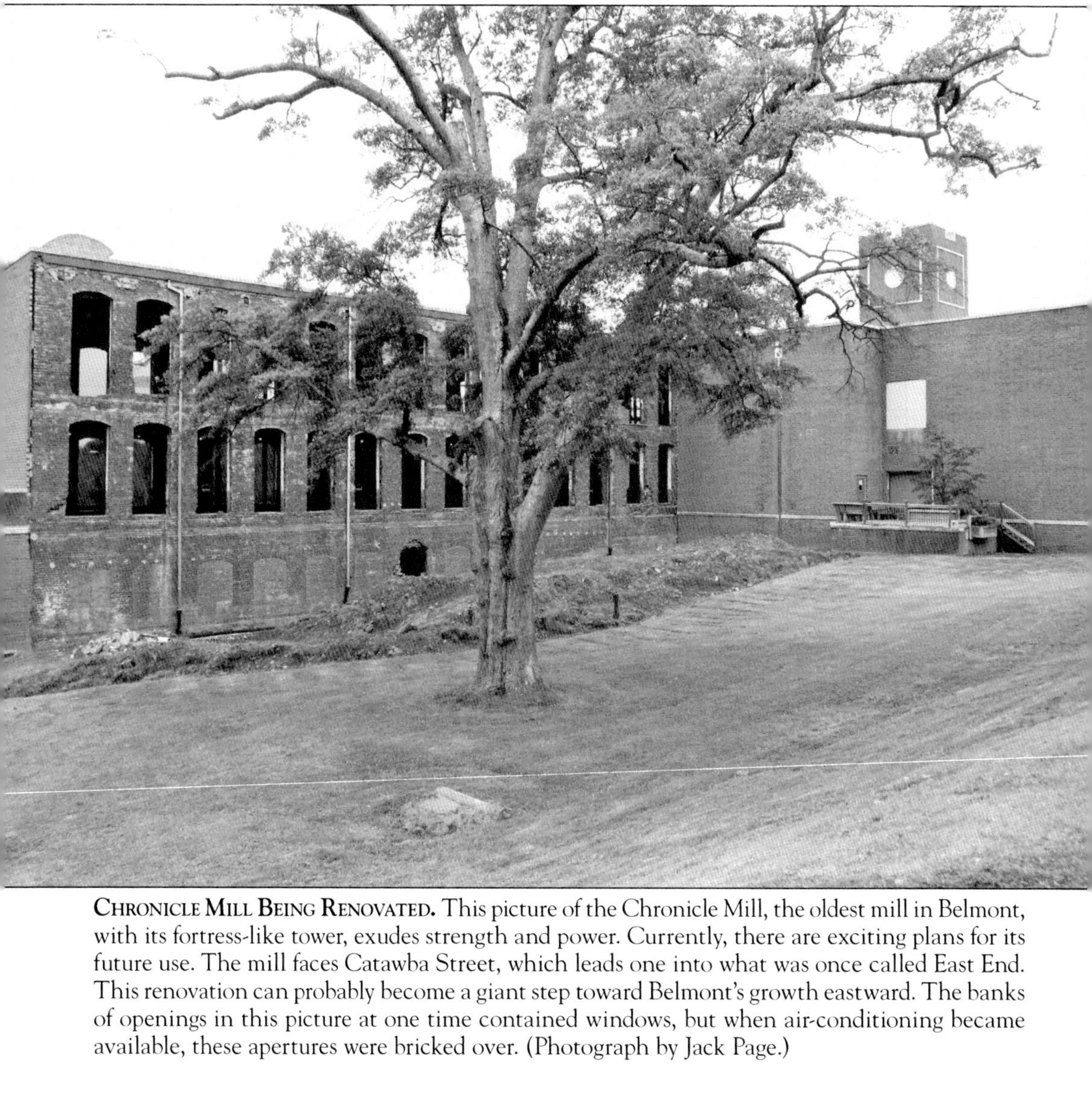

Chronicle Mill Being Renovated. This picture of the Chronicle Mill, the oldest mill in Belmont, with its fortress-like tower, exudes strength and power. Currently, there are exciting plans for its future use. The mill faces Catawba Street, which leads one into what was once called East End. This renovation can probably become a giant step toward Belmont's growth eastward. The banks of openings in this picture at one time contained windows, but when air-conditioning became available, these apertures were bricked over. (Photograph by Jack Page.)

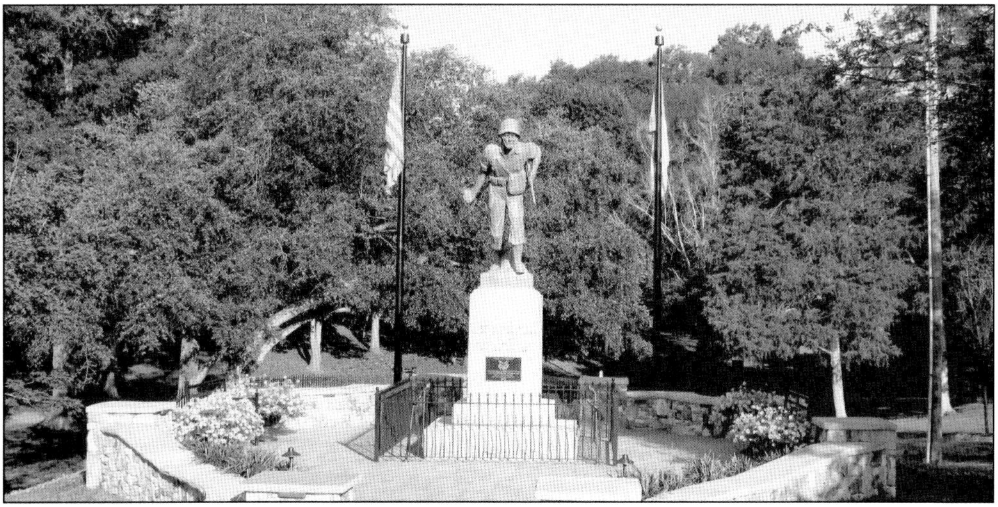

SPIRIT OF THE FIGHTING YANK. The *Spirit of the Fighting Yank* now rests in its beautiful new setting in Stowe Park, downtown Belmont, where more people can view it and better appreciate the veterans of all the wars in which brave men from this area fought. (Courtesy of Jack Page.)

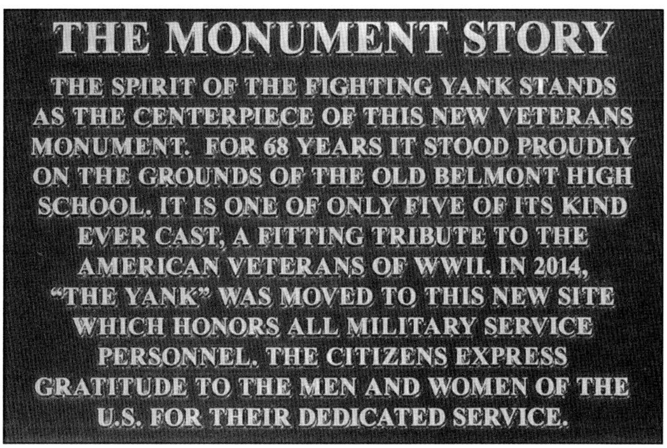

VETERANS MONUMENT. This move of the monument in June 2014 is one of the most recent innovations in the evolution of the city of Belmont. (Courtesy of Jack Page.)

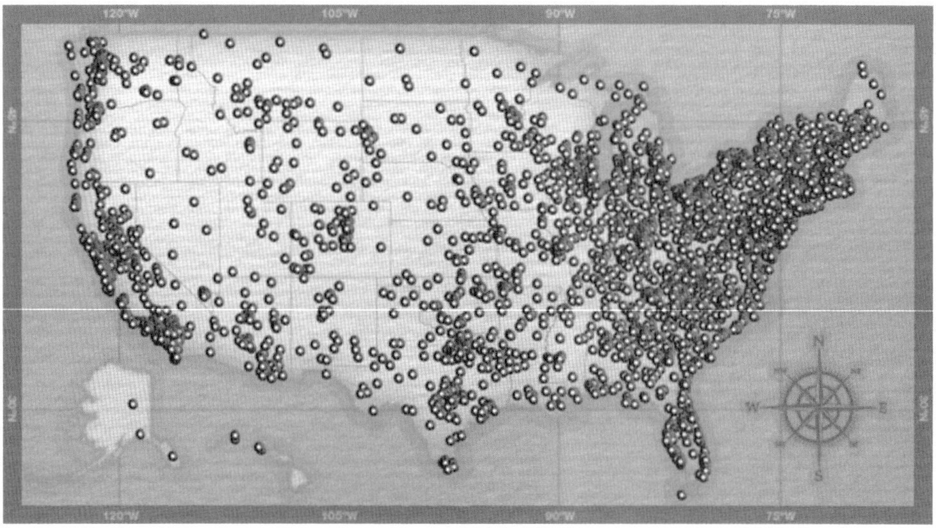